BETWEEN EVERYTHING
and NOTHING

BETWEEN EVERYTHING *and* NOTHING

The Journey of
Seidu Mohammed and **Razak Iyal**
and the Quest for **Asylum**

JOE MENO

Counterpoint Berkeley, California

BETWEEN EVERYTHING AND NOTHING

Library of Congress Cataloging-in-Publication Data
Names: Meno, Joe, author.
Title: Between everything and nothing : the journey of
    Seidu Mohammed and Razak Iyal and the quest for asylum
    / Joe Meno.
Description: First hardcover edition. | Berkeley, California :
    Counterpoint Press, 2020.
Identifiers: LCCN 2019039301 | ISBN 9781640093140
    (hardcover) | ISBN 9781640093157 (ebook)
Subjects: LCSH: Mohammed, Seidu, 1993- | Iyal, Razak.
    | Ghanaians—United States—Biography. | Ghanaians—
    Canada—Biography. | Ghana—Politics and government. |
    United States—Emigration and immigration—Government
    policy. | Canada—Emigration and immigration—
    Governemnt policy.
Classification: LCC E183.8.G5 M46 2020 | DDC
    966.705/40922—dc23
LC record available at https://lccn.loc.gov/2019039301

Jacket design by Donna Cheng
Book design by Wah-Ming Chang

COUNTERPOINT
2560 Ninth Street, Suite 318
Berkeley, CA 94710
www.counterpointpress.com

Printed in the United States of America
Distributed by Publishers Group West

10 9 8 7 6 5 4 3 2 1

For family, friends, and the others we pass along the way

BETWEEN EVERYTHING
and NOTHING

Begin with sound. Begin with light. Seidu Mohammed stands on the side of the road, unsure whether he is alive or dead. Beside him the frigid highway points back toward North Dakota—unbroken, unchanging. An abiding darkness has settled over everything. There are no other cars, no trucks, no traffic. The wind swallows every noise. He wonders if it is better to cross at night. It is less likely they will be seen, yes, but it is so much colder. Seidu—twenty-four, dressed in a sweatshirt and several jackets—turns and faces an empty field, covered in deep snow, intense in its whiteness, leading north toward the border. Somewhere on the other side of this frozen landscape is the town of Emerson, Canada. Beyond that, freedom. Or other kinds of tragedy.

Razak Iyal stands beside him, staring at the barren stretch of field, taking in the inconceivable distance, unsure if they should go forward or turn back. The thirty-four-year-old adjusts his hat. Both men murmur to each other—their voices captured by the biting wind—before finally descending into the field of snow. In a moment it covers their feet. A moment after that it is up to their knees. Walk toward the light, *they have been told.* Stay on the left side of the highway. If a vehicle approaches on the right, it will be the immigration patrol. Hide, lie on the ground. All you need to do is get across the border. Then ask for help. The journey will only be one half hour.

Both of them keep walking, searching for the lights of the border. The land glistens before them but the border is nowhere in sight. They glance at each other, knowing they are lost, but all they can do is put one foot in front of the other, marking their way through the deepening drifts.

Although they can still make out the shape of the highway some-where on their right, there is no sign of anything up ahead, no faint glimmer of movement, only the cold reach of the wind.

Everything has become cold and black, and the snow—up to their waists now—makes their hands and feet numb. One walks ahead, the other—ten, twenty yards behind—follows. Sometimes there are skeletal trees to hold on to, but just as often the land mysteriously opens up and there is nothing but the unsettling flatness of the fields, bisected at the horizon by the black sky overhead. It begins to snow again and the wind, rushing at thirty miles an hour, cuts across their exposed faces, burns the places where their clothes do not hide the skin.

By then Seidu has fallen behind. Once or twice a vehicle approaches along the highway and both he and Razak are forced to lie on the ground, waiting for it to pass, the headlights crossing over them, then vanishing into a blur of silver.

Each time they are forced to lie down, the cold creeps further into their clothes, through their jackets, in the spaces between their gloves and pants and shoes. Seidu's eyelids have begun to freeze. Tears run down his cheeks and turn to ice. He wipes at his eyes with his bare hands, then calls out to Razak for help, following the sound of the other man's voice.

One hour, two hours later they are lost, having disappeared com-pletely into the snow.

What do you do when you have nothing left? Nowhere to go? What kind of person are you forced to become?

In the spare bedroom of his brother Kamal's house in Ohio, Seidu quietly put his things into his backpack, going through his belongings, searching for clothes and the documents he would need. He placed his soccer cleats on the bed, then checked the Minneapolis weather on Kamal's laptop once again. The forecast said it would be between eight and ten degrees Fahrenheit on the day he'd arrive, December 23. He had never been anywhere that cold before, and so he began putting aside extra sweatshirts, a light jacket, an extra pair of gloves, as many socks as he could fit into his bag.

Somehow Kamal got the money for the trip north the next day—taking out a loan from a local bank. He drove Seidu to the bus station near the center of Youngstown, bought him a bus ticket, and waited with him until the bus arrived. The gray and silver lobby seemed sterile, silent, like the waiting room of a hospital. The two brothers had been apart for eleven years before Seidu had arrived in the States. Now they would be separated once again.

The men smiled at each other, knowing they would not see each other again for some time.

Everything is going to be okay, Kamal said. *Just be careful.*

After an hour, the bus approached. Seidu looked at it hesitantly, then turned to his older brother and stood.

Don't worry. We'll see each other again soon, Kamal said. Seidu gave his brother a long hug, then climbed onto the bus. The pneumatic doors closed with an exultant sound, signifying the end of one world and the beginning of another.

Outside the glossy pane of the bus's windows, there was a tumult, a clatter—the wind rattling the windows as if some shapeless, unidentifiable darkness were in pursuit. By the border of Indiana, he was certain that the catastrophe he had attempted to flee had somehow followed him, that someone had his name and photograph and was only waiting to see where he was going, what he intended to do.

You must go, a voice told him. *Keep running. Do not stop moving until you are safe.*

Over those two days, Seidu rode through five states, tracing the shape of the country through its arterial roads and highways. Shadows flashed past upon the bleary window like faded images from an out-of-date movie. The snowy terrain, the long expanse of uninterrupted expressways, cities that appeared and receded into the late December grayness. The towering, tattered billboards along the road cited biblical quotations condemning homosexuality and abortion, and then a few miles later there were advertisements for adult bookstores. The meek-looking aluminum houses, all the different kinds of trees, the water towers in their muted colors, the automobiles abandoned in transoms along the side of culverts, the old steel bridges and discolored flags, the other people on the bus with their strange manners, all of it was so unlike home.

Twice he changed buses, and was able to grab some chips and a bottle of Coca-Cola. He thought about calling his brother, wondered if the government had a way to listen to the phone lines, and so decided against it. He climbed aboard the bus again and tried to get some sleep. In the back of the vehicle a young woman was singing. A child was crying. Over the last two years, ever since he had left Ghana, Seidu had traveled almost entirely by foot or bus through South and Central America. He had seen the same faces again and again; all over the world, the forlorn, the stubborn, the dispossessed were forced to wear the exact same expression.

He had seen something online days before, a Facebook post that said if you could make it across the border into Canada without being stopped by the U.S. Border Patrol, you could apply for asylum on the other side, regardless of your status in the United States. The post had said that the Canadians were more fair than the Americans, and even offered free legal representation to non-citizens. All he had to do was get across.

Ten hours later the bus pulled into another city. From behind the smudged window, Seidu could see the glass exterior of Minneapolis rising against a bleak sky—just before the bus quickly descended beneath the shadows of high-rises and office buildings.

Cold settled in once he stepped off the bus, first hitting him in the face, then burning his hands. He buried his fists into the folds of his coat as he asked for directions. The Minneapolis bus station was a busy place on the afternoon of December 23. People were hurrying to visit loved ones—the working poor, other migrants, the dazed, angry faces of Americans, shoving bags and luggage, carrying packages, dragging children by the hand. In a parking lot he asked for directions again and headed south.

He had called two days before to get a room at a nearby Motel 6, but when he arrived at the run-down building in a seemingly abandoned part of downtown, he discovered the room was $200 a night, which was much too expensive. He was also worried about being reported by the clerk, concerned that if he paid in cash and used a fake name he might be found out. He stepped back outside onto the dimly lit street, then crossed back again to where he'd started.

Upon feeling the cold air making his lungs tighten, he decided to return to the bus station, to see if he could find a bus to take him closer to the border.

No one knew him in the city, but he felt certain that if he stayed, the authorities would find him. Better to keep moving than to stop and wait, to be found out, to get caught and sent back to Ghana.

It was not yet snowing, though everything was daunting, unclear, faint.

The bus station was nearly empty at 9:30 p.m. Seidu took a seat on a grimy metal bench and looked around. For a moment, the world revealed itself in all its amazing, tired complexity. The fluorescent lights looked false. The glow of the vending machines, with their insistent hum; the overhead screens announcing departing buses, flickering regretfully; someone across the way coughed, sounding as if they belonged in an emergency room. The only other black person he saw was a round-faced man sitting alone, staring into the distance. He could tell by the man's appearance, by his body language, by the color of his complexion, and by his clothes—two jackets, a hoodie, and blue jeans—that he was African, that he was not from Minnesota, and he too was not used to the frigid weather. The man looked to be in his early thirties, with wide shoulders and a closely shaven beard and an amiable expression. Something about this other man's face, his features, seemed familiar. Seidu decided to say something and so stood up and crossed the bus terminal.

"Hello."

The other man looked up and said, "Hello."

The accent was recognizable.

"Where are you from?" Seidu asked.

"Ghana."

Seidu smiled. "I'm from Ghana too."

Both men grinned widely. From there, they began to speak in Hausa. The other man began: *"Menene sunanka?"* *What's your name?*

Seidu.

I'm Razak.

Someone—some disbeliever, some journalist, some political pundit, some sociologist, someone who did not understand the silent realm of migrants, asylum seekers, and refugees, someone who had never fled their home, someone who did not understand the bizarre coincidences, the signs and markings of being an individual thousands of miles from the country you knew—would think this meeting was entirely improbable. Only consider the tens of thousands of asylum seekers who enter the United States each year. But, having made the long odyssey, first from Brazil, then to Mexico, then to the U.S., having met émigrés from other African nations, including Ghana, all along the way, having heard the familiar tongue, the language of their homeland during their internment in Mexican and U.S. detention facilities, having seen others who, like them, were all searching, the fact that both men spoke the same local dialect, that both men were Muslims, that both men were from the same country, the same city, the same neighborhood of Nima, seemed like a marvel and an inevitability. It made perfect sense that they would find another lost country-man to help them make their way on this, the final part of their journey. Because it soon became clear that both of them were try-ing to cross into Canada.

"*Nada ka?*" Razak asked. *Where are you going?*

I'm going to the Canadian border, Seidu replied.

Razak smiled. *I'm also going to the border.*

Seidu asked, *Who are you waiting for?*

Nobody. I've been sitting here since this morning, trying to come up with a plan.

Seidu nodded. It occurred to the two men that they might be able to make it to Canada together, just as each had relied on companions, fellow asylum seekers, and other strangers since first leaving their homes years before.

Seidu thought, *Okay. We can do this. We can make this journey together.*

Outside the bus station, a black taxi with no identification on its doors pulled up beside the two men. The driver rolled down the passenger-side window and asked where the two men were going. The driver's face was unreadable, hidden by a dark baseball cap.

They told the taxi driver that they wanted to go to the U.S. border.

"Grand Forks," the man said knowingly. From the tone of his voice it sounded as if he had made the trip before.

Both men were surprised, not knowing the name of the town in North Dakota where they were supposed to be going.

"Each of you need to give me two hundred bucks," the cab driver said.

Seidu and Razak felt this man knew what he was doing and did not ask any questions. At any moment, they could be stopped—by police, by an ICE officer, by an overzealous Trump supporter—so the decision was made without any other discussion. Razak climbed into the front of the cab beside the driver while Seidu climbed into the back.

The taxi driver, face still shadowed by his hat, asked for the money right away. Eager to be off, the two men handed it over. Then the driver pulled away from the curb.

"How long does it take to get to the border?" Razak asked.

"Four hours or so," the driver answered, looking back at the road. It had begun to snow, adding to the large drifts that had already accumulated along the city streets. Neither Seidu nor Razak had seen so much of it before. Even in Ohio or New York it never snowed like this. In Minneapolis, the snowflakes themselves looked larger, like paper cutouts, turning the urban sidewalks into hillocks of inordinate whiteness. In the end there was just too much of it. The buildings, the parked cars, the stop signs, all of it seemed to dissolve into immobile shapes. Passing along the edge of the city, the black cab navigated among the colossal drifts and finally took a ramp onto Interstate 94, heading north and west.

Others had come this way before them, the driver assured them. He mentioned driving Ethiopians and Haitians to the border only a few days before. These asylum seekers had exploited a flaw in the U.S.–Canada Safe Third Country Agreement, which allowed migrants who crossed into Canada on foot and presented themselves to the Canadian authorities the opportunity to apply for refugee protection, regardless of their immigration status in the United States. The recent election of Donald Trump and his proposed shifts in U.S. immigration policy had transformed the upper Midwest, and one of its northernmost cities, Grand Forks, into a borderland that migrants had begun to pass through with more and more frequency, with the hope that Canada was more welcoming.

Both men listened and nodded at each other, glad to hear they were headed in the right direction.

Everything around them began to fade to a somnambulant blur, a territory of suburban sameness, the houses growing farther and farther apart, the intersecting rings of the Twin Cities dissolving into interrupted fields of fluorescence and then forests, appearing and disappearing in circular permutations beneath the highway lights. The car's heater continued to roar as the temperature outside dropped to eight degrees Fahrenheit, then six, then five as they drove farther north.

Passing over a bridge, both men watched the flurries as they continued to fall. The taxi slid and swerved once or twice. In the distance, up ahead, the highway seemed to fade beneath the accumulation of ice and snow. Razak looked out the passenger-side window as the cab maintained its erratic progress, hopeful the vehicle's momentum would carry him far from the difficulties of the past.

Before they knew it, three and a half hours had passed. Razak and Seidu remained silent at the beginning of the journey, then began sharing stories about how they had arrived in the United States and the paths of their individual journeys. Both men had been born in the neighborhood of Nima in Accra, both had been forced to flee to Brazil, both had survived the dangers of traveling through

Central America, both had been detained in the same Mexican immigration detention facility, both had presented themselves at the U.S. port of entry in San Ysidro. Both men had faced the systemic depravations and ignominy of lengthy detainment in the U.S, both had lost their asylum pleas, and both were certain they were about to be deported. An eerie calm engulfed the cab as it hurtled along the highway. In the front seat, Razak prayed. When he finished, he kissed the pocket-size Koran his friend had given him many years before, then quietly put it away.

It was around one in the morning when a green and silver sign appeared along the side of the road, announcing their approach to Grand Forks, North Dakota. Sometime later, perhaps a half hour or more, the taxicab pulled to the side of the road. Neither Seidu nor Razak had any idea where they were. In reality, the car was parked along the side of Interstate 29, somewhere north of the town of Joliette, many miles from the U.S-Canadian border.

The cab driver told Razak and Seidu how to proceed, that they should stay away from the right side of the highway where there was a river and where border agents were known to patrol, that they should go to the left side of the highway where the open fields led north. *Look for the lights of the border. Hide yourself in the snow whenever a vehicle passes. It will only be twenty minutes to get across, a half hour at the most.* Together both men thanked the cab driver and began to put on their gloves and hats. Outside it looked quiet, calm, as if the entire world had gone to sleep. The display on the car's dashboard said it was four degrees Fahrenheit. Seidu looked over at Razak, who had begun to zip up his coat.

The two men climbed from the cab. It was unlike anything either of them had seen before: a frozen wasteland, cold and shimmering, extending in every direction. Seidu and Razak began to walk toward the left side of the highway. Wind shook the cab as it slowly pulled away.

Everything before them—the unbroken sky, the bleakness of the icy terrain—seemed treacherous. But on the other side of those fields, everything would be different. The other world Seidu had dreamed of for so long existed just beyond the edge of his peripheral vision. Soon it would open up before him in unequaled glory.

Part One

Far from Home

1

Even as a boy, Seidu was aware that life in Ghana was a series of contradictions, and in order to survive, you had to keep moving to avoid every obstacle, every incongruity. The nation seemed to be a collision of postcolonial failed state and twentieth-century democracy, an explosive clash of modern politics and age-old traditions, of Western ideals and enduring tribalism, a country of dangerous, oftentimes irreconcilable paradoxes. Known formerly as the Gold Coast, Ghana was a former British colony that did not receive independence until 1957. With its extensive manufacturing, mining, and shipping operations, it was a country that had always struggled with its identity; first as a community of adjacent tribes oppressed by the British, then as an independent nation with a series of unsettling military coups, then as a democracy approaching the new millennium with a well-documented history of bribery, political cronyism, police corruption, and drug-smuggling. The people of Ghana witnessed these tragedies with the same patience that many citizens of the world are forced to employ whenever their political system blatantly favors one social group over the other. When it was the other political group's turn in office, old indignities resurfaced and the same cycle of recriminations played out, regardless of the acronym of the party.

Ghana continues to be a contradiction—caught somewhere

between its need for economic development and its complicated colonial past. It is a nation ruled by commerce and trade, some of which is illegal—drugs, guns, counterfeited goods—while at the same time, it publicly aspires to be seen as a fervently religious nation, with 68 percent of the population identifying as Christian and another 16 percent identifying as Muslim. Ghanaian politicians often invoke God in their speeches, while public laws leverage the majority's Christian beliefs. Although most Ghanaians speak several local dialects, children in schools throughout the capital of Accra are taught to read and write in English. Even more surprising, members of Ghana's parliament operate within their interpretation of the British system of self-rule, an outdated form of representative government that, even in the United Kingdom, favors the wealthy and well-connected.

Accra is one of the country's greatest paradoxes—a sprawling, relentless metropolis that calls many of these unresolved differences into focus. With over 2 million people, all situated on the Atlantic coast of West Africa, this capital city is the most populous region of Ghana. Many of the political elites, the military, and the wealthy inhabit the East Legon neighborhood, bringing money back from a number of extralegal sources abroad while hundreds of thousands of other Ghanaians live only a few miles away in the neighborhood of Nima, one of the fiercest slums in the modern world, oftentimes without access to clean drinking water or electricity. Open sewers carry human excrement past residential dwellings. Muddy orange roads are sometimes overtaken by piles of garbage. In those parts of the city, children, entire families who migrate from the rural parts of the country, sleep in wooden sheds or out on the street.

Gold-filigreed Mercedes rarely pass these neighborhoods, where fried yams, boo-froot, and akkala bake in the sun in open-air markets. As Seidu hurried through the market as a boy, it seemed to him that everything was for sale—spools of fabric, used tires, appliances—the stalls echoing with the joyous ferocity of his country, though for the families of Nima, there did not seem to be any sense of change, any hope for the future, no matter what was being bought or sold.

Today 25 percent of Ghanaians live below the poverty line, making it nearly impossible to escape the economic class they are born into. You can live in a free country, but you are not truly free unless you have the opportunity and financial means to express that freedom. And unless you are a politician, in the military, or have money, the state—which purports to be a democracy—has no use for you. This glaring disparity between wealth and poverty affects every transaction, informs every conversation, every glance.

The city, the country itself, resists resolution. You will not find its center anywhere on a map, because it exists in past, present, and future tense, always changing, always going backward and forward at the same time. Try to locate Ghana, try to find the spirit of the country and its people, and you become lost, because it is not nor has ever been one thing. By its very nature, it ignores interpretation, simplification. If there is a center to Ghana at all, it is a paradox itself, an unopened flower in a nest of nettles, a diamond buried in a hill of refuse, a beautiful song echoing from a dark alley.

Born in Nima in 1992, Seidu was a quiet though energetic child. As a boy, he recognized some of the disparities that surrounded Ghana and decided he would devote himself to football, practicing every day after school, certain the sport would be the thing that would help him transcend the difficult circumstances of his family's economic situation.

During the 1990s, Seidu's father, Mohammed, worked at a local travel agency where he prepared visas and other documents while his mother, Hawa, had a vegetable stall in the market. Together his parents made just enough money for the family to survive. Their house had one bedroom—Seidu shared a bed with his brothers, Kamal and Faisal, while his sister, Ayisha, slept with their parents.

The year Seidu turned ten, he surprised all of his classmates when he volunteered for his elementary school's football team. Before class and during recess, he would often sit and watch the other boys playing football, studying how they moved, what they did with their bodies. In the shadows of the Kanda Estate school building, with its failing roof and collapsing plaster walls—the paint fading and peeling in the shape of gladioli—he dreamed of being a professional football player, a champion like Ghanaian superstar Abedi Pele. He never played football at school because he knew if he got his school uniform dirty, he would be beaten by his teacher.

Playing for the interschool team finally gave Seidu the opportunity to show his classmates and his community just how committed to football he was. On the day of the match, he was assigned to defensive midfield, the position he most enjoyed. He looked up, saw his older brother, Kamal, sitting in the stands, and grinned. Although the game was a tight one, Seidu worked hard to keep the ball away from his team's goal, sending it flying back each time it came near. He began to get tired, but stayed focused, trying to follow every instruction his coach shouted from the sideline. Seidu's team eventually scored and won 1–0. When the game was over, Seidu looked at the sidelines again and saw Kamal, standing on his feet, cheering.

After the success of the interschool team, Seidu started playing at local soccer academies, in pickup games with friends at nearby fields, and in scrimmages against neighbors in the street. He continued practicing on his own until, at age thirteen, he was invited to play for a Division Three soccer team, the Montreal

Football Club. During his first season he helped the team win the league championship, scoring three goals as a midfield player.

That same year, Seidu's parents separated and the family continued to struggle financially. Not long after, Seidu began to have terrible stomachaches. The pain lasted for several days. One morning he couldn't stand up and could only crawl on his hands and knees. A strange abscess had formed along his stomach. Before long he began to vomit blood. Seidu's mother brought him to a clinic and then by taxi to a hospital, where he was given a CAT scan. At first, local doctors were unable to identify the reason for his illness. He was hospitalized for seven days without food or water. While there, nurses were instructed to try to drain the fluid that had formed around what they suspected might be an abdominal tumor. They extracted a yellowish pus, much to Seidu's horror and disgust. Finally, a surgeon arrived and, recognizing the protrusion as an umbilical hernia, operated, returning the tissue to the abdominal cavity, leaving a large, hook-shaped scar along the boy's belly button.

Seidu's mother was convinced the illness was no accident, that it was spiritual in nature, so she took the boy to a healer, an elder in the community. Although he had been raised as a Muslim, Seidu's family, like many other Ghanaians, often relied on traditional spiritual practices as well. That day, Seidu sat before the elder, who studied him, asked questions, then looked at his body. The spiritualist determined someone in the boy's extended family had put a curse on him, though he would not reveal who it was. He told Seidu that he was lucky to have survived. He gave the boy a special soap—mixed with traditional herbal medicine—to gain protection from further spiritual attacks, a short prayer to repeat each night before bed, and a charm—a small scroll of paper wrapped in white string—which the boy was to place beneath his pillow to keep evil spirits away before he went to sleep.

Seidu treated these objects seriously, believing in their power, using the soap, repeating the words, sleeping with the charm under his pillow, to avoid endangering his future.

When Seidu was fourteen, Kamal—ten years older—met someone online, a Greek American woman named Maria. Through their correspondence, the two developed a romantic relationship and decided to meet in person in Greece. After spending several weeks together, the couple decided to get married. Kamal called home to Accra and announced the news. Seidu and his family told Kamal that they loved him and supported his decision. Days later, Kamal returned to Ghana and went to the embassy to obtain a visa and soon joined his wife in Florida in the U.S.

The United States became something real for Seidu then, more than just a place he sometimes saw on TV or in films—something faraway, distant, but possible, attainable. All he needed to do now was to keep practicing, playing as hard as he could.

By the age of fifteen, Seidu had gotten his primary school certificate and had secretly stopped going to school, concentrating all of his energies on football. That same year his father, Mohammed, emigrated to the United Kingdom to try to make money to send back home. Attempting to ignore his father's absence, Seidu committed to physically pushing himself harder than ever, training before and after grueling practice sessions and games with local teams. One day, his uncle Danjuma came from Spain to watch him play. After the match, his uncle called Seidu's father in England and told him his son was going to be a star. Not long after, Seidu's father sent a pair of soccer cleats from the U.K. to help spur the boy on.

Seidu's mother would still wake him to go to school. Oftentimes he would put on his school uniform but would then go play soccer at the football club instead. One day there was a PTA meeting, which Seidu's mother decided to attend. There she learned that Seidu had not been to class in months. When she returned from the meeting, she beat him. Seidu apologized for lying, but said it was because he had to.

It's because you've been playing football, his mother said. *Tell me the truth.*

I can't.

I'm not going to give you food, if you don't tell me the truth. Why are you not going to school?

Seidu admitted it was because he had been going to practice football.

You can do both, she told him. But Seidu knew it was unlikely. To go on to secondary education, he needed money to pay for high school. Seidu's mother called his father, who said they could not afford it at the moment. Seidu understood then that football was the only thing he could do to support himself and his family, although, at that moment, he was still not being paid to play.

Seidu continued playing for Montreal FC for another two years. Somehow the family survived with very little income, as did many families in Nima. Every few months they would call Seidu's father to ask for help, but there would be long periods when he was unable to send anything.

At the age of sixteen, Seidu was invited to join the Golden Tulip Football Club, a Division Two team, named after a local Lebanese hotel that was its sponsor. The Golden Tulip manager offered Seidu a new pair of cleats, a pair of socks, a set of jerseys, a bag of rice, and some money to take home to his family. Playing for a Division Two team would give Seidu a better opportunity to be seen by international scouts, as the team manager had helped other young men transition from playing for local clubs to playing for European teams. Team managers and team owners in Ghana both have a financial incentive to help place young football players in European or South American leagues, as they receive a bonus or percentage when the player's contract is sold from their club to a better-funded international team.

During a preseason game at Legon, the team manager put Seidu in as striker because of his height—at sixteen, he was taller than most of the other boys. It was the first time Seidu ever played that position, and he performed well, scoring a goal.

After the match, a European scout for a Scottish football club gave his business card to Seidu's manager. He wanted to talk about the possibility of Seidu playing in Europe.

Seidu was overjoyed. He and his manager called the scout, who explained that he wanted to help Seidu come to Scotland to play for a local club. The man promised to take care of Seidu's future in the European leagues. He then asked if Seidu had a passport.

"I don't," he told the scout. The man told him to apply for a passport and then paid the substantial sum required to have it processed, more than $100. Seidu prepared to go to Europe. A few days before he was set to leave, the scout called again, having discovered Seidu was only sixteen. Based on what he had seen on the field, the scout couldn't believe it.

"I thought you were nineteen. Your manager said you're nineteen. You play like an adult. Are you sure you're not older? Are you sure there's not some mistake?"

But it was too late to lie. Seidu's passport documented his birthdate, and no matter how much he would have liked to say otherwise, he knew there was nothing he could do to change it. Seidu was crushed. After the deal fell apart, he yelled at his coach, "Why? Why did you do this? Why didn't you tell me what you had done?"

Soon after, Seidu stopped going to practice, saying he had

injured his leg, believing his coach had lied in order to get a bonus for selling Seidu's player contract to a European team. Seidu
attended the first game of the season and watched his team win
from the sidelines. Eventually he reconciled with his coach, who
apologized for deceiving the Scottish scout.

Seidu continued to push himself harder and harder on
the field, even though he was almost never paid for his efforts.
Other, older players on the team inspired Seidu to continue to
outperform—players who themselves had played on the country's
premier teams. Like Seidu, these older players felt trapped by the
contracts at their clubs and were unable to advance in their profession due to the unfair practices of the GFA, the Ghana Football
Association, which favored the rights of team owners and managers over the rights of the players.

The Golden Tulip squad won second place in the league that
year and qualified for the playoffs, making it to the Division Two
finals, but lost during its single-elimination match. Afterward, a
prospective investor offered to help sponsor the team, and suggested offering cash bonuses for players and even purchasing a
new team bus. But the owner of the team declined, unwilling to
give up his percentage of the team's profits. The players once again
felt betrayed by the limitations of their team and the GFA and
soon stopped going to practice. All of Seidu's hard work seemed to
have been for nothing. Not long after, the Golden Tulip FC team
disbanded and Seidu would not play soccer competitively again
for half a year.

2

Six months passed. Seidu was playing in a local football tournament when an agent for a Division One team—Accra Great Olympics FC—offered him a spot in a two-week tryout. Great Olympics FC was part of the premier league in Ghana—the highest level of professional football in the country. It was an immense honor, and after many setbacks, Seidu felt he was once again moving closer to his goal of supporting himself and his family by playing football. As trials for the twenty-seven-man squad began, Seidu was determined to make the team. At every practice, he pushed himself to his physical limit, leaving everything on the field.

The team owner came to watch the last day of tryouts. Seidu outperformed some of the other players on defense while the owner was watching—clearing the ball out of the post in a confident, aggressive manner. Later the owner called the eighteen-year-old over, asked Seidu his name, and told him he was playing very well. Seidu was surprised, knowing how talented the other competitors were.

At the end of practice, the coach began reading the names of the squad; Seidu waited but did not hear his name. Finally, he was the nineteenth player to be announced. He was overcome, happy to be playing for such a well-known club.

The owner got Seidu's player card from the defunct Golden Tulip team and gave him a new contract.

Preseason began for the Division One team with Seidu making it to the starting eleven-man squad, playing against D'International at the Accra Sports Stadium, the biggest football venue in the city. Thirty-five thousand supporters came for the first preseason game, more people than Seidu had ever played in front of. Before the game, Seidu looked around the field, dressed in his blue and white uniform, nervous for the first time in his life. He was no longer playing midfield, but defense, in position five. The grass was stiff, the pitch hardened by years of play.

As the game began, Seidu lost himself in the movement of bodies and the velocity of the ball. Fans began chanting his name. At the eighty-seventh minute, just seconds before the end of the game, Seidu gave a quick pass to one of his teammates at midfield, who then passed it on to the striker, who finally scored a goal. The preseason game ended 1–0. Afterward, the coach congratulated the team and the president gave each of the players a cash bonus.

Once the league started in earnest, however, Seidu was benched. During the team's first regular season game, he watched anxiously from the sidelines. After the first half, the coach told Seidu to warm up. When one of his teammates on defense suffered an injury, Seidu entered the game as a substitute. Seidu had no idea what kind of magic they expected of him. The other team was already up 1–0. The Olympics team missed a couple of chances and soon lost the match, their first home game of the season. The fans, the coaches, everyone was furious. Walking out of the stadium, Seidu hid beneath his hooded sweatshirt in shame.

Coming back from that initial loss, the Greater Olympics team won the next five games in a row. Greater Olympics FC went on to have a triumphant season, and within two years, Seidu had become a fan favorite.

Seidu kept advancing through the Division One league, team by team. In 2014, at the age of twenty-two, he was playing for the

Nima Lenient International Football Club when he was asked to try out for the Criciúma Football Club in the city of Criciúma, Brazil. It was the first time he had been invited to go overseas for soccer. By then, Seidu was ready to make the leap to playing for a team outside of Ghana.

Criciúma was a highly regarded South American team that competed in the national league of Brazil; the club was famous for winning the Brazil Cup in 1991.

Tryouts would begin in June and last several weeks. Seidu would be accompanied to Brazil by the Lenient FC team manager; both the manager and the team owner would benefit financially if Seidu's contract were sold to the Brazilian club. After playing for so many years, Seidu felt an incredible pressure to succeed on behalf of his family, his team owner and manager, and his community.

While he was packing for the trip, he decided to leave the charm he had been given as a boy under his pillow. He had been told it would lose its protection if he tried to take it over a body of water.

As he landed in Brazil, he was certain his life was only beginning.

But he also carried a secret with him that threatened everything.

Seidu always knew he was attracted to other boys. At six, he developed strong feelings for Jamal, a boy from his neighborhood whom he sometimes played football with. Often the two boys would take a ball up to the pitch and practice or simply sit and talk. The feelings they had were unclear, yet powerful. Both eventually realized they were interested in more than a typical friendship.

Seidu was also aware of the danger and social stigma of being gay or lesbian or bisexual or transgender in a devoutly Christian and

Muslim country. Homosexuality of any form is illegal in Ghana, with mere accusations of being gay often leading to public beatings and harassment by other citizens and the police, sometimes ending in torture and even death. Once indicted, LGBT people in Ghana are subjected to a minimum of three years in prison, though sentences are often much harsher. Seidu had heard stories of other men accused of being gay being dragged from their houses, beaten by their neighbors, and later brutalized by the police.

In 2011, when Seidu was nine, anti-gay sentiment in Ghana seemed to intensify. Paul Evans Aidoo, the Western Region Minister of Ghana, ordered all LGBT people in the west of the country to be arrested, accusing the opposition party of signing up queer people for the upcoming election. Aidoo publicly called on family members, landlords, and neighbors to inform on citizens they suspected of being LGBT. News of Aidoo's statements reached the city of Accra and the neighborhood of Nima: "All efforts are being made to get rid of these people in the society."

That same year, John Atta Mills, the president of Ghana, pledged to never initiate or support any attempt to legalize homosexuality in Ghana. A few months later, in March 2012, a gang of men assaulted nine individuals they believed to be gay in Jamestown, a neighborhood of Accra. Innocent people were pulled from their homes and beaten with canes and sticks in the street. Although several of the victims filed complaints with the local police and a number of human rights organizations, no arrests were ever made.

When Seidu was twelve, a man from Nima was accused of being a homosexual. He was arrested and beaten by the police. Seidu saw the man's photograph in the newspaper; later, he passed the man on the street. He watched him limp away on a leg that had been ruined during the brutal police interrogation; it seemed his entire life had been destroyed. Even at that young age, Seidu

understood that this person could not change who he was, and
that no amount of force or terror or pain could force him to become someone different.

The same year Seidu was playing soccer for Juventus, a local
team for boys under the age of fourteen, one of his teammates
stopped coming to practice. It was as if the boy had simply vanished. Several days later, when the boy returned to practice, it was
clear that he had been badly beaten. His head was bandaged, his
leg and ankle fractured. The young man explained he been tortured by the police after being caught with another boy. The coach
listened sorrowfully, as did Seidu, who did not understand why a
child of any age would ever be tortured.

As Seidu got older, he recognized the very real threat of violence, the possibility of abandonment by his family, and the near
impossibility of finding work or a place to live if his secret were
ever discovered. He also understood that the country, the city,
his neighborhood of Nima were all a series of overlapping circles,
where the support of one's family was at the center. Individual
desires, including matters of sexual orientation and identity, were
considered unimportant when it came to the honor and approval
of the family.

Seidu and Jamal agreed that their relationship must be kept
hidden. They would go to the football pitch, knowing no one
would question their relationship if they were practicing soccer.
Sometimes they would stand on a darkened corner, speaking in
hushed tones. If they wanted to kiss, they would meet at night and
hide in the bushes. If they wanted to be intimate, they could be together in Jamal's room at his house whenever the situation allowed.

At fifteen, Seidu realized he was interested in girls as well. He
started dating a young woman named Ayisha. Sometimes Seidu
would spend hours with her, and Jamal would become jealous.

During these years he was careful to spend an equal amount of time with both Jamal and Ayisha. He had no doubt it was possible to love two people equally. He texted them frequently on his cell, and became intimate with them both. Although Jamal knew about Ayisha, Seidu was terrified when Ayisha asked why Seidu spent so much time with Jamal. Afraid his football career and his future would be ruined if she ever found out the truth, he denied everything, preferring instead to keep his bisexuality secret. Eventually, at the age of sixteen, Ayisha brought up the prospect of marriage. Seidu quietly argued that until he could support himself and a wife, marriage was out of the question. He had no plans for his personal life, other than to keep dating both of them. Everything about this felt natural. It was who he was, at heart. He did not feel he was lying.

But in Brazil, something went wrong. Everything came to light.

After several weeks of tryouts in Criciúma, he made the mistake of believing that he was his own person, that he had become someone else entirely. Living in the hotel near the soccer stadium, he thought he had left those feelings of fear and desperation somewhere far behind.

One morning, after his soccer trials had been completed, he found himself in bed with another man. Lying beside this stranger, Seidu enjoyed the sound of unfamiliar birds outside the window, their names not yet known. The light slanting through the window, bright and warm. The feeling of someone else's breath upon his cheek. He could imagine a life of freedom, of acceptance, of quiet possibilities. Then there was the knock at the door and the unexpected voice of his team manager shouting, after which nothing would be the same.

~~~~~~~

A half hour later, the landscape continued to appear infinite, its harshness made more imposing by the freezing cold. Between several violent gusts of wind, Seidu looked down at his watch. He turned to Razak and remarked on how far they had already come. *We've been walking for more than a half hour*, he said. *It doesn't feel like we're getting any closer. There still aren't any lights.*

Razak nodded. *He said for us to keep going until we saw the border.*

What if he was wrong? What if we went the wrong way?

Maybe we were farther than he thought.

Should we turn back?

Razak shook his head, pulling the knitted cap down over his forehead. *We can't go back. Let's walk for another twenty minutes and see where we're at.*

Okay.

Just don't stop moving.

Seidu nodded, unsure if Razak could even see it, and then continued on.

Where are you going? What are you doing? What have you done to yourself?

One foot in front of the other, step after step, the wind obscured everything before Seidu's eyes. He pulled his ball cap down over his face and braced himself against the forceful blasts of frigid air, searching for a flash of gold, of silver, of any color, of any kind.

But the world before them, and behind, was white, plain, and unkind. There were no border lights anywhere. It seemed unlikely, but somehow they had gone the wrong way. Now they were lost, alone in the cold.

Up ahead the drifts of snow rose from their thighs up to their waists. They descended deeper into the accumulation of wintry ice. Seidu felt his legs, his hands begin to shiver, his eyes and mouth no longer able to move. He had never felt so far from what he knew and was afraid of what lay ahead.

A moment later another torrent of wind swept across the icy plain and blew Seidu's baseball cap from his head. Both men turned and watched it fly high into the dark and then disappear somewhere behind them. *My hat! My hat!* Seidu cried. Razak turned and dug around in the snow.

It's gone, Razak said. *I'm sorry. I don't see it anywhere.*

Seidu silently cursed. Razak put a hand on his shoulder. *We need to keep going. We have to be close.*

Seidu nodded and put his gloved hands over his ears and at the same time surveyed the frozen wasteland, feeling the frigid temperatures begin to creep into his muscles and bones. All he could do was let his body take over, doing what it had always done, letting his feet, his momentum carry him toward a fate not yet known.

An hour later, it was almost three in the morning and they were nowhere near the border. An hour and a half had passed since the two men had left the warmth of the vehicle, fighting against the wind and snow, only to arrive at nothing. It was now clear that not only were they lost, they had also been taken advantage of. The taxi driver had left them out in the cold to quit or falter or die, miles from any sort of help. It was also apparent they were still far from the lights of any border.

As the wind continued to blow about them with a fierce chill of minus twenty degrees Fahrenheit, the air temperature continued to drop, sending a torrent of blistering cold against their unprotected skin. Both men were underdressed for the weather, even with extra layers on. Nothing in their experience—traveling from Ghana to South America, then up to the States—had prepared them for this.

Even at its worst, Ghana, an equatorial nation, rarely got much colder than seventy degrees Fahrenheit. The other countries both men had passed through on their way to the United States were also tropical, with rainy and dry seasons, but nothing resembling the kind of frigid air they were now confronting. Neither man had ever been this cold before nor had ever experienced walking through the wind and snow at such dismal temperatures.

It was their disbelief that kept them moving, perhaps; the shock, the indignity of finding themselves in a situation so outrageous, so grim.

Razak prayed as he kept marching forward, forcing his way against the cold. *Please forgive me for whatever I have done. Please help us get to our destination safely.* Again and again, as a young man, he had found himself in trouble for questioning the way things were in Ghana, but had always discovered a way to press on. In truth, surrounded by the limitlessness of the snowy fields, he now felt like giving up. There was no way to know how far they were from the border, or if they would ever reach it at all.

One foot in front of the other, they continued on.

One half hour after that, it began to snow once more, the night becoming a cascading curtain of fearsome white. Beginning with soft, large flakes, the precipitation soon turned brittle and icy. It collected everywhere—on their faces, on the shoulders of their coats, in between their wrists and gloves.

At first it was beautiful, an unfamiliar miracle. But soon their vision was totally obscured and their boots and shoes were soaking wet, as were the rest of their clothes.

Out of nowhere the night itself had become a fortress, a mountain, an obstacle they had to pass through. Razak carried on, looking back often for Seidu. Wind carried the precipitation in great gusts, in peaks and valleys of blowing ice against his face. What had only moments before appeared as a flat boundary—frightful in its equanimity—had now taken on three dimensions, was now a vortex of swirling, jagged sleet. It seemed impossible to keep going.

At some point, a fierce gust of wind sent Seidu's gloves flying from his hands. It was surreal, almost mythical, to see both gloves fly away into the darkness. It made no sense that the wind should be so strong, so unforgiving, like something from a folktale or children's story. Seidu immediately cried out for help. Both men searched for the gloves but were unable to recover them. Razak watched as Seidu shoved his bare hands beneath the armpits of his coat and trampled on.

Later the younger man's words interrupted Razak's thoughts.

We're lost, Seidu said, stopping suddenly. *We should back go to the highway.*

No. We have to be getting closer, Razak argued.

It's been too long. The cab driver lied to us. We're going to die out here. We have to go back to the highway.

No, Razak said, shaking his head. *They'll send us back. They'll send us home to Ghana. Do you want to get sent back?*

No.

Then we need to keep moving.

Razak made his way forward as Seidu fell behind once again. On and on they went across the frozen plain. Their shadows, the figures they made as they crossed through the sheets of falling snow, the repetitive physical movement of the young man walking behind him, the eerie, impenetrable silence all called forth a single memory in Razak's mind. Between the cadaverous husks of fallen trees, he stumbled onto a scene he did not recognize, bringing to the surface a single, forgotten image from the past.

3

The body was lying in front of a neighbor's house, before a closed metal gate, dressed in military garb—black boots, green field pants. Although someone had covered its face, a small crowd of twenty or thirty people had already gathered and were standing on the street, quietly staring. Razak had been walking to school. He was thirteen years old and living at his grandmother's house in Santa Maria, a neighborhood in Accra. It was 1996, and his parents were traveling in Nigeria. When he awoke each morning, he put on his school uniform, a white shirt and blue pants. His uncle—his mother's younger brother, Danjuma, a year older but shorter than him—also got ready for class. When both boys stepped outside that morning, they saw that the road was muddy.

It was 10:00 a.m. During the rainy season, school always started later to allow extra time to travel along the slippery roads. Other children—whose parents could afford the five dollars per month for the school bus—waited near the bus stop, while Razak and Danjuma began the long walk, passing these luckier classmates in silence.

A few blocks later, they saw a crowd gathered in front of a three-story building, which was surrounded by a fence with a wide, metal gate.

Razak had noticed the house before, admired its height, had seen the fence and locked gate, had always assumed a politician or member of the military lived there. But now a body was lying beside the front gate. People on their way to the market or work paused to look at the odd shape the body made. Mothers led their children quickly past, chastising them for staring. But Razak and his uncle were on their own. Razak stepped closer and realized what he was seeing, that the shape was not moving, that it was a body now and no longer a person.

The boys moved even closer, sneaking between the adults to take in the uncompromising mystery, to make sense of the vital distinction between life and death. Elders were gathered there, also watching, and cut their eyes at the boys, telling them to get back. But Razak kept looking and thinking.

Why?

Why is this body lying here?

This man, he works for the government. How did a military man get killed in front of his own house?

How did this happen?

Other onlookers whispered but Razak did not look away.

For almost all of Razak's childhood, politics in Ghana had been an armed battle, marked by instability and violence. After gaining its independence, Ghana experienced a series of coups, with elected officials frequently replaced by military commanders, usually with dire economic consequences.

In 1978, Lieutenant General Frederick Kwasi Akuffo led a coup against the elected head of state, General Ignatius Kutu Acheampong. One year later, on June 4, 1979, a junior military commander, Flight Lieutenant Jerry John Rawlings, led a counter-coup against Akuffo's regime. The coup was at first unsuccessful and Rawlings was arrested and sentenced to death. A speech he gave during his trial appealed to many of his countrymen, and sometime later, a number of his military counterparts helped Rawlings escape from jail. He then led a second coup, which resulted in the death of Akuffo and left Rawlings in charge. Afterward, Rawlings, along with his political and military associates, formed the AFRC, the Armed Forces Revolutionary Council, and attempted to address the social inequalities and corruption that had gripped Ghana for so long.

"We of the Armed Forces Revolutionary Council, during our short stay in power, have demonstrated openly what many people had only suspected before, namely that the holding of office in government in this country had, in almost all cases, been used to plunder the wealth of the nation," Rawlings publicly stated.

At first, the Ghanaian public appeared to be largely in favor of the AFRC's second coup. Elections were held in 1981, organized by the AFRC. AFRC candidate Hilla Limann won, though months later, the AFRC would overthrow his regime and install Rawlings in his place. That same year the Constitution of Ghana would be officially suspended. All political parties were banned and the country descended into chaos.

Under pressure from a nationwide hunger strike and prevailing international disapproval, Rawlings finally approved a second Constitution of Ghana but did not allow elections until 1992, ten years later. Rawlings, with the support of his political party, the NDC—the National Democratic Congress—won the election amid complaints of vote tampering. He was reelected again in 1996, continuing more than twenty years of social inequality, bribery, cronyism, military rule, and corruption—serving as the political and social backdrop for Razak's entire childhood.

Are all countries like this? Razak had often wondered, seeing the inequities in his neighborhood. Now, staring at the body before him, it was difficult to look away. Everything that was wrong with his country was lying there at his feet. Other boys from school appeared and joined the crowd but Razak hardly noticed.

After a while, Danjuma nudged him and said, *Come on, we're going to be late.*

One by one, the boys made their way down the road, talking to each other.

One boy said, *I never saw a body before.*

Another boy said he had been afraid of the body. But Razak felt frightened for other reasons.

He remembered the expressions of the Ghanaian soldiers on parade each week, crossing through town, singing songs, carrying their rifles. He thought of how you were not supposed to move until they passed, how you were not supposed to speak to them unless they spoke to you, how the best thing to do was to remain still and silent.

He also recalled being forced to climb down into the gutter whenever a military vehicle crossed. He knew if he and his friends refused to give up the road, the soldiers would climb out and beat them.

The other boys kept joking as they walked, but Razak had begun to think.

If a member of the military can be killed and left in the road, in front of his own house, then who will be safe in this country?

He was late for school. There was a sense of gloom in the sky and his heart was heavy, but not because of the impending rain.

4

Even as a child, Razak recognized an essential unfairness in many of the disparities of Ghana as they manifested themselves in everyday objects, in the struggles of daily life. Extension cords crisscrossed the sky in neighborhoods where electricity had to be improvised. Used gasoline jugs carried drinking water. Clouds of exhaust from motorbikes rose from the nearby market. In Nima, the crime rate was dramatically higher than in other parts of the city. Every Friday he would attend prayers at the Nima Central Mosque. The front of the impressive building would be crowded with beggars. As young as he was, Razak could sense an inherent inequality that informed his entire upbringing.

When Razak was six, his father, Mohammed, a former truck driver and enterprising trader in food items at the market, took a second wife. Polygamy is legal in Ghana, and the production of healthy children is a signifier of familial and financial success and also offers a more functional purpose. Children are expected to care for their parents in their old age, providing both economic and emotional support. Razak's mother, Safiya, was often sickly, sometimes had fevers, and had been unable to produce any other children. She agreed with Razak's father when he suggested taking a second wife. Razak's father married Hija Kandy Ali, whose brother was connected to a number of local politicians in the NDC party. Razak soon began to call his father's new wife "Mami."

The growing family moved into a compound house, a rectangular, one-level building that featured a small open-air area in the center, surrounded by a series of individual rooms. Bisecting laundry lines crossed the center of the building where cooking and other household tasks were usually performed. Razak's father intended to be egalitarian after they moved into the compound house, drawing up a schedule so that he would spend one week at a time with each wife.

But Razak—more than six years older than the younger half-siblings who were soon born—struggled for his father's attention. Razak's mother's status was greatly diminished once Razak's siblings appeared—first a boy, Mubarak, then another boy, Jamal, then a third, Baba, and eventually two younger sisters.

One day when Razak was thirteen, his two mothers had a fierce argument, shouting at each other, calling one another names while the children were at school.

When he came home, Razak's mother, Safiya, told him what happened. *She said I am useless as a wife because I can't give him children.* Razak was incredibly disturbed, certain that something monumental had shifted within the family. Some time later, Razak approached his father and said he needed to speak with him about what was happening in the house. His father was furious.

You are not the person to come and ask me about this, his father said. *It's not your place. I am the head of the family. Who are you to question me?*

One of Razak's neighbors in Nima had a television: their son had emigrated to Austria and had sent one back from Europe. After school, Razak would go by his neighbor's house and catch a soccer game or watch music videos. One day, American hip-hop was playing on the small screen. Razak studied the images of men and women partying, dancing, enjoying life.

The man who owned the TV looked over at Razak and said, *Look. Americans are always happy. Look at how they laugh. They are black like you, having fun.*

Razak continued to stare.

Look at us, the man said. *Look at us here in Ghana. We don't feel that way.*

Razak watched the screen and slowly agreed.

At some point near the end of his childhood, Razak's father had begun investing in local land, buying ten acres east of the inner city in Abokobi. The land took on mythical dimensions in the family's life; it was sometimes mentioned but never discussed outright. Razak wondered if the property had anything to do with the tension in the house between the two families.

When he was seventeen, Razak decided to move out and live with his best friend Haziz's family. Each night he would return to the compound house to have dinner with his mother, whose health continued to be difficult. It was during this time that Haziz presented him with a small Koran, which could fit into a pocket. Razak was deeply moved by the gesture.

You've given me something that I've needed in my life, he told his friend.

The book became something he would always carry with him as he navigated the unpredictable situation between his parents and half-siblings. It was something that gave him stability and peace.

Months later, Razak needed $200 in order to take the qualifying exams to continue to the next grade level at school. He was afraid to ask his father and instead went to his father's business partner and told him he needed money to take the test. Chagrined, the business partner gave the boy the exam fees. The next day Razak hurried to school and paid the deposit for the test.

Later that same day, Razak's father appeared in the headmistress's office, deeply aggrieved, looking for his son. Razak was called down to the office and stood before his father.

Why did you ask my business partner for money? his father asked.

Razak was unable to answer at first. Finally, he said, *Because I needed money for the exams.*

Humiliated, Razak's father demanded the school refund the money and the headmistress was forced to oblige. Razak wandered home, crying, and told his mother what had happened. Over the course of the next few days, she was able to borrow from relatives and sell just enough at the vegetable stall in the market to pay for his exams.

But that deep pang of embarrassment and hurt, knowing Mohammed had refused to pay for his schooling, caused a deep rift between Razak and his father. Worse, the resentment he felt toward his half-siblings was building. *What is fair about a system of schooling that allows for only those wealthy enough to be educated? What is equal about a country where only those with political power and money are allowed to survive?*

Eighteen years old, Razak did his best to ignore the unfair practices of his house and homeland and left school to get a job working at a barbershop, cutting hair and cleaning up. He started to dream about owning his own business. At the time, Razak's friend Ahmad, who sometimes performed in local hip-hop shows, mentioned how he could repair anything electric. Razak saved up money for two years and was able to rent a store down the road from the barbershop. The shop, called Razak and Ahmad's

Electronics Store, opened when he was twenty. Together the two friends repaired refrigerators, microwaves, and electric toasters. Local music would play from the store's speakers and men from the neighborhood would pull up chairs in front of the shop and spend the day, chatting, talking politics. If there was a customer at the barbershop, Razak would run down the street, cut his hair, and then run back.

One day Razak's father stopped by the repair shop, asking him to come to dinner at the compound house. It was the first time his father had been to the shop. By then his father stayed with Razak's stepmom, Hija, exclusively, which further complicated Razak and his father's relationship. Seeing the opportunity to mend their broken trust, Razak agreed to dinner. It seemed as if his father was attempting to recognize him as an adult. Over the next several months, Razak continued to grow his business, zipping back and forth from the barbershop to the electronics repair store on a motorcycle. Accra was like another place then. All the songs on the radio, people calling out on the street, everyone excited about the possibilities of living.

When Razak was twenty-one, he rented a room in a compound house in the neighborhood of Kanda. One day after work he was in his room when a young woman appeared. She was there to meet Eva, the landlord's daughter. The unknown girl with a young, bright face was wearing jeans and a T-shirt, her head covered with a blue scarf. He watched as she said goodbye to her friend.

Razak immediately approached Eva and said, *I saw your friend. Do you know if she has a boyfriend?*

Eva was suspicious. *She's single. What do you want from her?*

I just wanted to talk to her. I know she came to see you. I was just hoping to get some more information. Can you tell me her name?

Cynthia.

There was something about the girl's name that was both pleasing and serious, the sound of someone you could rely on.

Sometime later Eva told Cynthia that Razak had asked about her. Cynthia seemed intrigued and told Eva to tell him hello.

Three or four days later, Razak was in his room when he noticed Cynthia had once again come to visit. After hanging out with Eva for a while, Cynthia finally introduced herself.

Hello.

Hello, Razak said. *I saw you last time but I didn't have a chance to talk to you. I talked to Eva and she said you were single. That's why I wanted to talk to you.*

What did you want to talk about?

I just saw you and I like you. I'd like you to be my girlfriend.

She looked at him and said, *That's not going to be easy. All men are liars.*

At first Razak was taken aback and didn't know how to respond. Finally, he said, *How can you know unless you give me a chance to prove myself?*

Okay, I'll give you my number. We can talk and see what happens.

Soon the two began texting and speaking on the phone, getting to know the intimate details of one another's lives. Cynthia was raised as a Christian but had grown up in Nima, where she lived at her grandmother's house. Cynthia's parents had passed away years before, first her father, then her mother, both from unknown illnesses, and so, like Razak, she had been unable to continue going to school. At that time, Cynthia was a waitress at a restaurant and was going to hairdressing school, working hard to support herself and her family.

Over weeks and months, the two young people became a couple. They would go to Frankie's for fast food a few times a week. They would walk together and get shawarma, which it turned out Cynthia loved, from a nearby restaurant. They talked about religion and family. He explained his faith to her. Whatever cologne he happened to be using, she would want to try it out. Soon his friends began to ask why he was spending so much time with her. He ignored their questions. Although he made sure to eat dinner with his mother as often as he could, Razak was making plans, thinking about expanding the repair business, even opening a second location.

Three months after they started dating, Razak introduced Cynthia to his family during a marriage celebration for one of his relatives at his father's compound house. Bravely, Razak introduced Cynthia to his grandmother as his girlfriend.

His grandmother stared at him and said, *You know in Islam, girlfriends are not allowed?*

Razak nodded. *I know, but I want to marry her.*

You want to marry her? his grandmother repeated.

Razak never said anything like that out loud before. Certainly Cynthia had heard, but she hadn't said anything. Everyone seemed surprised by Razak's admission.

Days later, Razak's grandmother called Cynthia on the phone and said, *Do you know what Razak told me?*

Cynthia pretended not to know. *No.*

Razak's grandmother repeated his intention to marry Cynthia. Later, Cynthia called him and asked, *Are you serious? You're thinking about marriage?*

Of course, he said.

After that, Razak began saving money to pay for Cynthia's dowry, which was 1 million cedi, equal to several thousand dollars.

When Razak's mother returned a few weeks later from visiting her sister in the neighboring country of Togo, Razak explained his intention to get married. His mother, having not yet met Cynthia, offered to help pay a part of the dowry. The engagement moved along quickly.

Razak called Cynthia and said, *Look. We have different traditions. As a Muslim, I need to send my people to meet your family.*

Okay, I'll talk to my grandmother and aunt.

The women from Razak's family—his mother's sister and his father's sister and his two half-sisters—went to meet Cynthia's family to discuss the terms of the marriage. As was the local tradition, Cynthia's family had a list of requirements—mostly goods and objects—that they hoped Razak's family would buy in exchange for Cynthia's hand in marriage. Razak's family agreed to everything, except their request of alcohol, which as Muslims they chose not to purchase. Instead, they settled on paying the equivalent in cash.

Later his family members brought the list of requirements to Razak and his mother and together they went through each request, deciding what he would buy and what she would help him acquire. His life began to find a shape then, all things falling into place.

After more than two hours of wandering in the snow, the men were still lost, still some unknowable distance from the border. Razak glanced back and saw Seidu holding his bare hands over his exposed ears, forcing himself to carry on.

The temperature continued to drop to minus two degrees Fahrenheit with a wind speed of twenty-five miles per hour. As the two men marched ahead, they began to feel the punishing effects of negative wind chill—the dire consequences of air speed and frigid temperatures upon the surface of the human skin. Blood in the skin radiates a thin layer of warmth along the surface of the body, so that someone facing seventy-five degrees Fahrenheit without wind can actually have a skin temperature higher than the surrounding air. But if wind carries the heat away, a person experiences heat loss more quickly than their body can produce it.

The colder the temperature and the more forceful the wind, the greater the heat loss from the surface of the skin. The human brain and its nerve endings quickly perceive this loss, closing down blood cells in the extremities and skin, signaling for more blood to flow to internal organs in order to stay alive. This shutting down of cells in the extremities often leads to the ghastly phenomenon of frostbite, the condition in which skin and the tissue below the skin actually freeze.

At a wind chill of minus twenty-seven degrees Fahrenheit, these body parts—hands, toes, ears—will freeze in approximately half an hour. The skin itself will not start to freeze until it is below thirty-two Fahrenheit, as most skin cells contain a number of compounds, including salt, that help lower their freezing point. But with the persistence of wind and surrounding subzero temperatures, any exposed skin and the tissue beneath it can begin to freeze within thirty minutes, with permanent damage occurring within ninety minutes.

Neither Razak nor Seidu had ever heard of frostbite; they had no idea of the mortal danger they were now facing. After more than two hours out in the cold, they had entered a liminal zone, had just passed the point at which their bodies might never recover.

Burying his gloved hands in the armpits of his jacket, Razak marched on, feeling a sharp pain in his toes and ankles with every step. It felt as if the skin, the tissue itself was burning with a dolorous sensation. His body, after more than two hours in the frigid air, had begun the initial stages of hypothermia, his core temperature dropping far below normal levels, his physical coordination and mental functions becoming weaker and weaker, yet he did not know it.

At some point Razak heard a sound far behind him. It was Seidu's voice echoing from somewhere in the distance. By then the younger man had fallen dozens of yards behind. Razak looked back into the darkness, wind whipping at his unprotected face. He adjusted his hood and then squinted. Seidu had stopped moving and was bending over, holding his bare hands over his eyes. Razak slowly trekked backward through his own boot prints and then began to help wipe the snow from Seidu's face.

It was unlike anything Razak had ever seen—an image from a horror movie, some terrible dream. Seidu's eyes had become completely frozen, his face crusted over with snow. Without his baseball cap, without a hood, there was nothing to keep the snow and ice from covering Seidu's eyelids. Now that his gloves were also gone, there was ice and snow frozen between Seidu's fingers and he could no longer bend them.

Razak murmured to him, huddling close. *The border has to be up ahead. If you can't see, call out to me, okay? Just follow my voice. This is how we're going to make it. We can do this together.*

Seidu nodded and Razak started off, leading the way once more. Moments later, a faint light appeared somewhere up ahead, then vanished just as quickly.

Did you see it? Did you? Razak called out.

The light flashed again.

Do you see it? Razak shouted.

Seidu was unable to respond. He dug at his eyes, clawing the snow from where it had settled, freezing his eyelids shut. His hands were curled into cruel talons, ice and snow creeping between the fingers to bind them together. The younger man looked up again. A point in the distance began to tremble. He began to move faster now, calling ahead to Razak.

I see it! I see it!

The wind began to intensify, pushing hard against their bodies. Each step sank them deeper into the snow. Every time they set a boot or shoe down, their foot would become buried and they would have to use their bare fingers to dig their feet out. One by one, step by step, they dragged themselves through the snow, their hands and feet burning from the cold.

As they climbed along toward the distant flash of light, a particularly volatile rush of snow and wind blew Razak's gloves from his hands, the two objects being lifted high into the sky before vanishing into the dark.

Somewhere up ahead the darkness broke again. A color, the faint flash of light, then it was gone.

5

Months after Razak's engagement, when he was twenty-two, a devastating flood tore through Nima during the rainy season. Many people were displaced from their poorly constructed homes, which were unable to withstand the overpowering rain. Razak spoke to some of the people from his community and decided to go to Mustapha Ahmed, the member of parliament (MP) who represented the Ayawaso East region, to ask for help in arranging temporary housing.

When he arrived at the government building, Razak could see Mustapha, with his black glasses and short black hair, sitting in his office behind a thick pane of glass. Razak watched as Ahmed talked to the security guard, who then came out and told Razak that Ahmed was not there. Razak began to complain vigorously and the security guard forced him to leave, threatening to call the police. It was just another example of how the political structure in Ghana did not seem to serve the people, as if the MP somehow existed in some other world, beyond the complaints of his constituents. Razak began to wonder how he, and the other people in his community, could confront such an unjust system. It was only the beginning of his problems with Ahmed.

By the time Razak was twenty-four, his half-siblings had become involved in local politics. Razak's father's second wife, Hija, had a brother with close connections to the NDC, the National Democratic Congress, the political group who held power at the national level during most of Razak's youth. His three younger half-brothers followed their uncle's lead and volunteered on behalf of the NDC. Before every election, his half-brothers would put up signs throughout the neighborhood, appear at rallies, and organize other young people to vote for Mustapha Ahmed, the NDC candidate for parliament. Although the voting age in Ghana was eighteen, the youth in Nima—sometimes as young as fourteen—were encouraged by certain candidates to vote illegally, using forged or improper voting cards. Because there was no central, computerized data infrastructure in Ghana, voting fraud was rarely prosecuted.

The political system in Ghana is rife with irreconcilable tensions, which often escalate into violent personal disputes, sometimes within the same political party. Mustapha Ahmed, who served as a dental officer in the Ghana Armed Forces before being elected to parliament in 2000, seemed to capture the country's inherent sense of discord. After a few years of contentious infighting within the NDC, Ahmed's personal Land Cruiser was vandalized during a primary election in 2006. NDC leader Jerry John Rawlings called Ahmed the same day to say, "It's fortunate your car was only broken into and not burnt," which suggested pro-Rawlings supporters were responsible for the damage—this from the leader of Ahmed's own party and a former president of the country. These kinds of intense provocations, often carried out by underage supporters of individual candidates, were not uncommon.

Razak was aware of his siblings' political ambitions but had no interest in politics himself, having never belonged to a single political party. It seemed no matter which group was in power, very little changed—the same politicians and military families thrived while the rest of the country, especially the neighborhood of Nima, continued to struggle.

In the repair shop, Razak would often discuss the state of the country and the lack of accountability for politicians. Razak was quick to criticize Ahmed's lack of interest in the neighborhood's nonexistent infrastructure, the uneven roads, the crumbling local school. But no matter how much he complained, every election still ended with the same result.

Mustapha Ahmed seemed to represent everything that was questionable about politics in Ghana. For years, Ahmed had been given a number of ministerial positions, although he had done little to confront the high levels of crime, illiteracy, unemployment, and difficult living conditions within his own region. The press frequently accused Ahmed of manipulating the youth from his constituency. In the 2008 election, it was said groups of young people from his region were taken to other parts of the country— to the Volta and Ashanti districts—to vote illegally and to help prop up failing NDC candidates. Ahmed was also accused of distributing computers to select schools in his district and doling out laptops and clothes to supporters. There were also a number of accusations of Ahmed illegally transferring property to NDC delegates and volunteers. Still, Ahmed won election after election, while Razak was once again frustrated by the acceptance of corruption by his half-siblings and others within the country.

A few months after the 2008 election there was a community meeting with several local community leaders and Ahmed as the region's MP. During the meeting, Razak got up and began to speak, criticizing the state of the local school.

You are taking care of yourself but not the community. Just look at the building, he said.

Ahmed grew angry. *Who are you to criticize me? What about the majority? Every time there's an election, I win it. The neighborhood and the people in Nima, they like me.*

By then Razak had given up almost any possibility of social equality for his neighborhood or his country.

In 2009, Razak's father became ill. Although he was only in his early sixties, he had developed diabetes and was facing several other mounting physical troubles. While his half-siblings were busy with politics, Razak did his best to come home and visit his father as often as he could.

At the end of that year, Razak and his father visited the land his father had purchased in Abokobi—ten acres, with each acre as big as seven or eight city blocks. It was enormous, and some of it was already being tended by local farmers. Razak could see how much the land meant to his father and what it would mean, one day, for him and his siblings.

Razak's father was hospitalized a few months later in January 2010. Doctors were unable to come up with any kind of specific diagnosis. Mohammed wanted to return to Bimbila, the small rural village in the north of Ghana where he had been born, to meet with a spiritualist to receive treatment. It was a day-and-a-half drive. Razak arranged to drive him north, staying for two weeks with his father, then returned to Accra to manage the electronic repair business.

On January 20, 2010, Razak received word that his father had passed away. Razak called his siblings and together the family organized a burial in the village near Bimbila. Razak's mother and stepmother did not attend, as local Islamic custom requires wives to mourn for their husbands for 120 days by staying within the family dwellings.

After his father's burial in Bimbila, Razak and his siblings returned to Accra. The family held a meeting to discuss their father's affairs. By then it was clear Razak's father had never drawn up a will. All the necessary documents regarding Mohammed's property were in Razak's stepmother's possession. Razak hoped the land could be divided equally, without contention. But neither his siblings nor Hija seemed willing to share the essential documents.

With his father dead, Razak had little connection to his father's second family. The fault lines and fractures within the family, their political disagreements and differences, soon became disturbingly apparent.

Islamic law in the region requires that no inheritance may be disbursed until one year after the death of a family member and that all property and assets must transfer from father to son, bypassing the female heirs of the family, including wives and mothers. All Razak could do was wait.

By the end of the year, his life would be in danger and the cloud of Ghana's political system would overshadow the entire world he had come to know.

By October 2010, ten months after Razak's father's death, the discussion with his siblings over the property was at a standstill. Unable to legally divide the land without their consent, and without his father's documents, Razak had no sense of how to plan for the future. He recognized the land had the power to change his life but felt trapped by the outdated system of laws his country ascribed to. It was as if he were constantly forced to live tied to the past.

On October 22, 2010, in the city of Aflao, on the border between Ghana and Togo, a cabdriver tried to cross from Ghana into Togo and failed to stop at a routine security check. Military intelligence officers pursued the cab on motorcycles and pulled the driver from his car. On his knees, the taxi driver begged for mercy. One of the intelligence officers, who worked for Ghana's immigration service, fired two rounds, one into the man's lower abdomen and the other into his back.

Local radio stations broadcast news of the incident. The community responded by blocking all major roads, setting trash and tires ablaze, damaging military intelligence vehicles, and chasing military intelligence officers from town with cudgels and knives. Rioting continued along the border for seven hours until the Ghanaian army was called in.

Razak, like many in the country, watched in horror as the scene was captured on television and later in the newspapers. He was certain the military intelligence officer would not be held accountable, would be released without an investigation. It was another reminder of the unfair system of justice in Ghana.

In January 2011, one year after his father's death, Razak called a meeting of his half-siblings to discuss the sale of his father's property. Local Islamic custom places the responsibility of disbursement of property upon the eldest son, and Razak took this responsibility seriously. He carefully argued the need to divide the land equally. By then each acre of land was worth $15,000 by itself, an incredible sum by the standards of the local economy. But Mubarak, Razak's half-brother, refused to entertain the thought.

No. We can't talk about the land, he said. *We can't divide up the property now.*

Why not? Razak asked.

There are six of us and you're only one person. We're not going to divide it.

Why?

Razak suspected Mubarak and his other half-siblings were working with Mustapha Ahmed, whom Razak believed planned to buy the land from his half-siblings for development, cheating Razak out of his inheritance. The initial discussion ended in insults and shouting.

After the argument, Razak did his best to explain the situation to Cynthia. She was concerned to see him so upset.

Why are they fighting you about the land?

This is a family issue. I don't want you to have to be dragged into it.

No. I'm part of the family now. I want to know.

I know, but I don't want you to be in danger if anything happens.

By then more than three years had passed since the couple had begun dating. Though they had yet to be married, Cynthia had moved in with Razak's mother to help care for her. The young couple was planning their wedding for December 2012, so that some of Cynthia's family could travel from Nigeria to be part of the ceremony. With the sale of the land held up, the couple's hopes and plans had become uncertain.

To help settle the dispute, Razak appealed to his mother, then his father's brother, Baba. The siblings met a week later with their uncle at the compound house.

Razak is right, his uncle said. *This is how we share our property, in the Islamic way, in the traditional way.*

We are not ready to share the property.

It's not about if you are ready. That's the law. It doesn't matter if you're ready or not.

No. We are not going to share the property.

Uncle Baba said, *Why are you saying this?*

This is what we decided.

Mubarak and the other half-siblings began to insult Razak's uncle, and once again refused to turn over the legal documents.

It doesn't matter if you have the documents, Razak's uncle said. *You can't take advantage of the land. The eldest son must be the one to sell it.*

Further discussions went nowhere. Afterward, Razak's uncle suggested that he go to the police. Razak began to fear that perhaps his siblings intended to harm him physically or remove him from the financial equation altogether. He had never had any involvement with the police before. Anxiously, he went to the local police station and presented his case.

I'm here to report a difficulty between me and my family members sharing property.

The police officer looked over at Razak and said, *We can't take care of this. Go back to your family yourself.*

What about if someone gets killed?

No one is killed so we cannot get involved. Go. Go back.

Razak went to the local Islamic community leader and explained what had been going on. In front of him, the community leader called his siblings, but none of them would pick up the telephone. The community leader recommended Razak return to the police.

Razak returned to the police station a second time and reviewed all the steps he had taken in order to resolve the land dispute.

A police officer looked at him and said, *Okay. We can take care of this. If you give us twenty-five hundred dollars, we can start an investigation.*

Why do I have to pay you before you investigate?

We don't want to involve ourselves in a family issue.

What are you here for? You're here for families. What if someone is killing his wife? What if someone is killing his son or daughter? You say you're not going to get involved because of a family issue? How can I pay money to you before you've even taken my statement?

Razak became suspicious that the police officers had been bribed by his siblings or Mustafa Ahmed. Razak went back to the Islamic community leader to report what had happened. The leader assured Razak he would get involved. Once again, the imam tried to call his siblings. Once again, none of them answered.

A few weeks later, Razak went to visit his mother at the compound house. He was sitting in front of her room when he saw his siblings arrive.

You think you can do something stupid by going to the police? We will end your life.

Razak's mother became incensed. *Why are you saying this?*

You better keep your mouth shut, one of his siblings replied.

You can say anything to me, Razak said. *But I'm not going to allow you to talk to my mother like that.*

One of his half-brothers, Jamal, punched Razak in the face. Razak began fighting back. Some of the neighbors arrived and tried to break up the fight.

We will end your life, one of his half-brothers shouted. *We will end you. We will show you we have the power.*

6

Even after several months, even after the physical dispute that led to his half-siblings threatening to end his life, Razak could not let the question of the land go. His mother, his aunt, Cynthia, all of them asked him to please forget it, to please step aside. For some reason he could not explain, he was unable to do so.

Certainly it had something to do with obeying local Islamic tradition. Certainly it was part of his right as the eldest son. Certainly he would be able to use part of the money from the sale of the land to help his business prosper and also to begin a life with Cynthia. But because he had grown close to his father in the remaining months before his death, because together they had reached an understanding, because he had come to know him as a father and not just another unjust authoritarian figure, Razak found it difficult to move on.

There was also a question of fairness. In a neighborhood, in a city, in a country where basic human rights were often ignored, where such rights were systematically disabled, Razak felt that dividing the land equally was the only way to proceed.

In November 2011, Razak went to the police for the third time to try to settle the dispute. This time he brought his mother, so she could witness how he was treated. When they arrived, the police commander asked, *What are you here for? You remember what me and my boys told you last time?*

Razak was enraged. He turned to her and said, *Mom, have I ever lied to you before? I told you this is what is going on.*

The police officers only shrugged. Defeated, Razak and his mother left. Outside the police station, his mother pulled him aside.

Nobody there will fight for you, she said. *Are you going to try to do this by yourself?*

Razak thought for a while and said, *If the police are not willing to help me, I don't have a choice. I'll have to do it on my own.*

You can't do this alone. You need money and you need other people to be involved.

I talked to the police, I talked to the community leaders, everyone witnessed everything, Razak said. *No one else is willing to help.*

A week later he took a bus out to the land and walked down the road to where the loamy red fields extended off into the distance. Ten acres of land, parts already being farmed. There were no buildings anywhere in sight. Since his father had passed away and he had attempted to confront his siblings about the land, Razak had not been back to see it.

That day he stood in the middle of the field, watching a few farmers attend to their crops of lettuce and corn. The afternoon sun peaked high as Razak surveyed the land before him.

An odd group of men appeared somewhere along the right side of his field of vision. Some were carrying sticks and some had knives. One had a machete. As guns were illegal within the city, Razak assumed these men must be out hunting.

Slowly the group made their way toward Razak until one asked, *Who are you and what are you doing here?*

Razak immediately responded, *Who am I? What kind of question is that?*

One of the men stepped forward more forcefully and said, *We asked you—who are you?*

Another man asked the man beside him, *Is this the brother of Jamal and Mubarak and Baba?*

Another answered, *Yeah. That's him.*

Something shifted in the air. Razak immediately thought that these men had been hired to do something—to intimidate him, to beat him, to possibly murder him.

Razak stared at them and said, *I'm their brother. And this land belongs to my father.*

One of the men spoke again. *Why are you here? They told you not to step on this land.*

Razak's heart quickened. *Who told me not to step on this land? Who has a right to tell me not to step on my property?*

Before he realized it, one of the men crossed behind Razak and hit him with a large stick. Razak shouted for help. The other men beat him, pummeling him with their weapons. Razak fell down, feeling the blows on his legs and shoulders, then against the back of his head. Across the field he saw some of the farmers running toward him. Before he knew it, the sky tilted and became black.

In a local hospital, Razak awoke with a severe pain in the back of his head. Everything slowly blinked into a lazy white focus.

A nurse appeared and Razak, dazed, asked, *Where am I?*

The hospital.

Razak was startled to see she was telling the truth.

What happened?

A group of people brought you here. She produced Razak's cell phone and said, *Can you please try to open your phone? We tried yesterday but it was locked. Can you open it so we can call your family?*

He opened the phone and gave the nurse his mother's number.

Razak believed the men in the field meant to murder him—that although they did not have guns, they intended to beat him to death before the farmers intervened. If it had not been for them, Razak was convinced he would have been killed. He recalled a case from the 1990s where a police officer in Accra was killed by his siblings and buried on the land in a dispute. Other, more recent cases had made the newspapers, quarrels over land leading to violence among relatives. Razak lay in his hospital bed and felt lucky to be alive.

Some time later, Razak's mother arrived with Cynthia and his aunt Rabi. His mother looked at him and started crying, seeing his wounded face. *I told you, Razak. I told you this would happen.*

Mom, stop saying that.

These people, they want to kill you. Please. I told you. They mean it. You need to stop.

I'm never going to stop talking about the land. I want justice. I want justice to be served.

How can you get justice when there's nobody there to help you? The police, nobody's going to help you.

Razak, too, began to cry. *Mom, I can't stop. I can't.*

Look at what they did to you. They're going to kill you. You need to leave the country.

I was born here. I'm not leaving.

A doctor came in and told the family Razak needed to rest.

After his relatives left, nurses checked his wounds and gave him additional medication. Some time later, he told the nurse he wanted to speak to his mother.

His mother came back in and sat across from him.

After several moments of silence, he spoke. *Why? Why are they doing this? Was there something that went wrong between you and my dad?*

I don't know, she answered. *I don't know what's come over them. Their mother isn't talking to me. I don't know why they're doing this.*

Razak believed it was because they could—because of the inequities of the political system, because of the corruption of the police, because of their relationship to Mustapha Ahmed. He remembered what Ahmed had said: *Who are you to criticize me?* In that moment, Razak was sure the MP was behind all that was happening. He believed the MP had an interest in the land, which he intended to help Razak's siblings develop in exchange for his part of the inheritance. Years later, after his political ouster in the elections of 2015, Mustapha Ahmed would be accused by *The Ghanaian Times* of illegally acquiring large tracts of land for sale and development, though no criminal charges would ever be made.

One week later, Razak was released from the hospital. The doctor looked at him and said, *Please. You have to stay away from your siblings. I don't want to see you in here again.*

Razak stayed with his mother while he recovered from his injuries. His aunt and Cynthia continued to plead with him.

Your mother wants you to leave the country, Cynthia said. *She's worried about your safety.*

Why should I leave the country?

Your siblings might end up killing you, his mother said.

Cynthia looked at him and said, *Your mom is right. I don't think you're safe here.*

Razak looked at them and asked, *Where? Where am I supposed to go?*

One day in December 2011, his half-brothers went to his mother's room looking for Razak, while he was out. Believing she was hiding him, one of his brothers pushed his mother aside, knocking her down and breaking two of her ribs, and then searched the room. A neighbor called Razak, who then rushed to the hospital where she had been taken.

His mother looked at him severely and said, *You see what I've been telling you? They nearly killed me. Stop. I want you to leave. You have to go. Please. Please. Please.*

Mom, I've never traveled before. I don't have anybody. I don't have anywhere to go.

Please. If they say they're going to kill you, they will.

Believing his life was in immediate danger, Razak spoke with a number of friends, who all agreed he needed to leave. One of his oldest companions, Haziz, said, *You know how this country works. You have to go.*

Razak explained to his business partner, Ahmad, what was happening. Together they decided to dissolve their partnership so that Razak could have money to travel.

Razak went to stay with his aunt across the border in Togo while his mother made preparations for him to acquire a visa to travel abroad. Razak's half-siblings kept looking for him, sending threatening text messages to his aunt:

> *We know he is in Togo*
> *Even there we can hire someone to make sure they are*
>   *done with him*

Terrified, Razak's aunt showed him the texts and offered to help any way she could. After three weeks of hiding in Togo, Razak decided he had to go back to Ghana to finalize the dissolution of his business. He returned to Accra in February 2012 and stayed with friends to avoid being discovered.

Razak's mother sold some of her jewelry. She went to a travel agent to get a visa to Germany—she explained that she wanted to get her son to get as far from Ghana as she could. Unfortunately, there were no visas available for anywhere in Europe, but Brazil offered a year-long visa which was relatively easy to obtain. Knowing no one in the country, and unable to speak the language, Razak was confronted with the decision of staying in Ghana and being killed or fleeing to a part of the world he knew nothing about. Unwilling to ignore his mother's and aunt's and Cynthia's wishes any longer, Razak agreed to go to Brazil in April 2012. He would fly from Ghana to Turkey and then to São Paulo.

Before he left, Cynthia said, *I know you're leaving but I will always be here. Don't think just because you're leaving I won't be there for you.*
      I still don't know why I have to leave the country where I was born.
      I know it's hard but we want you safe. You know the people your siblings work for.

In the airport on the edge of Accra, Razak broke down, for the first time in as long as he could remember, losing control of his feelings. He had never been on a plane, had never traveled overseas. *I don't know anyone where I am going. I don't have anyone. Who am I going to meet? What is my life going to be?*
      On the plane, he sat and waited, listening to the music playing in his headphones, holding the Koran his friend Haziz had given him. He had $1,500 from the sale of the electronics store, his passport, and a one-year visa. He was leaving everything: his family, his fiancée, his business, his country. The only possibilities left were halfway around the world, in some unknown city, in some unknown land.

~~~~~~

The light was there.

It appeared, then disappeared once more.

It moved like an object, something you could almost touch, floating in the air, and then vanished. Razak held his hand out, forcing himself to walk into the path of the harsh wind. Behind him, Seidu called out, blinded by the snow again, struggling with every step. Razak shouted back, *Two feet to the left. Follow my voice. It's there. It's just ahead.*

All they had to do was keep moving. All they had to do was get to the light.

Part Two

Brazil to the United States

7

In Criciúma, Brazil, twilight was an explosion of pink and purple. Seidu stood by the hotel window, cell phone in hand. It was July 4, 2014. Several weeks after arriving in Brazil, Seidu had finally completed the training camp for Criciúma Esporte Clube. He texted his boyfriend, Jamal, and then his girlfriend, Ayisha, back in Accra, saying he had done his best. He felt certain he had made the team.

My trials are over. I'm happy about my performance. I think the staff likes me.

Both of them texted back, saying they were praying for him. Seidu was aware of the life-changing importance of the moment. The president of Nima Lenient football club had paid to fly Seidu along with his team manager, Aminu Pele, to Brazil for the trials. If Seidu failed, it would be an embarrassment for everyone. He sent one final text to his sister back in Accra and stood by the windows of the hotel at dusk, watching the lights of Criciúma come to life.

In a celebratory mood, Seidu decided to go out to see the city, as he had been in training camp for the last several weeks and unable to take in anything more than the stadium. Tall silver and glass buildings reached higher than thirty or forty floors, unlike anything he had seen back in Ghana. The city felt modern but also familiar, quaint, with fewer than 200,000 people, set several miles inland from the ocean and framed by the green mountains of Santa Catarina. Seidu appreciated the city's beauty, believing he would be happy there. By then it had become night and the streets were starting to cool off. He walked farther and stopped, seeing a gay nightclub with a name in English spelled out in round lights. Having never been to a gay bar before, or any kind of bar as a young Muslim man, and having just finished one of the most grueling trials of his life, he decided to go in.

It was unlike anything he had experienced before. There were men dressed in women's clothing sitting at the bar, laughing and drinking, women dancing with each other, people throwing their arms in the air and expressing themselves with their bodies to lepo-lepo music.

He sat down at an empty table and ordered a bottle of Coca-Cola. He saw a tall man sitting by himself a few tables away and Seidu, always willing to start a conversation, said, "Hola."

"*Hola,*" the man replied. "*Tu ta bene?*"

"Good." Seidu repeated, "*Tu ta bene?*"

The man smiled. Seidu picked up his phone and used an app to translate from English into Portuguese.

What's your name? he asked, holding up the phone.

The man typed something and held up his own phone. *Nome es Ronnie.*

Seidu nodded and typed. *Where do you live?*

The other man responded. *I live around this area. What about you?*

I've been staying here for two months and will go back soon once my time is up.

We should go dance, the man suggested.

Seidu read the words and half frowned, holding up his phone. *I don't know how to dance.*

Moments later, Ronnie got up to dance by himself. Seidu sat

and watched. It was now past midnight. A few minutes later, the man returned and the two continued their conversation through their phones. Seidu typed, *I think I am going to leave.*

Where are you going?

I am going to my hotel, right around the stadium.

Why are you here?

I am from Ghana. I am here for the football trials for Criciúma.

Okay. That's nice. Criciúma is very good.

Somehow both of them were walking now, out into the darkness. He had barely noticed that they were strolling side by side, the nighttime punctuated by a streetlight here and there.

So how did the tryouts go? Ronnie asked with his phone.

I don't know yet.

Seidu looked over at Ronnie and made a decision, stopping in the darkness between two of the streetlights. *It's late,* he typed. *Why don't you come to the hotel?*

Ronnie agreed and the two men started off again.

Quietly they passed through the lobby of the hotel, where Seidu led Ronnie into the elevator. On the third floor, he paused, knowing he had to walk past his team manager's room. He was certain Pele was asleep, but still he hurried into the room with Ronnie, quickly locking the door behind them.

Once inside, the two men talked and drank orange juice. As a practicing Muslim and as an athlete, Seidu never drank alcohol. An awkwardness, a tension filled the air. Unsure what to do, Seidu put on the television, switched on the news.

Ronnie smiled and then changed the channel.

Seidu said he liked to watch the news.

Ronnie said okay, and changed the channel back. Together they sat before the screen and texted back and forth to each other. Soon they fell asleep. Sometime later they woke up and had sex.

Afterward, they both went to sleep again, Seidu half nude, his arm around Ronnie.

By eight in the morning, Seidu had forgotten about room service, which brought him breakfast every day—vegetables, rice, juice, and tea. One of the maids knocked on the door. Ronnie put on Seidu's shirt and let the maid inside while Seidu stayed in bed in his underwear. The maid brought the food in and promptly left. Together Seidu and Ronnie ate breakfast and talked to each other through their phones. The day felt new, the beginning of a number of unknown possibilities.

Forty-five minutes later, Aminu Pele entered without knocking. The door had been left unlocked when the maid brought breakfast. Pele had come to deliver the news that Seidu had not made the Criciúma team. Before he could speak, Pele saw the two men in their underclothes. Immediately he began yelling. Already angered by the fact Seidu's contract would not be sold to Criciúma—that they had wasted several weeks and would not make any money—Pele was overwhelmed with fury as he saw the two men in their underclothes.

"You are a wicked person!" he began to shout. "You are a dirty person! You are a disgrace to your country and your community! I will make sure your career in football is over! I will tell the Ghana Football Association and everyone you know that this is who you are. This is who you are and what you have been hiding!"

Panicked, Ronnie grabbed his clothes and hurried away, still wearing one of Seidu's shirts. Seidu got up to speak but Pele shoved the door closed and stormed away.

Everything came crashing down in that moment. Seidu was deeply frightened, shivering, shaking, more scared than he had ever felt in his life. He was certain the team manager would make good on his threats to expose him, and if he did, the life he knew, the life he had worked so hard for, would be over. There would be inquiries by the police, the newspapers, his neighbors. Jail. Torture. Even the possibility of being put to death. A black cloud settled over him, occluding the past, present, and future. Unable to come up with a plan but unwilling to wait and experience the horrible consequences of what might happen, Seidu did what he had always done to survive. He grabbed his passport, his cell phone, his remaining money, his documents, as many of his clothes as he could, and put it all in his backpack. He ran down the stairs—because he did not want to be delayed by the elevator—and out through the lobby, passing the hotel manager he saw almost every day. Overcome with embarrassment and fear, he was unable to look her in the face.

He ran to a nearby park, lowered himself onto a bench, and felt himself shiver as the sun continued to rise. Everything was laid out before him, the entire world—broken and trembling—at his feet.

8

Humankind's survival has always depended on its ability to move. One of the fundamental shifts in the development of the species was its strange capacity to stand up on two legs, to place one foot in front of the other, and to walk upright. Modern anthropologists are still unsure how and why this particular evolutionary trait developed, but nearly everything followed from those first uncertain steps. The capability to track herds of animals across miles and miles of territory, the resourcefulness to search for stronger material for better tools, the competency to seek richer and richer lands to plant crops—all this was dependent on humankind's willingness to wander.

Beyond several physiological consequences, this shift in mobility also led to a number of emotional and social developments, most noticeably an unwavering curiosity—a profound need to explore—that defines who we are as a species. Our nervous system is hardwired for fight-or-flight response, much more so than other primates, a psychological and physiological reaction that relies on our ability to escape danger by fleeing on foot when necessary. Our potential to start over, to begin again among a new set of circumstances, may also be tied to this unique physical adaptation.

Beginning with the movement of *Homo erectus*, who first

traveled from Africa to Eurasia 1.75 million years ago, and later followed by the migration of *Homo sapiens* from Africa to Asia, Australia, and Europe 270,000 years ago, humankind's progress has been defined by its ability to negotiate unfamiliar landscapes and the difficult promise of the unknown.

Early migrations—across Indo-Europe and Asia—were often caused by inadequate food supply, shifting climates, and war. Later mass movements—the Indu-Aryan migrations and the Greek and Roman empires—led to fundamental shifts in both culture and language. As humans traveled from one part of the world to the other more frequently, entire civilizations vanished while others were forced to adapt to ongoing changes in climate, politics, and social arrangements.

The Age of Exploration, beginning in the fifteenth century, only intensified this pattern of mass human migration to colonies across North and South America and Africa. In the sixteenth century alone, nearly 250,000 Europeans landed in the Americas. Many local populations found themselves displaced, conquered, or systematically destroyed. In addition to the persistent rise of colonialism, forced migration at the hand of the international slave trade gave rise to another form of human movement. By the end of the nineteenth century, three hundred years later, the number of migrants from Europe to the Americas had exploded to an almost unfathomable 50 million.

The customs, the land, the peoples of both North and South America were permanently changed by this unprecedented influx of other humans, tools, weapons, and political and religious beliefs, leading to a collision of cultures from which our modern national identity emerged.

At the start of the twentieth century, industrialization throughout the United States and Europe inspired millions of people to migrate to new countries and new cities, seeking

economic prosperity. Eventually World Wars I and II led to
the largest migration of the century, with the displacement and
resettlement of nearly 20 million individuals. Other political
conflicts—the end of the Ottoman Empire and the partition of
India—added to this exponential increase in human movement
across the globe.

This enduring fascination with physical mobility is celebrated
in many of our best-loved myths, and is at the very center of the
stories we tell each other about what it means to be human. The
Odyssey, the Bhagavad Gita, the Old Testament, the Koran all fea-
ture narratives that capture elemental ideas of identity, agency,
and change. In epic story after epic story, someone is always going
on a journey, always searching for something that may help them
save themselves and save the world. There is an old, hard truth in
these tales that we must reconcile ourselves with. Who we are,
why things are the way they appear to be—all the answers we
seek are rarely close at hand. You must be willing to become lost
in order to become free.

Hours after running from his hotel, Seidu sat on a park bench,
staring down at his hands. He felt as if somehow, somewhere in
the contour and creases of his upturned palms, there must be an
answer. Some time later, he looked up and saw a group of three
men—Haitians, he thought from their accents. The men were
sitting nearby, speaking a patois of Portuguese and French. Seidu
could not understand everything they said, but there was one
word he recognized, which they repeated over and over again.

America.

Seidu walked over, holding his cell phone. He began to type
rapidly: *Hello. Where are you from?*

One of the men typed into his own phone. *We live two blocks
away.*

Seidu typed. *I need help. Please. I need somewhere to go. I need somewhere to stay.*

The men looked at each other. One of the men translated on his phone and said, *Who are you? What happened?*

Seidu took a moment, then typed, *I'm from Ghana. I'm lost.*

The man typed back, *Give me your number. We will call you. We might be able to help.*

Seidu obliged. They exchanged numbers and soon the men left. All afternoon Seidu waited in the park. When it became dark, he found a shabby hotel for a few *reals* a night and slept there. In the morning he waited again, knowing he could not pay to stay in a hotel much longer and that he had to come up with a plan.

By day, he floated through the city in search of the other men, looking for some sign of how to move forward. He was afraid his team manager might be looking for him, that if he was found, he would be sent back to Ghana and put into prison.

Days passed without any word. Seidu texted and called the Haitians but got no response. He was down to less than $200. He was checking out of the hotel when he received a text asking, *Where are you?*

I'm in a hotel.

We'll come meet you.

The men brought Seidu back to the apartment they were renting. It was meager, with three bedrooms and very little furniture.

We don't have a bedroom for you but you can sleep on the couch.

That's not a problem. I just want a place to lay my head on.

Okay.

Later the next day the men were talking, sitting at the kitchen table. There was the word again. *America.* A feeling. A sense of hope. The three men were planning on making their way north to the United States.

Seidu's brother, Kamal, lived with his wife in Florida as a permanent resident. It could be a solution. All he had to do was go north.

How can we get there? Seidu asked.

We have some friends who left a month ago. They can tell us how they've done it.

Okay. But how can I go? I don't have money.

We don't have much money either, one of the men said. *But we can help you with some food.*

How much do I need?

One thousand at least. You need money for a flight and bus fare.

Seidu thought and came up with a plan. Sometime later, he called his sister Ayisha back in Accra. He told her everything that happened—finishing the trials, meeting Ronnie, the team manager's discovery and his threat to ruin him.

I'm so sorry. I have kept this secret forever, he told her and then asked if she could send whatever money she could. Ayisha was able to sell two of her sewing machines and sent the money to a friend in the U.S., who forwarded it on to a Western Union in Brazil, where Seidu used his passport to cash it, as Ghanaian law prohibits money transfers through entities like Western Union. It was $300 American, 1,500 *reals* in Brazil. Seidu showed the money to the Haitians, who reluctantly agreed that it would have to be enough.

Two days later, Seidu took a flight with the three Haitian asylum seekers from Criciúma to Quito, Ecuador. Ecuador did not require a visa, so the four men could enter the country and make their way north and west into Colombia without having to wait for any kind of paperwork. The flight cost fifty dollars and allowed the men the opportunity to travel in plain sight, without the difficulty of having to negotiate with human smugglers.

Once they landed, one of the men told Seidu to wait at the airport while they went to find another group of friends who were also heading north. Seidu sat at the airport for several hours, getting up to check the time, watching the airplanes take off and land. A security guard approached him and said he could not spend the night in the lobby. Seidu reluctantly agreed and put his backpack over his shoulders.

Outside, both the temperature and the humidity felt hostile. The long, flat airport building was surrounded by the city of Quito, with its dense, squat architecture and stubby mountain rising in the center of the city, framed by the green Andean foothills. Facing the unknown country of Ecuador alone, unable to speak the language and without any contact to help him proceed, Seidu felt utterly sorry for himself.

He took a taxi to a cheap hotel and slept there, becoming numb to his situation. He counted his money, then counted it again. In the morning he spoke to the receptionist and asked how to get to Colombia.

The young woman directed Seidu to a bus station, and even went so far as to call a taxi for him. He was moved by this small act of kindness and told her he would not forget it. He paid the cab driver twenty pesos and looked around the near-empty bus station, then bought a ticket to Colombia. The clerk at the ticket counter told him the bus would not arrive until midnight. In a stall in the dank bathroom, Seidu divvied up his remaining cash, putting two hundred of it under the soles of his shoes. The rest he put in his pocket to have at the ready. Then he took a seat in the bus station and waited, watching the colors of the Ecuador day fail, then fade into night.

At midnight, Seidu climbed aboard the bus and sat near the back. The bus pulled away from the small city and began its journey down the uneven road, deep into the dark, foreign territory.

From his seat he could feel the bus fighting against the hills, the florid density of the Cayambe Coca jungle reaching out into the night.

Only a few miles from the city, the bus was pulled over at a police checkpoint. Seidu began to tremble, unsure what to do with his hands. Back in Ghana, he never had to deal with the police, was never interrogated or searched. He waited as, row by row, two police officers made their way through the bus, asking for passports and IDs. One of the police officers inspected Seidu's passport, saw he had a Brazilian visa, but not one for Ecuador or Colombia.

Where are you going? the policemen asked in Spanish.

Seidu replied in English. "I'm going to Colombia. I'm going to the border between Colombia and Panama."

The policeman looked down at the documents and then shook his head. He told Seidu to get off the bus. Even though Seidu did not speak Spanish, from the grim look on the officer's face, he understood he was in danger.

Several seconds later, in the middle of the humid Ecuadorian night, Seidu stood on the side of the road, facing the two police officers. One of them stepped forward and asked, *Where are you from?*

Seidu searched the other man's face for the answer he thought he most wanted to hear. He believed the police officers had seen many people, men and women and children like him, pass this way on the journey north to the United States. Seidu answered slowly in English. "I'm from Brazil. I'm Ghanaian. I'm going north."

The other policeman nodded and said, *Dolar. Dolar.*

Seidu did not understand the word at first. "What is *dolar*?"

The other police officer held up his hand, rubbing his fingers together and Seidu immediately understood. He carefully removed ten dollars American from his pocket and handed it to the police officer.

"No, not enough," the other officer said.

Seidu shook his head and said, "I don't have anything. I don't have any more money."

Dolar. Dolar.

Seidu shrugged. "This is it. This is all I have."

The two men, expressionless, said it again. *Dolar. Dolar.*

Seidu hung his head. "I don't have anything else. You can kill me if you want, but I don't have any more. I don't have anything else."

The two police officers stared at him, perhaps stunned by his bravery, and said, "Go, go, go." They handed him his passport, then waved him back on the bus.

After an hour of the police interrogating other passengers, the bus hurtled back into the dark. Soon the sun appeared, a smudge on the glass. Sometime later, near the border of Colombia, a second pair of Ecuadorian police officers pulled the bus over. Once again, the officers made their way through, seat by seat, reviewing everyone's papers. By now, Seidu was furious. *Why are they stopping us so often?* he wondered. A half hour later, the officers reached Seidu's aisle and asked for his identification.

"I'm going to the border. I don't have anything but a passport."

One of them looked at Seidu's passport, saw it was from Ghana, and then told him to get off the bus. Out along the road, beneath the cobalt blue sky, both police officers looked over his documents again and said, *Dolar, dolar, dolar.*

Seidu stared at them and said, *No sabe nada.*

The two officers shook their heads.

"You can search me, but I don't have any more money."

Maybe it was the fierce look in Seidu's eyes or the early hour or the sound of insects echoing each other inharmoniously from the nearby jungle, but neither man seemed willing to argue. One of the officers sighed and gave Seidu his passport, then sent him back on the bus.

On the way to the final stop before the border, a third group of police officers pulled the bus over and looked at everyone's documents once again. The officers glanced over at Seidu, who had tried to make himself appear unapproachable. By chance or providence, the police did not ask for his identification papers. The officers exited the bus after some time and the vehicle continued on to the border, where Seidu promptly climbed off. There at the bus station, he was searched again, as were his bags and the bags of his fellow passengers. Unsure of where he was headed, he crossed into Colombia alone.

9

In Bogotá, Seidu moved among the modern buildings interspersed with remnants of colonial architecture, passing the cobblestoned city center, the busy throngs of residents and travelers, all crowded out by shimmering skyscrapers and the shadows of the clouds cast off by the Andes. After nearly twenty-two hours on several buses, he walked around La Candelaria and was trying to figure out how to cross into Panama when he happened upon a group of odd-looking men—other asylum seekers—at a bus station. There was something about their expressions, their wearied, humbled appearance, that suggested they, too, had come from somewhere far away.

One man was from Ghana, just outside Accra, two were from India, and one was from Nepal. All of them looked worse for wear, their faces capturing the difficulties of their long journeys. Seidu was overjoyed that he would have someone to travel with, someone he could speak to, ask questions of. The men explained that the only way into Panama without a visa was by crossing the series of rivers that bisected the enormous Los Katíos National Park. It would be extremely dangerous, they warned him.

Los Katíos is part of the Darién Gap, a jungle consisting of 10,000 square miles of fearsome animal and plant life. A map of the region looks like the palm of someone's hand—blue lines demarcating narrow rivers and inlets, crossing back and forth, suggesting the perils of both fate and luck.

The jungle itself is dense and unnerving; a stretch of rain forests, swampland, and marshes widely known as one of the most treacherous places in the world. Human smugglers often use the Gap to transport asylum seekers and other undocumented migrants across the Colombia–Panama border. Throughout the 1990s and 2000s, FARC, an armed group of Colombian Marxists who committed thousands of murders, kidnappings, and political assassinations, used the nearly impenetrable rain forest of the Gap as their hideout. Backpackers and other travelers since then have been kidnapped and sometimes murdered, as FARC considers most of these outside travelers to be foreign operatives. In June 2015, the body of Swedish backpacker Jan Philip Braunisch was found in the Gap; FARC later claimed responsibility for his death, having incorrectly assumed he was a spy.

Beyond paramilitary operations, drug smugglers are also known to use the route. Their illicit operations pose an additional and ever-present human threat. Then there are the dozens of human smugglers—often called *polleros* or coyotes because of their ruthlessness and guile. In addition to moving thousands of humans through the jungle each year, these criminals have also been known to rob, kidnap, or kill the same migrants they have been contracted to escort, leaving the bodies to decompose wherever they may fall.

The rain forest presents a number of other unpredictable physical dangers. Jaguars, larger than a man, patrol their territories at night in search of prey. Venomous creatures like coral snakes and giant black scorpions move undetected in trees overhead and underfoot among rotted logs. Mosquitoes, human-size clouds of them, attack relentlessly—many of them carry tropical diseases and, according to local myth, favor dark clothes and dark hair.

Then there is the thick humidity, the drenching precipitation, the constant heat, the remoteness, the lack of food and fresh water. There is nowhere to run to and, once you have started, no way to turn back.

Together all five asylum seekers traveled north to Salaqúi, where they located a guide who said he would lead them through the Gap. The smuggler first told the men he wanted $300 from each of them, but the asylum seekers argued, saying they didn't have that much. Seidu told the guide the truth—that he had less than $200 left. The smuggler agreed to take $100 from Seidu but told him not to tell the others.

Before proceeding into the jungle, the guide took the men to a ruined building, without electricity, near a small branch of one of the region's many rivers. The building was part of a former refugee camp run by the military that had been abandoned years before. The human smugglers had taken it over. There Seidu met two another Ghanaians, both of whom were trying to make it to the States. One of these men, a soccer player named Razeem, was also from Nima. Seidu marveled at the coincidence, relieved to have found someone he recognized making the same journey.

For three days the migrants sat in the outbuilding, waiting for the human smugglers to arrive with boats. The smugglers would then ferry the migrants across one of the rivers and deep into the jungle. During these tense nights of waiting, sickening waves of mosquitoes invaded the building, making it impossible to sleep.

One night Seidu awoke to the high-pitched whine of the mosquitoes. One of the other men also awoke and went outside to urinate. A moment later he ran back into the building yelling, "Snake! Snake!"

One of the Colombians who lived at the compound and was

responsible for cooking for the asylum seekers arrived to investigate. He took out a flashlight. All the refugees could see was the end of an enormous black snake, possibly a venomous pit viper. Seidu hated snakes, had hated them since he was a boy. He watched it slither back into the underbrush. Seidu and the other asylum seekers took the snake's appearance as an omen and agreed they needed to keep moving. They had already paid the smugglers and believed that the longer they stayed in Colombia, the more likely something terrible would happen. They approached the smugglers and demanded to leave immediately. The smugglers made some phone calls and told Seidu and the other asylum seekers they would be leaving that evening.

The boat arrived in the dark—a large wooden canoe, outfitted with an outboard motor. By then there were twenty undocumented migrants waiting to board, and all of them were forced to climb into the single boat. The men were told to lie in the bottom of the canoe and were then covered with a large black plastic tarp. One of the smugglers explained that there were patrol boats that crossed up and down the rivers in search of ferrymen carrying migrants and drugs north into Panama.

In the absolute blackness, lying beneath the tarp, Seidu could hear the sound of the river, of night birds and other mysterious wildlife. He could also hear some of the men praying. The pilot of the boat shouted as some large creature—a crocodile or caiman, Seidu couldn't be sure—crashed into the front of the canoe.

Seidu began to pray as well. *God, please help us make this journey successfully. Please guide us.*

About an hour into the trip, Seidu could hear the motor slowly give out. From beneath the tarp, the men began to panic, again calling out for reassurance.

The pilot had more bad news. The motor was dead. They would have to wait for someone to come with a replacement.

Even in the darkness, Seidu could feel the current pulling at the small boat. He began to pray even harder, unsure if he would be heard. He listened to the smuggler speaking on a cell phone and felt lost again, wondering if he might die on the river. Time stopped beneath the black tarp, dissolving to the odors, the heat, the noises produced by the other men beside him. Back and forth, the boat quietly rocked, the men too afraid to speak. Unable to stretch his legs, Seidu imagined this was what it must feel like to be buried alive.

Four hours later, another boat arrived and the smugglers replaced the motor. From there Seidu and the other migrants were brought to a tiny village near the border of Panama, where a second boat would help them cross yet another limb of the river. By then it was almost six in the morning and the sun had begun to rise, although the sky and surrounding forest was still blue-black. Some of the villagers helped the migrants from the boat and into the jungle.

The migrants waited for the second boat and watched a villager use his flashlight to kill two large scorpions. Seidu had never seen a venomous creature before and kept staring at the ground, at his feet, checking to be sure nothing dangerous was nearby. Finally, a half hour later, the second boat appeared and took Seidu, Razeem, and the other migrants over the river and to the far side of the jungle.

Once they disembarked, two Colombian boys from a nearby village helped the asylum seekers cross the muddy banks into a seemingly impenetrable jungle. The boys, no more than twelve or thirteen years old, showed the migrants how to walk through the mud, where to place their feet, all of them moving deeper and deeper to a shadowy, quiet place, far from any sign of life, where the men were told to wait again.

As they were hiding in the thickets of intertwined vines and trees, one of the men noticed a large boa constrictor crossing among the limbs overhead. The men watched, transfixed, as it made its way to the forest floor. Seidu grabbed a stick to protect himself before the snake calmly disappeared into the water.

While they waited, the men spoke about the many dangers of traveling north. Some of the migrants mentioned how more and more people were leaving their own nations of origin. Seidu listened attentively as each of the other twenty men told their stories.

Beginning in 2010 and continuing through 2014, the civil war in Syria, the political unrest in Libya, and sustained violence in Central America all caused millions of people to seek better lives abroad in Europe, Canada, and the United States. At the U.S. border, there was an explosion of unaccompanied women and children from El Salvador, Guatemala, and Honduras in particular, with individuals fleeing unremitting violence from drug cartels, gang warfare, and food shortages.

Across the world, the number of refugees grew exponentially during the second decade of the twenty-first century, reaching nearly 65.3 million people by the end of 2015, according to the United Nations High Commissioner for Refugees. Twenty-one million of these individuals were refugees who had fled their homes, 40 million were internally displaced, and 3 million were asylum seekers who had already begun the asylum process in Europe, Canada, or the United States.

Seidu looked at the faces of the other men and realized he had become part of something much more complicated, much bigger than he had ever previously considered. It was terrifying to imagine all the men, women, and children forced to leave their homes, and how they all seemed to be moving in the same direction. In the end, his problems—which once seemed so extraordinary—were only a faint echo of some much larger question.

Hours later, another boat arrived and took the men across the Atrato River, which flowed north into the low hills of western Colombia, with several branches and tributaries bisecting the lush jungle of the Western Cordillera mountain range.

Opalescent shadows began to appear above the mountains to the north and west. Soon it would be dark. Seidu watched as the small boat crossed among fallen logs and shifting currents.

Only a few minutes into the crossing, the boat got stuck, lodging itself against the muddy bottom. The boys told the asylum seekers to get out into the river and push. Terrified, Seidu watched Razeem and the other men climb out of the boat into the murky water. Reluctantly he joined them and began to push, but the boat did not move. The boys told them to push harder. The men pushed, but the boat seemed only to sink deeper. They pushed again, finally dislodging the prow. Seidu looked behind him and saw a thin snake crossing along the surface, swimming in the opposite direction. Quickly the asylum seekers climbed back into the boat and slowly drifted to the other side of the river. On the opposite bank, Seidu stepped into the mud, seeking higher ground. He was still far from his destination, less than one quarter of the way to the United States.

The light appeared again in the snow-covered void and then vanished. A far-off flash, some glimmer of possibility, then it was gone. Razak kept on walking ahead unsteadily, trying to reach the break in the darkness.

From twenty yards behind he could hear Seidu calling out, still stumbling to catch up. The younger man was once again blinded, his face covered in ice and snow.

Razak turned and called back, *Twenty more yards. Follow my voice!* When he faced north again, the point of light trembled in the distance once more. He began to move quicker now, calling back over his shoulder.

Keep going forward. Follow my voice!

Seidu soon joined him at his side, putting a hand out. Razak cleaned the snow from the other man's eyes, his own fingers having gone numb hours before.

Do you see it? Razak asked. *The light. It's just ahead.*

Seidu stared out and nodded. He kept a hand on Razak's shoulder as they began to move forward again. Once they got closer, both men lay down behind a large snowdrift and glanced directly toward the source of the light. Razak could see the shape of some indefinable building, on top of which was a rotating searchlight—every three or four minutes the light passed in a slow, widening arc, tracing a faint triangular field of whiteness on the snow. Beyond the searchlight, behind the building, there was a low barbed-wire fence—the actual border—on the other side of which was their future, freedom, everything they had hoped for.

If they timed their movements carefully, hurrying a few feet across the snow, then burying themselves before the light came around again, they could make it. Both men decided to move far from the highway, deeper into the icy field, to avoid being spotted by the U.S. Border Patrol agents inside the station. As they did, the snow rose past their hips, past their waists. It was too much, too cold. Razak's entire body began to convulse, shivering uncontrollably. Even though they were so close to freedom, he felt could no longer go on. He fought the urge to quit, to capitulate, to give in, and instead pulled himself forward.

By then the light had become bright upon their faces. As it slowly swung back around, Razak and Seidu both dove down, hiding in the deep snow. Each felt their limbs writhing with pain. The icy ground on their bare skin sent sharp waves of discomfort throughout their bodies. Razak got up on his elbows and once again watched the rotating light.

Once it passed, he quietly called to Seidu and they quickly hurried forward. Before the searchlight could catch them in its beam, the men lay back down in the snow, allowing themselves to sink into the icy drifts.

After it spun around once more, Razak crept onward, disappearing into the oblong darkness.

10

Eight months after the attempt on his life and his flight from Ghana, Razak was living at a mosque in São Paulo, cleaning the building before and after morning, afternoon, and evening prayers. He stayed in a tiny room usually reserved for Muslim pilgrims passing through the city and ate his meals using the mosque's small kitchen. Five times a day he knelt and prayed with the other Muslim men at the mosque. Although each recited their prayers in Arabic, once these familiar recitations were over, Razak was unable to speak the other men's language—either Portuguese or Spanish. His enforced solitude slowly began to feel like prison.

Razak entered the country in late April 2012 with a one-year visa. For several weeks he stayed in a series of cheaper and cheaper hotels, going through his money quickly, realizing all too late that although the visa allowed him to stay in the country for a year, he had no way to get a work permit, was unable to make a living, and thus was unable to afford an apartment of his own. He worked construction for several weeks and lived with a man from Angola he had met.

Eventually, running out of money, he moved into the local mosque.

Because of his status and his difficulties with the language, he had become like a cleric or a monk, barely leaving the safety of his room. The Palestinians who ran the mosque allowed him to live there and share their food—they did not speak English—but they employed a translator who spoke both English and Portuguese. Razak explained his story to the owners through the translator and was allowed to stay indefinitely. He had no idea what to do once his visa ran out in another few months.

One day in March 2013, after prayer services ended and the other men filed out of the mosque, Razak remained deep in prayer, contemplating the series of events that had led to his escape. Two hours later a group of African migrants—from Somalia and Eretria and Ethiopia—entered the mosque for afternoon worship. Razak sat by the door and watched, recognizing them as fellow Africans. Once their prayers were finished, one of the men approached him.

As-salamu alaikum.

Wa-alaikum assalaam, Razak replied.

The other man was thin, of average height, in his thirties, with a friendly, inquisitive expression. In English, he asked, "Where are you from?"

"I'm from Africa."

It felt like the first time in months that someone had spoken to him in English.

"I know, but what part of Africa? Nigeria?"

"No, I'm from Ghana," Razak replied. "I live here, in the mosque. I left my country because of some problems."

"Are you asking for asylum here?"

"No."

"Then what are you doing here? You're just staying in Brazil alone?"

Razak did not know how to respond. The man introduced himself as Jabba, told him he was from Somalia, and motioned to the other men.

"Some of us are from Somalia, some of us are from Eritrea. We're going to the United States."

"Do you have a visa?" Razak asked.

"No. We're going to go by foot and bus."

"How can you do that?"

"A lot of people do it. Every day, they do it."

The thought had never even occurred to Razak—the distance, the length of time to travel, the food, the checkpoints, the possible pitfalls along the way—all of it seemed like some other world, some kind of fantasy.

"If you want to go with us, we can help you. We're going to leave in a couple of days."

Jabba wrote down a phone number, his name on Facebook, and the address of a nearby hotel where the men were all staying.

After they left, Razak stared at the piece of paper. It was the first time in months he had felt anything like optimism, even though it seemed fleeting, a cold, bright star.

He called his mother a few days later on Facebook and told her he had met some men at the mosque who were traveling to the United States. He explained they had come from Somalia and Eritrea and were willing to help him.

Are you sure this is what you should do? she asked.

I don't think I have any other choice. There's nothing for me here. I can't work, I can't afford to live here. It's no way to live a life.

What do you need from me? she asked.

Razak paused, feeling embarrassed about even having to utter the words. *I need some money.*

How much?
I'll find out.

The following day, a Tuesday, Razak met the asylum seekers at their hotel. He asked Jabba, the Somali who seemed to be the leader of the group, how much money he would need to join them.

"Three thousand dollars would be good, if you can get it."

"I don't know. I don't know if I can get that much."

Another Somali, older, in his forties and slightly overweight, said, "Don't worry if you can't get all of it."

Razak turned and faced him. This other man introduced himself as Mohammed Mamoud. He had striking black hair and spoke perfect English. There was something about his manner that was both thoughtful and kind. He looked at Razak and said, "We're all helping each other out. We're all going to travel together."

Razak went back to the mosque and called his mother on Facebook Messenger to explain the situation. When he told her how much he needed, there was a brief silence.

Three thousand. Okay. We'll find a way.

Later, Razak's mother and fiancée called him back to say that both of them were going to sell their remaining jewelry in order to help him pay for the trip.

I don't know what to say. I don't want you to have to do that, he told his mother.

But the conversation came to a close with Razak agreeing to accept their help. In the end there was no other way.

On Friday, Razak spoke with his aunt in Togo, who had gotten fifteen hundred from Razak's mother and Cynthia. The money was sent via a cabdriver, who carried the cash to Razak's aunt in Togo, and was then wired to Brazil through Western Union. Razak used his passport to claim the money, recognizing all that his loved ones had sacrificed for him was now resting in his hands.

Later Razak went to the hotel where the other asylum seekers were staying and told them he had $1,500 of his own money and five hundred from his family, declining to mention the additional $1,000. Mohammed Mamoud agreed that $2,000 should be enough. He told Razak they would be able to get him a visa and airline ticket for Panama, which would cost about $700. Razak complained about the price. Mohammed said he was welcome to go along with them and barter for a better price with the man in charge of making the arrangements.

In a large market at the center of São Paulo, Razak traveled with Mohammed Mamoud to meet the man, a tall, thin Nigerian with a large afro haircut and long beard. He was set up in an internet café in a back room, along with a few other Africans who had permanent residence in Brazil.

"Look, I'm from Ghana," Razak explained to the forger. "I want to go with these guys but I don't have a lot of money. I can give you five hundred for the ticket and visa."

"Why do you want to go to the U.S.? You have a Brazilian visa. You can stay here."

"I've been here for eleven months. I don't have any legal documents. I can't work. I can't do anything."

The Nigerian stared at Razak for a long time and then nodded. "Okay. When do you guys want to go?"

Mohammed Mamoud leaned forward and said, "Three or four days."

"Okay. The visas and tickets will be ready."

The Nigerian took Razak's passport and the $500 as well as materials from Mohammed.

Later the man called Razak for some additional personal information—his height, his weight. Two days later, he phoned Razak and said, "Everything's okay. Your visa's been approved."

When Razak went to pick up the tickets and visa, he saw the counterfeit stamp on his passport that the Nigerian had arranged. The Nigerian had also bought tickets for Avianca, a Brazilian airline, for the asylum seekers in groups of three and four.

Razak was put in the second group. He told Mohammed, "Look, you're the only one here who speaks good English. I want to go with you."

"Okay, no problem."

In order to reach the United States, Razak would have to fly from Brazil to Panama, then travel from Panama to Costa Rica by foot and bus, passing into Nicaragua and then on to Honduras, Guatemala, then finally through Mexico and on to the U.S.—a total of seven border crossings without documents. Crossing one border would be difficult enough, but seven seemed unimaginable. Although the other asylum seekers did not seem concerned, Razak went over the path again and again on his phone, seeing in the pixelated map the unlikeliness, the unpredictability of such an odyssey.

Two days later, on May 6, 2013, Razak traveled with Mohammed and Jabba to the airport in São Paulo, carrying his few belongings in a meager backpack. No one said a word as he passed through the Brazilian immigration checkpoint. It was a four-hour flight to Panama City. In four short hours, the journey that would take up the next four and a half years of his life would begin.

11

In Panama, there was trouble for the asylum seekers as soon as they landed. Officers from the Panamanian Immigration Service held on to their passports and forced the three men to wait for several hours as their documents were carefully inspected. Sitting outside the immigration office, Razak began to worry. He had used his real passport, while Mohammed and Jabba had used falsified Kenyan documents.

Finally, after three hours, Razak walked up to the Immigration counter and said, "We've been here for hours. Can you tell me what's happening? Is there some kind of problem?"

The immigration officer—a slight-looking woman—went to check on their documents, speaking with her supervisor in a small office. Razak watched the conversation, trying to get a sense of what was going on. Moments later she returned and told Razak he and his companions would have to keep waiting.

Afraid that if they were detained much longer they would be arrested or deported, Razak boldly decided to approach the officer who had initially taken their documents and question him directly. "Why are guys holding on to our passports? Is it because of how we look? Is it because we're black?"

"Take it easy."

"You have to be fair with everybody."

Other immigration officials looked around nervously and tried to calm Razak down. "Please be patient."

"I have a visa from Brazil. If you guys don't want me to come to your country, fine. Send me back to Brazil."

"It's not that way. Please just wait."

Moments later, the immigration supervisor arrived and spoke with Razak, impressed with his English. "Where are you and your friends from?"

"Brazil. We're here for a short visit. Two or three weeks."

The supervisor stared at Razak with an air of suspicion and asked, "How much money do you have in your bank account?"

"I have almost two thousand dollars. Do you want to see it?"

"No. I'm asking because I don't want you to come here and get stranded. A lot of people come from Brazil with fake passports, fake visas, and find themselves in trouble."

Once again, Razak decided to bluff.

"You can call your consulate in São Paulo and ask them, because we have the travel agent who got the visa for us. We have his number. Go ahead and call him."

"That doesn't matter, as long as you have money and the proper documents. What about your friends?"

"They all have money."

The supervisor studied Razak for a while and then said, "Okay. You're good to go," and stamped all three passports. When he had finished, the supervisor frowned and said, "I'm sorry for what happened."

"You need to explain why you took us aside for so long."

"Everyone here is just trying to do their job."

As the three men exited the airport, they were shocked to see that the Panamanian Immigration Service had arranged a taxi for them. Razak felt guilty then, seeing how apologetic the immigration officers were.

The driver—who was Jamaican Panamanian and spoke English—looked at the three passengers and said, "Africans. Where are you going?"

"We're looking for a cheap hotel."

"Okay. I know a place."

He brought the three asylum seekers to downtown Panama City. It was unlike anything Razak had expected—modern, Westernized, with tall glittering buildings, a bustling, cosmopolitan metropolis rising out of old colonial edifices, all of which revealed American and European financial influences. As a tax haven for the wealthy, the influx of foreign capital—in the gleaming, towering apartment buildings along the oceanfront, the expensive cars rushing past, the sleek advertisements for American products—was everywhere. Beneath this surprising surface, there was also another city, a city of shadows, the city of the working poor, inhabited by refugees and indigenous people who had left their villages, all of whom were struggling to survive. Along shadowy streets crowded with other migrants, the cabbie dropped the men off at a place that charged twenty-five dollars a night for a run-down room.

The plan was to meet another group of asylum seekers at the bus station the next day. Together the men would all buy tickets to travel north by bus to Costa Rica. After sleeping for a few hours in the flophouse, Razak followed the other men to the station, bought a ticket, and climbed aboard the bus.

Five hours later the bus stopped in some small, nameless village. Other travelers climbed off and bought food from the vendors in their stalls and on the street, but because Razak and the other two travelers were Muslim, they were not sure what they could eat. Eventually they settled on soda and cookies, and then, approaching a vendor, Razak bought two tacos. Although he had been living in Brazil for almost a year, he had never eaten a taco before. It was a brief joy, something miraculous, to taste something he had never tried before, to be able to enjoy a meal with other men, other people all moving in the same direction.

One hour later, around 8:00 p.m., the bus approached the border. Before they arrived, Mohammed Mamoud leaned over to Razak and said, "We have a connection. We need to get off just before the border."

The three men exited the bus at a nearby taxi station. Mohammed Mamoud telephoned a smuggler named Luis in Costa Rica, who told them he would send someone to pick them up. The jungle—with its dense foliage and strange sounds—rose up behind them, menacingly, as they waited. It felt as if any moment they could be caught, discovered by the police, robbed, or attacked by some unknown animal.

Thirty minutes later, an SUV pulled up. The driver asked, "Where's Mohammed?"

"I'm Mohammed."

"You talk to Luis?"

"Yes."

"Get in." The driver took the three men to a small house, which turned out to be the smuggler's own living quarters. It was oddly personal to be invited into this stranger's home. Amid the driver's mother and father and sisters sitting at the kitchen table, the smuggler explained that each of the asylum seekers would have to pay $300 to cross the border from Panama into Costa Rica.

Razak looked over at Mohammed and shook his head.

"Don't worry," Mohammed whispered. "We'll talk to him."

The driver's mother asked if any of the men wanted coffee. It became clear that the entire family depended on smuggling migrants as their main source of income. In a small room, there were five or six narrow mattresses laid out.

Mohammed and Razak sat down on the mattresses and tried to negotiate with the driver. "Listen," Mohammed said, "We can't pay three hundred. We don't have it."

"Then two hundred. It's the best I can do."

Razak talked slowly, tried to explain. "We took a flight from Brazil and got a visa and that was only five hundred. We can pay one hundred fifty for each of us and that's it."

"Two hundred, or you're not going," the man said.

"I can't do two hundred. Are you going to leave me at your house?"

The smuggler shook his head and left.

After waiting for more than twelve hours in the tiny room, the driver returned the next day around four in the afternoon and said it was time to go. They drove close to the border and switched to a different SUV, this one driven by an African Panamanian. A half hour later the new driver pulled over and said, "Everybody out. We're going into the jungle."

Under the cover of the darkness, moving among the dense foliage, the travelers were led into the nearly impassable forest, where three guides were waiting. Once they crossed beneath a swath of moonlight, Razak could see that one of the guides was carrying an AK-47. The other was holding a large knife. In a clearing up ahead, the third guide pointed a flashlight at the asylum seekers and asked, "Okay. How much do you got?"

Razak began to argue. "What do you mean? We already paid."

"If you can't pay, we can't take you."

"What do you mean?"

"If you don't pay, we'll leave you in this jungle."

Razak was incensed. "Why are you doing this? We already paid."

The other man did not respond.

Razak stared at the weapons, feeling the heaviness of their weight upon the air. "How much do you want?"

"Each of you needs to pay two hundred bucks."

"We just paid one-fifty to get here!" Razak looked at the other two travelers and said, "We can give you a hundred dollars each. Yes or no?"

The three smugglers briefly spoke in Spanish to each other. One of them finally turned to Razak and said, "Okay. Give us the money now."

"We'll pay you when we get to Costa Rica."

The man looked at Razak and then said, "Let's go."

From 6:00 p.m. to midnight, Razak and the other two men followed the smugglers through the Panamanian jungle. The darkness was complete, something you could feel moving against your skin. There was nothing to drink. Exhaustion began to set in. Razak felt himself grow more and more thirsty as he climbed through the underbrush. Sometimes there was a trail, other times it appeared as if no one had had ever crossed there before. The echo of birds and insects would be interrupted by the barking of dogs in the distance. At times the smugglers motioned for the migrants to lie down for two or three minutes, waiting for the noise to pass, then waved to them when it was time to start moving again.

In the middle of the night, one of the guides borrowed Razak's cell phone and called a taxi. Thirty minutes later they reached a small village. Climbing from the jungle, they saw a yellow cab approach along the side of the highway.

Two of the guides climbed into the front seat alongside the driver, while the other four men got in the back. The cab driver brought them to a gas station so that one of the smugglers could buy chips and water, which he passed out to Razak and the other asylum seekers. Razak then paid the smugglers. The cab driver drove the men through the tiny town.

In the near dark, Razak saw that the border of Costa Rica did not look much different than the border of Panama. Faded Coca-Cola billboards in Spanish, ramshackle, tin-roofed buildings, feral dogs patrolling overflowing bags of trash. The cab driver brought the men to a small house where Mohammed Mamoud called Luis again.

"Where are you?" Luis asked.

"At the border."

Luis asked to speak to the man who owned the house and explained he would be there to pick the migrants up in the morning. The owner agreed and showed the men to a room where they could rest on a number of bare mattresses.

It was a business, Razak was beginning to see.

While they waited, the men discussed the impending difficulties of crossing through Central America into the U.S. Razak, along with the other two migrants he was traveling with, had found himself caught in a complicated industry of human smuggling, an industry he had known nothing about before his journey began. Over the past thirty years a nearly invisible network of uncoordinated, small-scale smugglers had evolved into a highly organized enterprise. As the tide of migrants traveling to the United States grew throughout the twenty-first century, what was once a low-level, oftentimes family-run operation had become a multibillion-a-year business. Criminal organizations—including transnational drug traffickers—began to use human smuggling as an additional revenue source to support other illicit activities.

Human smugglers—often paid in advance and having little concern for the individuals they were transporting—led men, women, and children inside cargo trucks, shipping containers, refrigerated trucks, train cars, rotting boats, or on foot, all through stifling heat and perilous terrain. More than 4,000 migrants died worldwide each year in these human smuggling operations, though this number was only an approximation at best. Along the U.S.–Mexico border, more than four hundred migrant deaths—from hyperthermia, exposure, drowning, excessive use of force by Border Patrol officers, and killings by vigilante groups—were reported each year.

Since 2010, with the rise in the number of women and unaccompanied children fleeing from Central America to the U.S., there was also an increased threat of kidnapping, rape, extortion, and human trafficking—whereby migrants who paid smugglers for transportation north were abducted and sold into bondage, forced to become escorts and sex workers on both sides of the border.

Then there were the dozens, perhaps hundreds of people who simply disappeared, were never seen or heard from, nameless, faceless bodies that faded into an ever-shifting landscape of jungle or desert or sea.

Razak listened to these rumors quietly. The more the other two men spoke, repeating stories they had heard about the treacherous path ahead, the more improbable their passage became.

Before he fell asleep, he prayed along with the other men. Making their ablutions with water from a rusty pipe, kneeling on unfamiliar floors, the asylum seekers did their best to pray as often as they were able, asking for help on their journey.

The next morning, Luis arrived with two men, each on a motorbike. These guides gave Razak and his traveling companions a helmet each and then headed north along a narrow, foliage-covered route directly through the Costa Rican jungle. Howler monkeys, sloths, and venomous snakes all made their way in the dense trees above. From the back of the motorbike, Razak could see the forest around him was alive, constantly moving, a vital, breathing creature unto itself. Raindrops on leaves. Animal tracks in the mud. At the end of the journey, the asylum seekers each paid Luis $100 and then handed their helmets back to the smugglers. Razak looked at the narrow road ahead. Somehow the Panamanian border was now far behind him. He was now across the border of Costa Rica, more than halfway to the United States.

"From here you need to take a bus to San Jose," Luis said, smiling at them.

Razak nodded.

"When you're on the bus, don't talk to anyone. Take my advice. Don't do anything. Become invisible."

~~~~~~

The light bisected the night, splitting everything in two—the past and present, night and day, the United States and Canada. Each time the searchlight spun on its axis was another several minutes lying unprotected in the cold. Both men felt as if they were going nowhere. Their hands and feet were beginning to ache and flare with an intensifying pain. Gloves lost, hats gone, their skin, their faces burned each time they had to throw themselves forward and bury their limbs in the snow. Using every remaining bit of energy in their possession, both men lunged forward, crawling on their hands and knees when they found they were unable to walk.

But when Seidu finally looked up, digging at the snow that obscured his vision, it seemed the fence was no closer.

By the end of a half hour, they had gone only a few dozen yards. It was now close to 4:00 a.m. and the sky was still pitch dark. To make it all the way to the fence buried in the snow, it might take another half hour or hour. Seidu did not know if he'd be able to endure the cold much longer.

Besides, the U.S. Border Patrol building was right there. All he had to do was stand and walk and turn himself in, face whatever he was going to face, but at least it would be done, at least it would be over.

Still he crawled on.

Before long, both his and Razak's faces were covered with ice as they dragged themselves across the field toward the low-wire fence, hiding themselves from the light every few minutes. Seidu, nearly blinded again by the oncoming sleet, began to feel as if he were unable to breathe, unable to keep moving. For a moment both men cowered beneath the passing searchlight, trying to get their bearings. After it passed, Razak looked over at Seidu and finally murmured what both men had been thinking.

I don't know. I don't know if I can go any further.

What?

I don't think I can go on. Maybe we should go back to the highway. Maybe we should turn ourselves in.

Their voices, split by the wind, barely carried as far as each other's ears. The land around them was charged with the same palpable feeling of doubt, of uncertainty. It was as if their voices did not belong to them at all, but instead to the void, to the empty climate itself. The question hung in the air for what felt like forever.

No, Seidu finally said. *Come on. We have to keep going. We can't give up. This is for our lives.*

After some time Razak nodded. Once more the beam of the searchlight passed. The older man somehow managed to get to his feet again and took an unsure step forward. His boot sank so deeply into the snow that he had to use his bare hands to dig his foot out. Even though he wanted to, he could not run, could not go any faster. He went as far as he could before the searchlight came around again. Both men quickly fell to the ground.

After the light passed, Razak turned and saw Seidu had fallen behind. He was now some thirty yards back.

Where are you? Seidu called out.

The other man's eyes and face were covered in ice again. Razak watched as Seidu crawled through the snow as if swimming along the frozen terrain. Razak called out, *I'm here. Go on. Keep going.*

One hand after the other, stumbling toward freedom, both men continued on, having been brought lower than either thought was possible.

12

It took three days to cross the Colombian jungle.

Once Seidu and the other asylum seekers were on the other side of the Atrato River, it began to rain incessantly. Seidu followed a guide to a tiny village, deep inside the rain forest, where the asylum seekers were given shelter in a large wooden hut. Villagers—dressed in richly colored clothes, wearing bracelets made of fine, bright beads—welcomed them. There, squatting in the dark, Seidu met a number of other migrants from Ghana who had also crossed on the boat. Joined by Razeem, Seidu's fellow soccer player, the countrymen enjoyed the refuge from the rain and shared stories of their journeys, having no idea how far they actually were from the Panamanian border.

Some of the villagers had spent time in Panama City and knew how to speak English. They asked where the migrants were headed and offered the men food—mangoes, pawpaw fruit—all for free. Excited to see the travelers, they smiled and laughed, attempting to communicate with them by speaking a mixture of English and Spanish.

For two days, the asylum seekers suffered in the rain. When it wasn't raining, mosquitoes descended, making it difficult to sleep. Some of the villagers brought them mosquito nets, but even then a ripe humidity filled the air, forcing the men to sweat through restless, short-lived dreams.

One of the asylum seekers, who spoke some Spanish, asked a villager how far it was to the Panamanian border.

Ajar! the woman said. *You have to cross five mountains before you get to Panama!*

The guides—who were, in the end, only boys—told the men they would leave once it was dark. After some discussion, Seidu and some of the other migrants approached one of the boys and said they did not want to wait until it was dark—they wanted to continue the journey immediately. The boy nodded and led the men back into the jungle once the rain finally stopped.

All through the night the men walked. Some time past midnight, several flashlights appeared before them. Seidu and the other asylum seekers immediately stopped moving, the jungle echoing with their breath. Armed men suddenly emerged from the jungle holding sticks and knives, some wearing bandanas around their noses and mouths to help obscure their faces. Seidu backed away in fright but found that they were surrounded. There was nowhere to run, nowhere to hide. The armed men motioned with their weapons toward the migrants' backpacks. Seidu felt his stomach drop as he instinctively understood what the thieves were after. But he knew he could not give up his bag; inside were his passport and all his travel documents, everything he needed to prove his identity once he got to the U.S. Without the passport, he'd have no way to prove who he was. Could he run? Could he fight? One by one, the asylum seekers handed over their backpacks with a grave sense of embarrassment. The thieves drew closer. As the dread rose in Seidu's chest, he eventually recognized there was no arguing with the edge of a knife. Seidu felt one of the armed men take the bag from his hands before the robbers hurried back into the dark.

Benumbed by shock, physically exhausted, the men fell where they stood and decided to make camp there for the night.

In the morning, before the sun even had the chance to rise, other masked men appeared. It was another group of robbers, this time only carrying sticks.

Seidu awoke to the tumult of the men surrounding him. He looked up from the forest floor and saw that the asylum seekers were once again helpless.

"Shoes," one of the masked men said, and motioned toward Seidu's Converse sneakers. "Give them to us."

Seidu and a few of the other migrants quickly got to their feet and apprised the situation. The robbers did not seem very organized, and there were only five or six of them.

"Shoes," the masked man ordered again.

Seidu refused this time and knelt down to grab a large branch to defend himself. Some of the other migrants did the same. "No," Seidu said. "You're not going to take anything else from us."

The robbers glanced at each other, not knowing what to do. Seidu began swinging the branch wildly and shouting as loud as he could until the attackers rushed back into the jungle.

As soon as they were gone, Seidu felt his hands trembling from both anger and adrenaline. He carried the stick by his side the rest of the day, looking ahead and behind as he walked to be sure he and his companions would not be attacked again.

Hours later, somewhere near the Panamanian border, the boy guides refused to go any farther. They explained that there had been a terrible war between the Colombians and Panamanians. If they accompanied the men any farther, they could be arrested. There was a path, the boys said, that the men should follow. *Go straight through the jungle*, they said, handing one of the men a flashlight. Then the boys walked off into the foliage as if they had only been apparitions.

Seidu and the other migrants moved through the forest on their own. Along the way, the group of twenty men began to split off—some growing tired, others waiting for their companions and friends to catch up.

By the time darkness fell, there were only four of them left in the group—Seidu and three of the other Ghanaians, including Razeem. They decided to stop and try to sleep and start again in the morning. One of the men had a cigarette lighter and together they were able to build a small fire. In the dark, Seidu lay awake, listening to the screams of animals in the forest, fearing the worst. It was one of the longest nights of his journey so far.

In the morning, the four men continued on, following the heavily trodden path.

The sun was high in the sky when they all stopped to pray. There was no water to make their ablutions, so Seidu knelt down and put his hands on the ground, taking some dirt into his palms, and did the sacred gestures, using the dirt to spiritually clean himself before he began his prayers. Once he finished, he thought, *Please, God, make this journey easy for us. Let us pass through this jungle without any harm. You are the one guiding us. Please help us so I can get to my destination, so I can be safe, so I can be who I am meant to be.*

They walked until they were no longer able, deciding to rest in the afternoon. In the jungle, Seidu found he could not sleep. He felt unsafe, unprotected, and kept waking up, hearing the desperate noise of animals nearby and thinking of his loved ones back home. All of their food and water was now gone. After drifting off for a few moments, Seidu awoke and saw that Hamid, an older man from Ghana lying nearby, was also having trouble sleeping.

I haven't drunk anything for days, Hamid murmured, groaning with pain.

The other two men also woke.

What is it? Razeem asked.

Hamid muttered, *I need something to drink soon or I'm not going to be able to go on.*

You can drink your urine if you have to, Razeem replied. *There's a bottle over there if you want to use it.*

After some time, Hamid used the bottle to collect his urine but was not willing to drink from it. Seidu watched, afraid he, too, would soon be faced with the same terrible decision.

They would wait until the sun finally went down—when it was much cooler—to begin walking again.

Hours later, as they crossed through the unrelenting path of dirt, vines, and intersecting trees, Hamid collapsed. The men decided they needed to stop for the night and tried to get Hamid into a comfortable position. Seidu stayed up, keeping watch over the camp, holding the flashlight out before him. The noises from the surrounding forest seemed to grow in intensity the darker it got.

Seidu kept moving the light back and forth. The sounds constantly shifted—there was a far-away clamor, then the rattle of movement much closer. It seemed like something was approaching. Seidu leaned forward, holding the beam of light before him. He was terrified to see a shrunken, human shape, crawling on gnarled, hobbled legs toward the group of sleeping men. It looked like something out of a nightmare as it ambled forward. Seidu blinked the shape into focus and realized it was a black howler monkey, advancing aggressively, its fangs looking fierce.

Seidu looked around and found a sharp stick beside his feet and then held it up defensively, poking it in the monkey's direction.

The creature gave a wild screech and leapt forward, swiping at the branch. Seidu could see its pair of terrible fangs, could make out the shape of its claws. He banged the branch against the trees, waving his arms wildly, trying to frighten the animal off. The animal gave a final shriek and leapt into the dark branches above, its howl filling every corner of the night.

After the monkey's retreat, Seidu was too frightened to sleep. As the moon passed overhead, he kept the flashlight moving back and forth across the camp. At 4:00 a.m., he woke his friends so that they could get moving again. Seidu shook Hamid's tennis shoe but the older man didn't move. Seidu knelt down and studied Hamid's weathered face.

Hamid, he said. *Get up. It's time to go.*

The other man did not move.

Hamid?

Razeem came over and looked hard into Hamid's face. *He's not breathing.*

Seidu pulled off his T-shirt and began fanning his friend in the near dark. Razeem put out a tentative hand and felt Hamid's skin. *I think he's dead.*

Seidu knelt there, gazing in complete disbelief.

He's dead, Razeem repeated. *We can't wait any longer. We have to leave him.*

Seidu began to cry, feeling the sobs come up from some unknown place, mourning as if a family member or longtime friend had been lost. He never considered that someone might die along the way. He placed his shirt over the other man's face before the three men stood there and started to pray.

Seidu closed his eyes, hoping to offer some measure of peace. But there were no words to put to the grief, to the fear he now felt. The rain forest seemed to bear out this uncertainty. It appeared that at the center of the forest and of his journey there was an

inviolable blackness, a chaos that was inescapable, the same dis-
array, the same death, the same senseless suffering he had tried to
escape back home. It was the natural order of things, of humankind, which was no order at all—the strong over the weak, the
healthy over the sick. Even here, thousands of miles away in the
jungle, he had not been able to outrun it. When he finally opened
his eyes, everything was spinning, the cacophony of the jungle
humming in his ears.

He took one final glance at Hamid's body, then followed the
other men into the forest.

Over the course of that day, the three men walked on and eventually became two—Seidu and fellow soccer player Razeem—
leaving their friend in a clearing to rest. Hours later, they paused,
waiting for the other Ghanaian to catch up. But no one came, no
one followed, no matter how long they seemed to wait.

Let's keep moving, Razeem said.

We can't leave him, Seidu argued.

After resting for another hour, both men decided to continue on. Going further along the path, they became incredibly
thirsty—a burning sensation overwhelming their throats and
lungs. It felt like suffocating, drowning on the humid air. The
water they found as they walked—collected in small, muddy
puddles—seemed corrupt, unhealthy. Both of them looked back
and forth along the edge of the jungle for somewhere to get a
drink, for something to eat.

Outside the narrow path were a number of tin cans, their la-
bels still bright with popular colors and designs, advertising unknown foods, but all of these were empty. There were also a few
discarded cans of energy drinks. Seidu stepped off the path and
reached down to check inside one of the cans when he came upon
a shirt. A few feet from that there was a pair of pants hanging

on a low limb. Seidu followed the trail of clothes, hoping to find some food, something to drink, some useful supplies. A few feet on, there was another pair of pants, another shirt. And then he came upon a body lying on the dank earth. Backing away in terror, he saw it was not just one body but several, belonging to other migrants who had been robbed or killed, lying on the ground in a field of waist-high grass—four or five of them, some dressed, others not, all rotting alone, out in the jungle.

The odor of the open grave was rancid and Seidu gagged. Their clothes and belongings had been ransacked, picked over, discarded in the limbs of the low-lying trees. Although Seidu was unsure if the men had died from exhaustion, dehydration, or murder by FARC or other smugglers, he knew was it was not safe for them there.

We need to get out of here, Seidu said.

I can't, Razeem said, leaning against a passel of trees. *I can't keep walking.*

No. We're almost there, Seidu said, giving his companion a shake.

The other man nodded and pulled himself together, then followed Seidu along the path.

After four more hours through the jungle they found an enormous concrete pillar painted with a Panamanian flag. Seidu saw it and smiled, and together he and Razeem crossed into Panama. It had taken everything to get there, and it took everything to keep on going.

After crossing the border, Seidu and his companion walked six more hours through the Panamanian jungle. By then his thirst had become a painful jab with every one of his breaths. His head swam, his legs became weaker and weaker with each step. He felt that if he could not find water soon he would die.

Finally, a small village appeared before them as the jungle flattened and receded. Beside the village was a pond, fed by a narrow river. Seidu dove into the pond, drinking as much of the water as he could, ignoring whatever fears he had about its cleanliness. He sat down on the shore after some time, still feeling light-headed. Razeem yelled at him but he heard nothing. He looked up at the sky, wondering how he had traveled there, so far from what he had known, feeling as if he were floating. Blood pounded in his temples, and then everything went black.

13

Seidu came to on a bench in a small, dark room. He had no idea where he was or what had happened. He blinked himself awake and saw a number of worn-looking faces, other migrants—Indians, Somalis, Haitians, Nepalis—looking over at him. Two Panamanian army officers, identifiable by their faded uniforms, entered and brought Seidu into an interrogation room to search him and his clothing. The remainder of his money was hidden inside a secret pocket he had made in his pants. He was relieved when the officers finished their search and did not find it, though he had no idea what was going to happen now that he was in army custody.

By then Seidu realized he had collapsed on the river, had been left by Razeem, had been discovered by a Panamanian army patrol, and had been brought to an army camp for processing. It was August 2014, more than four weeks since he had begun his journey north.

The two officers brought Seidu into a bathroom. One put on rubber gloves and searched Seidu's body, found nothing, then left him alone to continue waiting.

For days, Seidu waited in the tiny cell. Although the camp did not have a wire fence surrounding it, there was a gigantic river that worked as a boundary, along with the edges of the insurmountable jungle. There were no roads, no cars, nowhere to escape to. After the fifth day, one of the Panamanian officers told Seidu that if he wanted to leave, he'd have to pay twenty dollars to be transferred to another camp farther north.

"We need petrol for our boat," the officer explained.

"I don't have any money," Seidu said.

Eventually the officers forced Seidu and twenty others migrants who being held there onto a narrow boat. Seidu squeezed himself beside the bodies of other people who had come from all corners of the world, all looking out at the perilous river with the same implacable stare, the same warring sense of disappointment and determination.

It took five hours to get from the army camp to a second military installation upriver. Forced to sleep outside without any shelter or blankets, disease-ridden mosquitoes swarmed the men at night. Some of the refugees complained about their living conditions. The army officers demanded, *Dinero! Dinero!* Seidu and the others were told they would have to pay an additional twenty dollars to be transferred to a third camp closer to Panama City.

In a shadowy grove beside the river, Seidu removed ten dollars from its hiding spot in his shoe and offered it to an officer.

"No. Twenty," the officer exclaimed.

Seidu shook his head. "It's all I have."

Then a group of Nepalis approached the officers. They were willing to pay the bribe required to keep the migrants moving north.

Once more the group of asylum seekers was ferried by boat to another army camp, this one near a bend in the river. Everything seemed to be dead or dying. Rotting fish, bloated animal carcasses, piles of garbage, streams of human waste, all floated by. The migrants were told to sleep by the foul-smelling river and given acrid beans to eat. They waited for more than four days while each was interrogated and photographed.

Seidu had fallen asleep on the edge of some river and woken up in a netherworld, a dreamland that kept repeating itself with no possibility of escape.

The fourth camp was an imposing series of permanent concrete buildings where Seidu met several other migrants from Accra—including a former teammate from a soccer club. Happy to speak Hausa and share the story of what he had seen, this sense of joy was short-lived. The mood of the detainment facility was one of complete desperation. The cell where he and the other Ghanaians were kept was stifling, with rusting bunk beds and a single privy in the corner. In the center of the detention facility was a court-yard where detainees from other countries often fought with each other—the Nepalis argued with the Somalis, the Ghanaians took exception to the Somalis—going so far one day as to assault each other and throw benches at their enemies. The army was called in and officers began to indiscriminately beat the detainees into submission.

Seidu was told he would have to wait another seven days in order to receive papers that would allow him to leave the country. After a week, Seidu and some of the other migrants were loaded onto a covered military truck and brought to the capital, Panama City, where they were told to sign a number of documents, which stated they had ten days to leave the country or face further imprisonment.

Seidu and his fellow Ghanaians wasted no time in finding their way to a bus station.

After spending almost three weeks in Panama, Seidu was eager to continue north as quickly as possible. All five of the men secured tickets to Costa Rica. When the bus finally arrived, they climbed aboard, laughing, talking, easing each other's sense of worry and uncertainty. One of Seidu's fellow asylum seekers had a cell phone and was trying to document his journey by posting brief clips on Facebook. Together the men passed the phone back and forth, seeing quick glimpses of themselves. The short videos gave proof of their struggle, the odd images, sounds, moments each man was being forced to confront.

For a day and a half Seidu and his companions rode the bus and then climbed off just before the Costa Rican border, afraid security forces would search them if they stayed on any longer.

By another bus station they found a makeshift shelter and waited, trying to come up with a plan for how to cross. An American man saw them and bought each a bottle of water, then wished them luck on their journey. Seidu was puzzled and touched by this stranger's generosity. Still the migrants watched, looking for a sign. By then they had come to understand part of the language— the symbols, the heuristics of human smuggling—the way someone would nod, glance, pass by in a vehicle multiple times. Later a Costa Rican man and a woman—both looking like Americans in bright T-shirts and shorts, with round faces—approached them at the shelter.

"We can help you," the man said. "We can give you a room and help you cross. Where are you from?"

One of Seidu's traveling partners told them they were all from Ghana.

"We can help you. We have a car. Come with us."

Seidu stared at the couple. There was something about their easygoing manner, their diffidence, their unearned friendliness, that seemed suspicious.

The five Ghanaians got into the SUV and the Costa Ricans drove them to a house near the edge of the jungle, right along the border of Panama and Costa Rica.

"We need three hundred dollars from each of you," the man said.

The Ghanaians negotiated to pay one hundred and fifty dollars each, as soon as they were safe in Costa Rica. The smugglers accepted and told them they would leave that same evening.

In the small house, Seidu and his companions joined five other refugees, sleeping for five hours in a room of deteriorating mattresses and broken light.

At midnight the Costa Ricans led the ten immigrants from the house into the damp-smelling rain forest. The walk seemed unusually long. After two hours the men began to complain.

"Don't worry. We're getting close," the smuggler said.

Seidu glanced over at his friends. They noticed every half hour or so the Costa Rican picked up his cell phone and called someone, murmuring conspiratorially.

I don't trust him, Seidu's friend whispered to him in Hausa.

Seidu nodded. *Me either*, he said. Both of them reached down and grabbed large sticks in case someone tried to rob them. The Costa Rican turned and saw Seidu and his companion arming themselves.

"You don't need any sticks," the man said. "Throw those down."

Seidu shook his head. "We just need them to keep walking."

The man stared at him and nodded.

One hour later, near four in the morning, they came upon a clearing and were told to sit and rest. Once again the Costa Rican made a phone call. Seidu stared out into the darkness, which seemed abysmal, pathless. He heard the complaint of a bird far in the distance.

Then something moved.

Several flashlights—four or five—approached.

Someone was running toward them.

In a momentary flash of clarity and clashing light, a group of masked robbers charged through the underbrush and surrounded the asylum seekers. It was difficult to know how many there were—five, six, or as many as ten. Some of the robbers held machetes, others brandished pistols. All Seidu could make out were interrupted images of menacing masks, imposing firearms, the glint of a blade.

He immediately got to his feet and ran without thinking, searching for refuge somewhere in the dark forest. Going as fast as he could, he groped blindly with his hands held out before him, feeling his way through the trees and vines until he was certain he was safe.

From several hundred yards away he heard gunshots. Hidden behind a copse of trees, he waited, trying to see what the robbers were doing. In the glare of several moving flashlights, Seidu watched as the robbers took his friends' backpacks, their money, their shirts, their shoes, then their pants, leaving some of the men half naked in the middle of the bush. One by one, they set upon the next person, stripping each migrant of his belongings. Seidu angrily witnessed the scene, unable to do anything to help, seeing the humiliation, the sense of powerlessness in each of his companion's faces. When the masked men had taken everything they could, they trampled back into the jungle. The Costa Rican who had been the asylum seekers' guide had also disappeared.

Twenty minutes later, when he was certain the danger had passed, Seidu returned to the open field, following the migrants' call for help. Seidu gave a shirt to one of the men who had been robbed. To another man missing his shoes, he gave a pair of slippers, and to a third man, a pair of pants. After going over their belongings and sharing their remaining clothes, the men realized one of their companions had gone missing in the panic. They called and called, but there was no answer, no sign of their friend. A hopelessness invaded Seidu's mind as it started to rain. Bleary precipitation obscured the path ahead. Still the asylum seekers started off, back into the jungle, unable to find anywhere to take cover. They kept on walking without any sense of direction, drifting into a haze of steam and darkness.

Eventually they came upon the edge of a farm, an enormous plot of land that bordered the jungle, where a gigantic tree grew like some otherworldly umbrella. Seidu and the other migrants gathered under the branches of the trees, watching the rain fall around them, shivering from the cold. In the quiet of the forest, in the near darkness, Seidu could hear waterfalls, monkeys, other wild animals. His heart thumped wildly. He was uncertain if he'd ever find his way to safety again.

14

Before the sun rose, an old man on a white horse rode out to meet the asylum seekers. He wore a white cowboy hat and seemed ancient atop the skinny animal, his face wrinkled, brows furrowed, eyes wise though gentle, like something from a myth or storybook. He made it to the gigantic tree just as the sun appeared over his shoulder.

"I heard a noise last night," he said. "Gunshots. I thought some of you might be out here. I'm an old man and live here alone. I couldn't come by myself. I hope you understand."

"Can you show us the way out?" Seidu asked in English.

The old man pointed north, and then gave further directions for the men to follow. Seidu and some of the others gave the old cowboy a few of their remaining clothes as a sign of gratitude.

Obligato, they said.

The old man smiled, taking the gifts. Seidu held up a hand and the old cowboy waved back, then turned on his horse. Watching him ride off, Seidu considered the kindness the old man had offered. It was enough to compel them to keep going.

One by one, Seidu and his companions stood and stretched, then followed the old man's directions through the jungle to a bus stop on the other side of the Costa Rican border.

•

In some ways Costa Rica reminded him of Accra. The ramshackle homes, the low-wire fences and tattered billboards with logos of gas companies, the advertisements for bottled water. He wondered at how strange it was to travel thousands of miles only to keep seeing the same tired faces, the same fallen places, time and time again. What did it say about the state of all these countries, the fate of all the people he passed, the direction the world turned, continued turning?

On a beach, Seidu and his compatriots met another pair of smugglers who agreed to lead them across the border into Nicaragua. In the middle of the jungle, they were robbed again, this time at knifepoint. Seidu did not hesitate to fight back. Once again he grabbed a thick branch from the ground and swung at his attackers as wildly as he could. Other migrants threw stones and eventually the robbers fled, empty-handed.

Seidu and the other migrants then paid a truck driver to transport them in the back of his semi across the border into Honduras. From there they took a bus to the interior and on to Tegucigalpa, the capital of Honduras. Sleeping in the bus station, a row of dark faces, strangers among the otherwise empty seats, another bus, this time to the Guatemalan border. Crossing again. Human smugglers who offered to help them get to the Mexican border in bicycle pedicabs. Thirty pesos each. The flow of air upon his face, fragrant blossoms of jungle flowers, the dark mountains of Guatemala glowering in the distance. What seemed disposable, almost forgotten, this brief feeling of freedom.

At Tecún Umán, near the border between Guatemala and Mexico, the men faced a wide, dirty river, the Suchiate. Avoiding a large concrete wall built by the Mexican government—intended to limit undocumented immigration—Seidu and the other men met a group of smugglers, shrouded by palm trees, ensconced in a small hut. On the bank of the river, several hastily constructed rafts—made of enormous black rubber inner tubes with pallets of wood attached to the top—sat waiting. No border patrol, no immigration officers, no police seemed to be surveying the scene. It was as public and as deliberate as boarding a bus.

Other migrants—some from Central America, some entire families—were already aboard the oddly shaped vessels, making their way across. Some people stood, some sat while the guides steered the rafts using long poles. Seidu paid his fare and climbed on top. For a moment in the middle of the river, the sun upon his face, it felt as if he was that much closer to safety, that much closer to the United States.

On the other side of the river there was Mexico and, somewhere in the distance, the Tacaná volcano. There was almost nothing to distinguish one country from another anymore. The sagging palm trees, their long leaves covered in dust; the rough, beige land; the cast-off clothes people wore; all of it was irreducible, continuous, a single continent that time had made plain by poverty. Dilapidated stores with metal bars covering their windows and doors, bleak-looking cell phone shops, travel agencies that appeared to have closed years before, all seemed strangely familiar. Shop after shop, business after business, built around the unending flood of migrants that passed along otherwise empty-seeming streets. It was an industry, Seidu recognized, an international enterprise connecting one country to another through a web of migrants, human smugglers, low-level criminals, robbers, drug cartels, human traffickers, the police, the military, and ordinary citizens who had all found a way to profit from human suffering. It was difficult to know how many millions of dollars these legal and illegal businesses accumulated each year, taking advantage of asylum seekers on their way north. But if prostitution was the oldest profession, then perhaps this—making a living off the displaced, the dispossessed—was the second.

Seidu followed the other migrants through the town. Each seemed to already know that they had no choice but to present themselves to the Mexican immigration authority.

Undocumented immigration is an administrative issue in Mexico, not a criminal offense. The Instituto Nacional de Migración (INM) is charged with enforcing migration law and does so with aggressive efficiency, armed with vehicles and equipment that have oftentimes been supplied by their U.S. counterparts, Immigration and Customs Enforcement (ICE).

Each country in South and Central America enforces immigration in its own way, with varying degrees of corruption and varying degrees of success. Many local police units seem content simply to keep asylum seekers moving north, often taking advantage of migrants who find themselves unable to cross a border without the proper visa or identification. Local police or border agents may require a bribe or turn a blind eye to an undocumented migrant passing before them. Enforcement in many of these countries is based on an individual officer's sense of duty and justice, rather than a federally mandated policy.

Mexico's INM, on the other hand, is a nationally coordinated agency, relentless in its mission to supervise all aspects of immigration within Mexico—aiding, apprehending, interviewing, registering, and detaining any migrants who pass through its boundaries. Unlike corresponding agencies in other Central and South American countries, the INM is federally funded with oversight from the secretariat of the interior. It is highly professional and highly bureaucratic, and its enforcement strategies seem to be strongly influenced by the politics and policies of the United States at any particular moment.

The INM building in Tapachula—a cubist, rectangular building with a green roof—is evidence of a highly organized, federally regulated program. The building is almost always busy. As Seidu approached it that afternoon, he saw a long line of asylum seekers already waiting in groups identifiable by their homeland. Seidu queued up along with a number of other asylum seekers, most of whom were men.

When it was his time to meet with an immigration officer, Seidu explained his case, speaking slowly in English, sketching out his hope to reach the United States. The official—a woman—asked to see his documents, all of which were missing. He explained they had been stolen along the way in Colombia.

"Very bad," the officer said. "We have to contact your consulate in Washington, D.C. You will have to wait here for sixty days before you can proceed to the U.S."

The INM detention facility in Tapachula was surrounded by a long white and green wall, shaded by tall trees of the jungle. From the outside, it looked more like the façade of a suburban subdivision than it did a prison.

Inside was less welcoming, though it still had the appearance of a public building. Cream-colored walls, concrete tables and chairs, metal benches, all seemed like they belonged in an outdoor park somewhere. Watercoolers were spaced at odd intervals. There was a large, open-air central courtyard where men, all dressed in their own clothes, some shirtless, gathered in groups by country of origin.

In the detention facility was a small soccer pitch where Seidu and other Ghanaians regularly routed teams composed of migrants from other countries. Bets were made. Ten pesos. Thirty pesos. Fifty pesos. Ecuadorians. Colombians. Haitians. Everyone playing. Eventually the other teams caught on and chose not to contest the Ghanaians.

You could wear your own clothes, watch soccer on one of the televisions, wash your laundry in the bathroom, control your own money, but it was still detainment against your will. Your cellmate had to use the bathroom in front of you. The odor of the building was stale, sometimes foul, musty with human fecundity. The food was foreign, mostly rice, beans, tortillas. Once a week there was chicken. A lingering sense of unease, of hope deferred, clung to the air. It was hard to imagine detention being any different.

He heard stories from some of the other men—Hondurans, Guatemalans—who said they were beaten by INM officers or placed in solitary confinement for lengthy periods of time. Others who had already traveled to the United States and had since been deported talked about being imprisoned in the U.S.—where you were not allowed to wear what you wanted, to carry your own money, to start your own business, to call back home whenever you wanted—but Seidu did not know if any of these rumors were true.

After thirty days in the INM detention facility, Seidu was finally released. "Your embassy has not responded to our request," an immigration officer told him, handing him his exit papers. "So there's nothing more we can do. You have twenty days to leave the country."

All along the main road of Tapachula, there were budget hotels that catered to migrants without documentation, some as cheap as ten dollars a night. Down a brick street wet with rain, Seidu took a room at a nameless inn and used the Facebook app on his cell phone to contact his brother Kamal in Florida. Seidu explained the situation—where he was, what he was intending to do. Without hesitation, Kamal sent him $300 through Western Union. The plan was for Seidu to buy a bus ticket and present himself to the U.S. port of entry near the border town of Tijuana.

Three more days on the bus. Sleeping. Eating chips and soda pop. Police frequently stopped the vehicle to check that migrants had their exit papers. The officers in Mexico never asked for money, only wanting to see his documents. Security seemed much tighter as the bus approached the U.S. border in California.

Seidu climbed off the bus after three days and followed the long line of other migrants into the San Ysidro U.S. Port of Entry building, just south of San Diego, a sprawling steel facility that looked like a modern airport. U.S. Customs and Border Protection officers, in stark blue uniforms, carrying pistols, were posted in groups of two or three around the facility. Seidu had no idea what to expect, had no idea what they would ask, was only certain that his documents had been stolen and that his life depended on him being allowed to stay in the U.S.

Once inside the building, he waited in line for several hours until a U.S. Customs and Border Protection officer, sitting at a small stainless steel booth, motioned him over. He took a deep breath and crossed over into oblivion.

~~~~~

Every five or ten minutes Seidu's eyes would be completely frozen and both men would have to stop to clear the ice away. Razak would then crawl ahead again, marking the way with his voice.

Keep going, he shouted. *Ten more feet. Eight more. I'm here. I'm right here. Follow my voice!*

Once the light made its way around, he would watch Razak rush forward. The fence seemed so close now, a tangle of unthreatening wire, half-buried in the snow. As soon as they were across, the ordeal would be over. All they had to do was find a Canadian immigration officer, signal to some vehicle on the highway, or call the police.

One step and then another, the silver wire, rusted and bent, rising weakly before them in the snow.

One step and then another.

Twenty yards ahead Razak was at the fence, touching it, pushing it down with his bare hands. Lifting one foot over, he turned and looked back.

Past the light now, beyond the reach of the U.S. Border Patrol, Razak called out, *Keep going. Keep going straight. I'm in Canada now,* he shouted. *I'm in Canada!*

The younger man lurched on, reaching out with his frozen hands.

Razak kept yelling until his voice was all but gone, swallowed by the bitterness of the wind and cold.

Eventually both men passed the snow-covered wire and stumbled through the dark into what seemed some other undiscovered country. Once they had climbed far from the fence, they looked back at the border, which had all but disappeared, as if the land behind them had never existed. Then they turned and faced north. The echoes—the emptiness of the wind, howling from somewhere ahead—was not what they had expected. In the air above, there was a huge flag flying, but they could not make out what was on it. It appeared as something black and menacing. Uncertainty and the fear of being remanded back to the United States forced them to keep moving, both men worrying that they might still be in some netherworld between the two countries.

On they went through the ankle-deep snow, but there was no Canada Border Services Agency building anywhere that they could see. No border patrol officers. No vehicles. There was no one there to help, nothing but the highway looming in the distance. It was around four-thirty in the morning. The sky was as dark as it had ever been. Frozen, exhausted, and out of breath, they fumbled forward together once more.

In the end, all they had done was cross from one kind of desolation to another.

15

More than halfway to the United States, Razak began to feel like
an outcast, as if he were marked, a target for smugglers and un-
sympathetic local police. On the bus to San Jose, the capital of
Costa Rica, he looked out the window and watched a police car
approach. Lights flashed and the bus pulled over. Razak and the
other men he was traveling with quickly hid their passports, tap-
ing them to the inside of their thighs. Costa Rican police—decked
out in regal blue uniforms—boarded the bus and walked straight
to the back seats where the asylum seekers had been sleeping. One
of the officers muttered, *Documentos.*

Razak handed the officer his voter ID from Ghana.

The officer looked at the ID and shook his head. *No. Docu-
mento. Passporte?*

"We don't have passports."

"Get your bags," one of the officers said, and led them off
the bus.

Outside, in the humid air, the officers searched the men, tear-
ing through their bags. Unwilling to present their passports, the
officers brought the asylum seekers to a local police station.

Inside the station, one of the officers asked, "Where are you
going?"

"We're trying to leave your country," Razak said. "We didn't come here to stay."

"You guys are not supposed to be here without passports. Where are you going?"

"Estados Unidos," Razak replied.

"You know that's against the law, to cross the border without a passport."

"What can we do? None of us could stay in our countries back home."

One of the officers fingerprinted Razak, then Mohammed Mamoud, along with a number of other asylum seekers. A second officer took their photos before interviewing each man. Expecting the police to ask for a bribe, Razak was surprised when one of the officers announced that the asylum seekers would have to go to the main immigration office to apply for asylum. Apparently, in Costa Rica, crossing the border without documents was not a criminal act, was merely an administrative issue, which helped to limit local police and political corruption.

After filling out a number of forms, the police released the men from their custody, then drove them to the bus station and instructed them on how to get to the main immigration office downtown. *It was strange*, Razak thought—the humility, the professionalism of the police. And still even he could see that, although polite, the police no longer looked at him like he was human.

At the Immigration Office in San Jose, there were migrants from all over the world waiting in line—from places as diverse as Thailand, Panama, and Chile. Razak had never seen anything like it. There was no way to know how many people, from how many different countries, how many different continents, were passing through on their way up to Mexico and eventually to the United States. Various Central American governments placed the number at around 150,000 each year, but other social organizations claimed it was as high as 400,000.

As they stood in line, Razak realized he and his companions were the only ones from Africa. There appeared to be a large number of migrants from China and Pakistan and other parts of Asia. For some reason, the other asylum seekers in line looked at Razak and his companions and laughed. He did not know why. Perhaps it was the way they looked—beaten, haggard, their clothes limply hanging on their bodies. Maybe it was their fatigued expressions or their failed attempts to speak Spanish. It could be that even here—in a long line of individuals who had almost nothing left to call their own—there was still the entanglement of race. It was also infuriating that among the cacophony of so many different languages, so many different cultures, the pervading distance, the relentless uncertainty, all of it made clear that so many people from across the world were fleeing their homelands, had chosen to give everything up, under threat of life and limb. What did it say about how the world, how these distinct nations organized themselves? How could so many people be so unhappy as to risk their lives in exchange for a chance of some other way of living? Was the world really that broken? He shuddered as the answer seemed to appear in the line before him.

The immigration office was completely overwhelmed. The Costa Ricans were attempting to confront the issue of migration with fairness and dignity, but there were just too many people passing across their border. After waiting in line for several hours, a translator from the immigration service came over to Razak and his companions and said, "I'm sorry. We can't help you. You have seventy-two hours to leave the country. You can take the bus to Nicaragua."

"That's what we've been trying to do."

From there the men took a bus close to the border of Nicaragua. Darkness turned the bus windows an unsettling shade of blue. Razak dozed for as long as he could. Once again, the men climbed off before passing across the border on foot.

In Nicaragua, the small cities and mountains looked washed away. The men hired a smuggler to take them through the jungle to the border of Honduras. While they were climbing through the forest, a number of armed men appeared with rifles and knives and started shouting, "Money, money." Before beginning his journey, Razak had never been robbed. It now happened with such frequency that Razak, overcome with exhaustion, simply gave whatever money he had left in his pocket—about one hundred and fifty dollars—having hid an additional $1,000 in his shoes. The armed men took the money and climbed back into the jungle, as if they, too, were only another part of the lurid landscape. It seemed that at any moment, someone could appear and take everything you had, even your life.

Passing the border into Honduras, the men gave another smuggler twenty dollars once they were safely across. They were told to wait for a bus into the interior of the country. Razak and the other asylum seekers stood along the side of the road and watched as a number of large semitrucks were loaded to carry goods back across the border to Nicaragua.

Moments later a Honduran police patrol vehicle made its way along the length of the border. Razak and his two companions ran behind a line of parked semitrucks. A truck driver who was waiting for his vehicle to be loaded saw them trying to hide and quickly waved them over, then opened the empty trailer for them. Razak and the other men hurried inside, thanking him for his kindness. The man was middle-aged and began speaking Spanish.

Razak shook his head. "No Spanish."

"You going to America?" the man asked in English.

"Yes, we are."

The driver nodded and went to watch for when the Honduran border patrol left, and then even went so far as to wave down a taxi. The man told the driver to take the migrants to the bus station, where they boarded a bus to the Honduran capital, Tegucigalpa.

One half hour outside the capital, the bus slowed for a police checkpoint. Razak looked over at Mohammed Mamoud and asked, "What are we going to do?"

Police officers boarded the bus, checking passports one by one as they moved along the aisle. Razak felt his face burning. One of the officers approached and asked for his documents in Spanish.

"English," Razak said.

The police officer eyed Razak and said, "Come with me."

The officer led the three asylum seekers off the bus and told the bus driver to go on. The men were put in the back of a police vehicle and driven off without explanation.

For an hour and a half the three migrants waited in a small police facility. Finally, a commanding officer who spoke English asked them where they were going.

"Estados Unidos," Razak replied.

"Where are your documents?"

"We don't have documents."

The commanding officer nodded and then offered, "Each of you have to pay one hundred dollars, American. Then we'll let you go."

"No money," Razak responded.

The officer grinned and said, "Then we're going to have to lock you up."

They began to lead Mohammed Mamoud toward a cell when Razak said, "Okay, we can talk. What if each of us gives you fifty dollars?"

The officers took the bribe and turned the asylum seekers free. As the men exited the building, other police officers they passed murmured, *Dolares. Dolares.*

Razak shook his head in anger. It was humiliating enough to be arrested, to be forced to pay to move freely from place to place, but to see the extent to which this kind of degradation was so ingrained, was such a part of the culture, was troubling. To them, all you were was an opportunity, a potential bribe.

One of the cops flagged down a taxi and put them in it, sending them onto Tegucigalpa, where they had to wait for a bus to Agua Caliente, a city on the western border of Honduras.

No documents were needed to buy a ticket, and the men had several hours before the next bus departed. As they waited, two Africans approached the ticket counter. One of them asked Razak in English, "Where are you from?"

"I'm from Ghana."

The other man began to laugh.

"Why, what about you?" Razak asked.

"Nigeria."

The second African shook his head and said, "Don't listen to him. He's from Ghana."

The Ghanaian introduced himself as Fred and told Razak he had been born in Accra, in Sabu Zongo, a neighborhood that was similar to Nima in its economic and political challenges. Together Razak and Fred and the other men shared stories of leaving their home and traveling through South America. Fred invited Razak and his traveling partners to eat with them. It felt good to be able to speak Hausa, to talk politics, to discuss football, though there was something tentative underlying their conversation, a note of gallows humor in the air.

The men finished their meal and returned to the bus station as a group, telling jokes and exchanging their plans for the future. Around 10:00 p.m., two police vehicles arrived. Dozens of police officers surrounded the station.

"Nobody leaves," one of the officers shouted.

The Honduran police rounded up anyone without papers and then put them in the back of a pickup. By now, Razak was no longer surprised, even at the indignity of being handcuffed. He sat in the back of the pickup, already certain of what was about to happen.

At another police station, a police officer called out each group of migrants by their nationality and then led them outside.

"Who is Cuban?"

"Who is Haitian?"

"Who is African?"

One by one, each group was told they would be transported to the immigration facility downtown.

At the central immigration facility, Razak and his companions were put in a large cell with a single toilet and several worn-out bunk beds. All night he paced back and forth. None of the asylum seekers had been fed, none of them had been offered water. Finally, Razak spoke up.

"Listen. We need water," he complained. "We need food. You can't keep us like this."

The other migrants told Razak to be quiet.

"No. We haven't eaten or had anything to drink," he continued.

A young police officer came over and asked what it was Razak wanted.

Razak looked at the young man and grinned. "I'll tell you what I'd like. I'd like a hot dog."

The other asylum seekers all thought Razak had gone crazy. *You're not serious. You are here illegally and you're asking for hot dogs?*

The young policeman looked at Razak and said, "A hot dog and what else?"

"A hot dog and something to drink."

The officer nodded and walked away.

A half hour later the officer returned with a greasy bag and handed it to Razak. Inside was a hot dog and fries. The migrants marveled at Razak's luck, all of them laughing and shouting.

You have to be willing to speak up, Razak said. *You can't be afraid to remind them you're a person.*

One of the other asylum seekers asked, *Are you going to share that?*

The police officer asked the other migrants, "Do you all want some?" and then made a second trip, returning with food for the other migrants.

In the morning, a Honduran immigration officer arrived and announced that Razak and the other asylum seekers would be released. First they were fingerprinted, then interviewed, and then one of the officers demanded each migrant pay $100 for their freedom.

Over and over again, Razak was forced to confront the same inequities, the same police corruption, the same blunt use of power that he had traveled thousands of miles to escape. Once more he had been rendered voiceless, powerless. Sitting in the dirty cell, it was becoming clearer and clearer to Razak that the West was entirely dependent on the clandestine industry of undocumented immigration and that few people were interested in seeing anything change. It was a secret everyone was aware of but no one was willing to talk about. Without migrants and other asylum seekers passing through, some of the people in these Central American towns would have few ways to make money. The smugglers, the corrupt police, the local politicians, all seemed to benefit from a complete lack of scrutiny when it came to immigration.

Other men he was traveling with also mentioned how these same countries benefited from undocumented labor in the United States—particularly Guatemala, Honduras, and El Salvador; how altogether these nations received more than $14 billion a year from money sent back home from the U.S., which, in turn, became an enormous part of their individual economies. It was to their financial advantage to keep all these determined men and women forever hiding in the dark.

Razak had seen enough. Unable to contain his anger any longer, he asked to speak with the commanding officer.

"We've been paying money since we began traveling. We don't have any more money!"

The commanding officer looked down and frowned with what seemed to be some degree of understanding. "I see. But if you don't pay, we can't release you."

Once he calmed down, Razak spoke with Mohammed Mamoud and Fred and the other asylum seekers. Eventually, all of the migrants agreed that they had no choice but to pay. They were each issued a travel visa—a piece of paper—that was supposed to guarantee free movement within the country for a period of ten days. They returned to the bus station and were finally able to take the bus to Agua Caliente, near the border of Guatemala.

Once aboard, Razak rested his head against the back window, feeling as if had fallen into some nightmare, one where he found himself endlessly walking in the dark, lost in a world where the borders were constantly shifting.

16

Nightfall. Through the jungle once again. The leaves glistening with precipitation, turning silver under the light of the moon. The muffled footsteps of the men, marching in a queue, passing over muddy ground, shuffling beneath the towering figures of trees. Shadows that were not shadows, simply the shapes of unresolved things—plants, vines, rocks, animals—the entire land changing, moving, whispering. Something hallowed, humbling about the procession, the movement of men, passing silently beneath the trees. Pilgrims on a journey to some unknowable country, walking right off a cliff.

Where am I going?

On the other side of the border was Guatemala, which at that hour was only a figment, a suggestion of night; they paid the smuggler $100 each after they crossed and then carried forth on their own.

Razak followed Mohammed Mamoud and the other migrants into a small border town, and the men once again found a bus station where they could sleep and wait for the next bus.

The country of Guatemala passed briefly from the corner of another bus window. He saw the round faces of people who had come down from mountain villages to sell their wares in the market.

The colors, the clothes, a baby slung on its mother's back, laughter from an outdoor stall, all of it unfamiliar though familiar. More and more, these faces gave way to the faces of other migrants, who began to crowd the back seats of the bus with the same benumbed expression of the uninvited. He awoke and the bus ride was almost over. Other people like him had traveled that way before and were still coming. Paths had been tracked all along the side of road, the direction of the wind and weather all pointing north.

He got off into a crowd of other migrants, trying to hide in a place where there was nowhere to be hidden.

At the border of Guatemala and Mexico near the Suchiate River, again, there were migrants from every part of the world. Hondurans, Nicaraguans, Haitians, Cubans, Africans, Asians, all heading north. It was September 2012, but he did not know the exact date. He had been traveling for two months, he realized as he faced this second-to-last border.

After some time, Razak and his companions were approached by a man in a van who offered to help them cross the river.

The man drove the migrants to a concrete building that looked as if construction on it had stopped years before. In the shadows of the building, other migrants had gathered and were negotiating the price of crossing the river.

"Each of you need to pay one fifty," the man said.

Razak shook his head. He had only sixty dollars left. He began to argue and the man threatened to leave. Mohammed Mamoud quickly intervened.

"We'll each give you a hundred pesos."

The smuggler agreed and led them through the jungle, under a long bridge, down to the banks of the Suchiate River, where a number of other migrants were all standing. Men, women, children, entire families, what looked to be a village of undocumented people, all waiting for the makeshift rafts constructed of wood and rubber. The migrants climbed aboard the enormous inner tubes and were transported across within moments, one after the other. It was chaotic. Razak crossed, having never exchanged money with any off the guides operating the rafts.

Once they had made it across to Mexico, one of the smugglers told them to walk to a nearby street before the INM officers arrived. The men hurried away into the night. Razak glanced at the town as they moved along the street. Concrete and plaster storefronts. Flat roofs. Signs announcing TORTILLAS 100% MASECA. Balloons, children's clothing, assorted plastic toys all hanging in see-through bags like at a carnival. A deserted main square with fading orange stucco. Graffiti on a bare wall that argued LOS MIGRANTES NO SOMOS CRIMINALES. SOMOS TRABAJADORES INTERNACIONAL. In the dark, the group of men discussed where they needed to go. There were no guides, no signposts. No one knew how to proceed.

Four young men eventually appeared from the shadows, one of whom spoke English.

"Where you guys going?"

Razak looked at their faces, saw no expression, then glanced down and realized that two of the young men were holding knives. One had a pistol. One seemed to be smiling.

Maleta! one of them yelled, motioning to the asylum seekers' backpacks. *Maleta!*

Another man said in English, "Give us your money! Give us your backpacks!"

By then Razak had been robbed and extorted so often that all he felt was an intensifying rage. All along the journey he had been taken advantage of, had been abused. Now, so close to his destination, some other group of assailants was trying to take all that he had left. The backpack contained the remainder of his life, all he had been able to hold on to—his passport, his voter ID, his birth certificate, his cell phone, his clothes. His remaining sixty dollars was hidden inside his sock, but without his backpack and his documentation, the money itself would be useless.

"Give us your bags!" the thief shouted again. The men held their knives to the asylum seekers' necks and faces. There was no way to fight, nothing to defend themselves with. One after the other, the exhausted migrants obeyed, slipping the backpacks from their heavy shoulders.

Furious now, but having no other choice, Razak regretfully handed the thieves his bag, knowing that in doing so, his life would be that much more difficult. It was like losing a piece of himself, some vital organ, some crucial part of his spirit, his hope.

The thieves grabbed as many wallets and backpacks as they could carry, then hurried away into the sweltering dawn. Razak paced back and forth, holding his hands to his eyes. He had nothing now, was dispossessed, had been stripped bare of almost everything. Standing in the empty street, the men were all in shock, did not know what had just happened, or what to do next. Even Mohammed Mamoud seemed shaken.

Later the men wandered along the street aimlessly until a taxicab pulled up and drove them to the nearby INM immigration facility in Tapachula, Chiapas. Razak paid the driver with twenty of his remaining sixty dollars and climbed out.

At that hour of the early morning, dozens of other migrants were already waiting. As he waited for his turn, Razak thanked Mohammed Mamoud and Fred for helping him make it that far.

Once inside the rectangular green and white building, the men were each processed separately, and each of them were given a number of forms to fill out.

What is your destination?

Razak wrote: The United States.

If you have any family in the United States, please list them there.

Razak wrote: I don't have anybody in the States.

A translator who spoke English explained that Razak and the other men from Ghana and Nigeria would all be detained for three months because they were undocumented and had no proof of their identity. There was no Ghanaian consulate in Mexico, and so the Mexican government would have to contact the embassy in Washington, D.C.

Razak grew upset. "Why do I have to stay for three months?"

"That's the process. You don't any have any ID. We don't know anything about your status."

That same night, Razak and some of the other men were brought to the INM detention facility in Tapachula. He had not been given a chance to say goodbye to Mohammed Mamoud or Fred or some of the other asylum seekers who had been sent to another detention facility. Once again he found himself alone. Beyond the low concrete wall outside the window of his cell, he could see the sun setting—pink, orange, blue, layers after layer of color. It looked like a fading flag.

17

In Mexico, Razak quietly acclimated to detention. The slow pace of institutionalized life, the laconic feel of the weather, was unfamiliar at first. The INM detainment facility had bunk beds that were built from concrete with narrow mattresses placed on top. Ten detainees shared a small room with a single toilet, though there was a larger bathroom at the end of the hall.

There were men from all over the world in detention, a collision of every kind of language and culture. Hondurans, Guatemalans, Costa Ricans, men from all across Africa, Asia, Haiti, the Dominican Republic. To look upon their faces in the courtyard or during meals, to hear them speak to each other in a clash of words and dialects, to be able to go from West Africa to Korea and then to Panama simply by walking down the hall or moving from table to table was both humbling and mystifying.

Each morning at six, the cell doors opened and the detainees were released, allowed to move freely about the facility. Every evening after dinner, the detainees were once again locked down. But the sense of openness, of some degree of freedom, was not what Razak expected.

When they opened the cell doors in the morning, most of the men ended up congregating to watch television in one of the common areas. The FIFA World Youth Championship were being broadcast. The tournament included teams from Ghana, Mexico, and the United States. Most of the detainees supported the U.S. team with an air of hope, having no idea what was going to happen to them once they actually crossed into America. Razak watched the matches and wondered.

After a month, Razak met a man from Honduras named Reynaldo, who had lived in the U.S. for nearly twenty years. He had been deported, sent back to Honduras, and had been making his way back to the U.S. when he was arrested by Mexican authorities. He had been in the detention facility for four months.

"You don't have to sit here," Reynaldo told him. "You have to do something. You can open a business. People like to smoke cigarettes here. You can sell cigarettes. You got any money?"

"I have forty dollars left."

"That should be enough."

Remembering his successful business back home, Razak went to the commissary and bought several packs of cigarettes and began selling single cigarettes for one peso each, a nearly five-dollar profit. Early each morning, Razak set up in between the facility's soccer pitch and basketball court with Reynaldo, putting the cigarettes out before them. Other Africans joined them at the table and soon it was much like the repair shop back in Accra—Razak becoming friends with a number of the different inmates and their factions, Guatemalans, Costa Ricans, Hondurans, anyone who could speak English.

Fumale, fumale, he called out. "I have cigarettes here!"

When someone asked one of the guards for a cigarette, the officers would all point toward Razak.

Soon he saved up enough money to buy calling cards for

twenty pesos—*tarjetas*—which he would then sell to other detainees for twenty-five or thirty pesos.

When he had saved up enough money, Razak bought a calling card and called his mother. The operator spoke in Spanish and Razak's mother quickly got confused and hung up. He then tried Cynthia's number and told her he was in a prison in Mexico.

It's been more than two months! she said. *We haven't heard anything from you. We've been terrified!*

It was unreal hearing her voice from the other side of the world. It was like leaving the prison as it appeared around him—with its cracked, stucco ceiling, fetid heat, and unpredictability—and stepping into something resembling a memory or a dream. It did not belong there, the soft timbre of her breathing. At first he did not know what to say, and only pressed the receiver to his ear, wondering what to tell her, what not to tell. How could he explain that he had been robbed, extorted by the police again and again, that his passport had been stolen, that he was being now detained in a foreign land, that he wanted to give up time and time again, and had no idea what lay ahead? How could he describe the precipice he now found himself standing on? How could he say all the things he was thinking, feeling, without breaking her, without ruining their future relationship completely? In the end all he could summon up were a few understated words.

It's been a very difficult journey.

There was a pause and then Cynthia asked, *How long are you going to be there?*

I think I have one month more before I'm released.

There was another pause as both of them considered what to say.

What will you do after they release you? she asked.

I'll go to the United States. I'm going to be okay once I get there.

The line was silent once again. He waited to see if it would break, if she would break. After a moment, she said, *Okay. I'll be waiting to hear from you.* He grinned. For days afterward he replayed the conversation over and over in his head.

As the weeks went on, Razak felt a sense of pride in the small business he had built. When other Africans arrived at the facility, they made it a point to introduce themselves to Razak. Although some detainees approached him looking for illicit substances—marijuana or cocaine—he shook his head, afraid trafficking in those items would delay his release.

After ninety days, Razak was released from detention. Immigration officers explained that there had been no response from the Ghanaian embassy in Washington, D.C.

"You are not seeking asylum here, so the only thing we can do is release you. You have twenty days to leave Mexico or you will be imprisoned."

Razak signed the papers before him and the officers gave him a copy to show to any police or immigration officers that might stop him.

After he was released, he counted up the money he had made from selling cigarettes and phone cards. It was nearly $300. He got a room at a small hotel in downtown Tapachula and called Cynthia and his mother from a pay phone.

Look, his mother said. *I have a brother. Your uncle. I haven't talked to him in some time. He's lived in the U.S. for the past thirty-two years.*

An uncle?

I have his contact information. If you're able to call him, maybe he can help you.

Razak's mother called her brother in New York that same evening and let him know her son would be in touch. The next morning, Razak called the number and his uncle Malik answered. His voice was kind, jovial, full of warmth.

I was expecting your call. Your mother told me you'd be in touch, he said. *The year that you were born was the same year I left. Where are you?*

I'm in Mexico.

Where in Mexico?

Chiapas.

So how do you plan on getting into the U.S.? Do you have a visa?

No, I don't. I have to go through the asylum process.

I don't know how that works. Do you need help?

I could use some money. I have a little but I think I need more for a bus ticket to get to the border.

Okay. I can help you with that.

A one-way bus ticket to Tijuana was two hundred and fifty dollars. Razak's uncle wired the money to Western Union in care of a local hotel owner, a woman who collected the money and kindly escorted him to the bus station. Razak was still missing his passport and documents but showed the bus terminal authorities his exit paper from the INM and was given a ticket on August 3, 2013.

After a two-and-a-half-day journey on the bus, Razak presented himself at the San Ysidro Port of Entry pedestrian lane on August 6, 2013. He had $600 in his possession, money he had saved from the business he had run in the INM facility with the addition of the money his uncle had sent.

Before him was the U.S. border, the flag mythic, unquestionable, gigantic—dividing the air on the other side of a long silver bridge. Razak passed groups of people camped out on the sidewalk, lying on blankets before makeshift tents all along the high concrete border wall. He entered a slate-colored building and took his place in a seemingly endless queue of migrants that looped back and forth in on itself, filling the entire lobby. Faces in all shades and shapes and sizes—old, middle-aged, children, infants—Africans, Asians, people from Mexico and South and Central America—entire families carrying luggage and presents—young men wearing nothing but backpacks—women with babbling infants on their hips—children gazing emotionlessly at the void ahead, holding their parents' unsteady hands—an unshifting mass of humans stretching far beyond anything he had expected.

Razak took note of the gender, the age, the countries of origin for all the people ahead and behind him. With more than 11 million unauthorized migrants living in the U.S., the largest percentage of individuals came from Mexico—more than 52 percent—followed by El Salvador at 6 percent, Guatemala at 5 percent, China at 3 percent, and Honduras, also at 3 percent. Fifty-three percent were men, 47 percent were women, and most of these people were between the ages of twenty-five and forty-five. It was like staring at the face of the world itself, endless in all its permutations and expressions, one body after the other, all arriving with their own stories, their own set of circumstances.

Hours passed, giving him time to consider each step he had taken that had led him to that point.

A U.S. Customs and Border Protection agent—an African American man—finally called Razak forward. The officer asked Razak where he was from. Razak gave him the document he had received in Mexico.

"This isn't what I want. I want your documents."

"I don't have any documents. I lost my passport. It was stolen."

"Stolen, huh? Where are you from?"

"Ghana. I'm here to seek asylum."

The officer nodded and asked his name, his age, and his date of birth. Razak answered truthfully, giving as much information as he could. When he finished, the officer told Razak to stand to the side where four other African migrants were waiting.

Moments later, two Customs and Border Protection officers appeared, carrying several pairs of handcuffs and leg chains. The officers told the men to turn around. Razak was bewildered and asked, "What's going on?"

"Turn around and put your hands back."

All throughout his journey, from Brazil, through Panama, Costa Rica, Nicaragua, Honduras, Guatemala, and Mexico, he had been handcuffed only once by the Honduran police, and even then, the restraints had been removed as soon as he was brought to the police station. He had never once thought that the U.S. officers at the border would handcuff him for presenting himself legally for asylum.

"Turn around," one of the officers muttered.

Razak tried to convince himself this was only part of the process, and placed his hands out for the officers to lock into place. It felt like some terrible, critical mistake had been made. He had followed the rules, had not entered illegally, wasn't a criminal. The cold steel bit into his wrists as one of the officers leaned down and put a waist restraint around his middle, then attached leg restraints to his ankles. Hands bound together, Razak closed his eyes and tried to prepare for what would happen next.

Part Three

Borderlands

18

The United States is a poem, a song, an apparition. Its power resides in the fact that it's largely imaginary. On paper it extends in a swath across the plains and mountains of North America, with its irregularly shaped states, its circles denoting major cities, its primary colors bisecting political districts by population, age, ethnicity, class. But its hills, its rivers, its valleys, all of them are essentially nameless, have gone for millennia without markers, without distinction. Only in the last few hundred years have these borders, these abstract lines, come to mean anything. Men and women have come to live and die, have learned to sacrifice by these boundary marks, which in the end are almost all invented. The thing that has always distinguished the United States from its very beginning is that it has always been more compelling as an ideal, a concept, a dream.

The power the United States holds over the imagination—especially in the twenty-first century—is particularly real. Its citizens are granted inalienable rights by the U.S. Constitution, which allows individuals the opportunity to express free speech in criticism of its leaders, access to an impartial judicial system, the ability to voice their concerns in the form of a representative democratic government, the right to a free public education, and the safety of a wide-ranging national infrastructure. The U.S. boasts some of the highest personal incomes anywhere in the world. Its influence—both political and cultural—is at the center of much of the international community's conversations.

For this reason, the naming and the granting of these rights and powers to an individual has always been a particularly fraught exercise.

The United States has a complicated legacy when it comes to the issue of immigration. By its very nature, it was a nation conceived by people who were migrants themselves—human beings willing to risk everything they had in order to search for something better. It has always been a nation of ceaseless movement, of people pursuing that which has yet to appear.

Before the country's inception, Native Americans roamed the expanse of North America, many following the migratory patterns of the animals they hunted. These same people, it's now surmised, traveled thousands of miles across land-bridges lost to the passage of time. Over hundreds of years, these tribes wandered, fought, built cities on the plains, only to move again with the seasons, to start over when necessary, in order to survive.

Before there was even a name for this nation, conquistadors from Spain landed along the southern territories while colonists from England and France and other parts of Europe made their way to eastern shores. These migrants found a land of bounty tempered by the harshness of the unknown. At that time, an American was any person brave or foolish enough to make the journey—entrepreneurs, religious fanatics, indentured servants—all fleeing to America in the 1600s, willing to struggle for economic opportunities, seeking freedom from religious difficulties, crawling to the rocky shores, wind-lashed and broken by months at sea. Then, being an American had to do with one's ability to risk life and limb for something improbable, to take refuge in the uncertain.

Once the colonies had formed governments throughout the seventeenth century, American citizenship meant being white and male—though to wield any sort of power, most men in political circles also had to be landowners, had to have been born into an aristocratic family with deep ties to England, or had to have adapted successful business ventures for the New World.

The forced mass migration of hundreds of thousands of Africans—transported against their will as slaves to the United States—challenged this narrow definition of citizenship with the eventual adoption of the Fifteenth Amendment after the Civil War in 1870, granting African American men the right to vote. Additional legislative acts like the Chinese Exclusion Act of 1882 attempted to place limits on where migrants could hail from, continuing to redefine what it meant to be an American. States, with their own political agendas, were allowed to pursue individual immigration policies until 1892, when the first federal immigration station opened on Ellis Island, leading to the first set of federal immigration guidelines.

When women were finally given the right to vote in 1920 with the passage of the Nineteenth Amendment, the definition of "citizen" once again dramatically shifted. As immigrants from Ireland, Germany, and Italy appeared in large numbers following the end of World War I, a quota system was introduced under the Emergency Immigration Act of 1921. For the first time, a numerical limit was placed on immigrants, as Congress once again sought to influence the characterization of American citizenry, hoping to impede immigration from Southern and Eastern Europe. In 1965, the quota system was replaced by the Immigration and Nationality Act, which removed racial and national barriers. Significant concerns about immigration continued, however, particularly in the wake of World War II, as the nation experienced a dramatic rise in economic prosperity throughout the 1950s and

'60s. Refugees and asylum seekers, searching for safety from catastrophes abroad, clamored to American shores, challenging politicians and citizens alike to once again reconsider the complicated notion of American identity.

The United Nations 1951 Refugee Convention and the 1967 Protocol began to clarify some of these otherwise unresolved questions, establishing asylum protections for any individual unable or unwilling to return to their home country due to a well-founded fear of being persecuted "on account of race, religion, nationality, membership in a particular social group, or political opinion." The U.S. Congress used a similar definition in its Refugee Act of 1980, which established two pathways for individuals to pursue refugee status—either through resettlement as a refugee abroad or as an asylum seeker making their way to the United States on their own.

The path for refugees begins with applying through a government entity abroad and is completely separate from the application process for asylum, although both are kept to the same legal standards. The U.S. federal government, through its various internal and external efforts, is able to control the total number of refugees it allows to enter the country each year. The Office of the President determines the total number of allowable refugees that can be resettled each year; through rigorous background checks and in-depth interviews, individuals are then granted refugee status. Approximately 70,000 to 80,000 individuals were granted refugee status each year between 2001 and 2010.

The path for asylum seekers is much more vulnerable to the shifting tides of history and politics. There are no self-imposed limits to the number of individuals who can apply for asylum each year. Under current UN protocols, anyone who presents themselves at a port of entry or from inside the country can apply for asylum as long as they put forward an application within one year of their arrival.

Like refugees, asylum seekers have the burden of proving they are eligible by demonstrating a "well-founded fear"—the notion that he or she or they fear for their life back in their home country. But this phrase, "a well-founded fear," has no precise definition in asylum law, which makes it incredibly difficult for migrants, fleeing their homeland, to document. Many asylum seekers, without court-appointed legal counsel, facing language barriers and the complexities of a foreign legal system, are unable to prove the merits of their case, regardless of the horrific details of their individual situations. Additionally, the vast majority of these migrants are confined to detention facilities, where the constraints of institutionalized life make it even more difficult to assemble a case. To be considered for "parole," migrants must be able to verify their identity, which can be exceedingly hard for asylum seekers escaping countries without a solid national infrastructure. They must also have family or contacts in the area, be able to pay a sizable bond, and demonstrate they will be financially supported while a decision in their legal status is being made. Detention presents its own series of challenges. Without access to the internet and long-distance calls, the chances of proving their cases are highly unlikely.

Over the past two decades, several dramatic shifts have additionally complicated how the U.S. handles immigration and how asylum seekers navigate the American immigration system. One of the greatest disruptions came from Congress's response to the September 11 terrorist attacks in 2001. Only five days before, President George W. Bush and Mexican president Vicente Fox had announced a comprehensive immigration agreement, which would create a temporary worker program and offer a process for legalization for most undocumented Mexicans living in the United States. Immediately after the attacks, President Bush and Congress shifted their immediate concerns to addressing issues of international terror and domestic safety.

In November 2002, Congress created the Department of Homeland Security (DHS), bringing together over twenty different agencies, including several immigration bureaus. The Immigration and Naturalization Service was reorganized under the DHS into three different divisions: Immigration and Customs Enforcement (ICE), Customs and Border Protection (CBP), and the United States Citizenship and Immigration Services (US-CIS). Asylum and immigration services suddenly became part of an organization whose mission was dedicated to protecting the nation from outside threats.

This seemingly nominal reorganization had far-reaching political and cultural consequences, immediately changing how refugees and asylum seekers were publicly viewed. Migrants—who for centuries were understood to be necessary to the well-being of the country as drivers of cultural, economic, and intellectual prosperity—were now being implicated as dangers to national security.

Other bureaucratic and legal ramifications were imposed, with a near doubling of deportations for non-criminals, exorbitant funding for border security, and increased scrutiny of asylum seekers. Previous to the attacks of 2001, asylum seekers, lacking a visa and without criminal backgrounds, were able to present themselves legally at ports of entry, apply for asylum, and be granted parole as they pursued the asylum process free from the encumbrance of lengthy incarcerations. By 2007, stricter parole guidelines had been created, placing tens of thousands of undocumented immigrants in the custody of DHS for months and years at a time. These dramatic legal and political shifts continue to have far-ranging consequences, greatly undercutting hundreds of years of American history and setting up an untenable legal fray, further complicating an outdated system of refugee and asylum assistance.

The second major shift has been the exponential increase of asylum seekers across the world and in the U.S. particularly. From 2001 to 2008, the U.S. saw a steady number of new asylum pleas, around 30,000 to 40,000 applications per year. Typically 20,000 to 25,000 individuals were granted asylee status—being granted permanent asylum—allowing them to eventually apply for a work permit, be granted public benefits like employment assistance and social services, and become integrated into American life.

Beginning in 2009, lack of employment throughout much of the third world, continued political strife in Afghanistan, Iraq, and Iran, and gang and drug violence in Central America and Mexico resulted in an explosion of asylum seekers at the U.S. border. Asylum applications rose each year, with affirmative and defensive filings reaching nearly 83,400 filings in 2012. During this time, the number of asylum applicants determined to have credible fear also exponentially increased. However, asylee rates remained relatively stable at 29,484. Although many more individuals were applying for asylum, a scant few of these individuals ever received it.

Immigration courts could not keep up with this drastic escalation. On average, only 25,000 applicants out of a backlog of more than 200,000 cases each year are ever granted asylum, and many of those awarded asylee status are those individuals able to afford a lawyer to help them win their pleas. It's estimated that only one out of ten asylum seekers without legal representation will ever receive asylum.

Over the past two decades, the asylum process in the U.S. has slowly become its own inviolable system, an abstract nation unto itself, an invisible country nearly impossible to escape.

19

Eleven months after fleeing Ghana, nearly three months after leaving Brazil, Razak reached the U.S. border and presented himself to a Customs and Border Protection officer to request asylum on August 6, 2013. Unable to produce any documents or identification, he was put in manacles and led away within moments of putting forth his plea.

In a separate interrogation room known as the Admissibility Enforcement Unit, CBP officers told Razak to take off his clothes, leaving him in his underwear. The officers then searched his entire body, forcing him to bend over, took the $600 he had hidden in his sock, and told him to get dressed. Among his only possessions was the pocket-size Koran, which he had carried with him throughout his travels.

Once dressed, he was handcuffed again and transferred to a holding cell to be processed. The cell was incredibly large and incredibly cold, institutional in its expansiveness, framed by floor-to-ceiling wire fences, fluorescent lights, metal benches, and concrete ground. The air conditioning blew constantly upon the migrants' tired faces. There were no bunks, no cots, no beds. No windows or evidence of the world outside. It was like being underground or on the moon. Thirty other men—some of whom had been separated from their wives and families—sat on the benches, speaking in low tones to each other about the temperature, their treatment, and how long they had been waiting. Some of them, having passed through U.S. immigration before, warned that this was how the process worked.

Hours later, no longer sure what time it was, some of the men began to complain about not being given food or water. CBP officers appeared in the middle of the night and handed out Taco Bell. Razak ate the greasy food, unable to finish his share. The officers gave each man two thin blankets, which many put on the concrete floor or used to cover themselves, all of them shivering in the cold air.

During that long expanse of time, Razak wondered, *Is this the United States? Am I in the right place? Is this a holding cell for criminals? Is this really what's going to happen to me?*

He glanced around and saw other men from Central America, from Africa, from Asia, and recognized he was with other asylum seekers, men without a home, people without a country, fallen into the hands of a nation that now held them with a fierce sense of suspicion.

The fluorescent lights, the cold air blowing, the suspension of belief and disbelief. Studying the persistent logic of your hands because there was nothing else to look at.

In the morning, there were burritos, a pulpy cup of lukewarm juice.

Razak soon learned, from speaking to the other asylum seekers, that in the United States, anyone could submit an asylum application either with an asylum officer or at a time of their choosing within one year of their arrival in the country as an affirmative request. If you presented yourself without a visa or passport, if you were detained at the border, or if you were apprehended somewhere in the U.S. and forced to stand before an immigration judge, you could submit an application as a defensive request. Once you made your application for asylum, an officer from the U.S. Citizenship and Immigration Services would interview you to establish if you had a credible or reasonable fear of persecution back in your home country. If the asylum officer decided you did not have credible fear, you would be deported and would not be allowed to reenter the U.S. for a period of five years.

If the asylum officer determined your fear was real, then you were granted "credible fear" status and allowed to continue on in the process. Eventually you would have to stand before an immigration judge to prove you deserved permanent asylum.

Even if your case was denied, you could appeal for an additional hearing, one of the men said. Razak imagined the entire process could take several weeks, even months, considering how long he had been detained in Mexico. He was also informed that entering the United States and applying for asylum without documents, without a passport, was considered a crime. By presenting himself at the port of entry without identifying papers, he would be charged with "alien inadmissibility" under Section 212 of the Immigration and Nationality Act. He had no idea how this charge would affect his appeal. He did not understand how it could be a crime to be robbed and then present yourself legally at the border to ask for asylum.

This ongoing confusion only worsened. For six days—unable to bathe, brush his teeth, or make a phone call—Razak and the other men waited, facing the numbness of the cold room and a persistent lack of information. Sitting on the bench or standing, time itself had become meaningless, a clock without hands. Some men paced, some prayed, some talked, some slept. On the floor, huddled together, they murmured rumors they had heard or had invented on their journey north:

We're going to be transferred soon.

They don't keep you here.
We're all going to be sent to other places.
Maybe that place will be better than here. Maybe there will be beds.

Razak glanced over and listened. No rumor could prepare him for the difficulties he was about to face.

During this time Razak was subjected to an extensive background check. His fingerprints were sent to the FBI. His name and birth-date were checked against databanks belonging to ICE, the FBI, the State Department, and the CIA. A special immigrant database, IDENT, was used to confirm his fingerprints as well. Each of these security checks was used for all the men awaiting their asylum interviews.

Eventually CBP agents transferred Razak to the Otay Mesa Port of Entry processing facility, where he was further interviewed by CBP officers. The building itself was institutional, nondescript. None of these places seemed to have any markings suggesting where their locations actually were. Razak was interviewed in a small room by two officers in blue uniforms. Given the choice to speak English or his native Hausa, Razak chose the latter. The officer conducting the interview made a call and two hours later an interpreter arrived. One of the officers then asked Razak if he was comfortable speaking Hausa and Razak nodded.

"Everything you say will be forwarded to the judge reviewing your case," the CBP officer explained. "The judge will be the one to decide whether your asylum plea is valid and whether or not you'll be allowed to stay in the United States."

Razak began explaining his story to the interpreter. No lawyer or social worker was present. During the interview with the CBP officers, the interpreter asked Razak if he had any family in the States. *Yes*, he told the interpreter in Hausa. *I have my uncle, I have his number and address.*

The interpreter relayed the information to the officer. One of the officers made a note of this in Razak's file and said, "We'll call him and let him know you're in our custody."

Razak was given a number of forms—an I-860, a list of pro bono attorneys, and an M-444. The interview concluded, although the CBP officers made no mention of how long the asylum process itself would take or how long it would be before his first formal credible fear interview with an asylum officer.

After the interview, Razak and a number of other asylum seekers were brought to a small detention facility, where they were finally allowed to shower and brush their teeth. Among a holding cell of forty beds, he wondered when he would be allowed to speak to his mother or Cynthia or his uncle. Once again, there were no windows, no way to mark location, the passage of time, whether it was night or day.

20

When he awoke the next morning, on August 12, 2013, Razak was transferred from CBP custody to ICE along with the other men he had been waiting with. ICE officers began calling out the detainees' names one by one. Each detainee was then asked to sign a piece of paper and was told that they were being transferred to a permanent detention facility that evening. "Read this document before you sign it. If you don't sign it, we can still take you anywhere we want to."

At that moment, Razak had no idea where he was going to end up or for how long. When his name was called, he stood and read the piece of paper. The document was a transfer agreement, declaring that the U.S. immigration services had decided to remand Razak into custody while he awaited asylum proceedings. The transfer stated he would be moved to Eloy Detention Center in Arizona. He had never heard the word *Arizona* before. He knew of California, New York, New Jersey—he had seen all these places in films and on television. But Arizona seemed like a complete invention. Before him the world became blurry, spots of confusion and rage erupting out of the corner of his vision. He approached an ICE officer and said, "Can I ask any questions?"

"Yes."

"I don't know where Arizona is but my uncle lives in New York, in the Bronx."

"So?"

"So that's where my uncle is. I don't know anything about Arizona. I don't know if it's possible to be sent to New York . . ."

"No. You don't choose where we take you. We can send you wherever we want to."

Frustrated, Razak recalled the feelings he had faced back in Ghana, unable to negotiate the corrupt bureaucracy, the systems of power that had been put in place. He had traveled thousands of miles only to find, once again, his life beset with obstacles put down by outside forces, controlled by a faceless government. *We can send you wherever we want.* He looked at the document again, holding it tightly in his hand.

"But I have no idea where you're taking me."

A number of migrants saw that they were also being sent to Arizona, while some of them were being transferred to detention centers in Texas. The remaining few would be detained in various facilities throughout California.

Later that afternoon, each detainee was given an orange jumpsuit to wear over their clothes. Razak looked around the large room and saw all of the asylum seekers putting on the coveralls. Half an hour later, ICE agents dragged out several large crates. Razak stared at them and watched as an officer began calling out the asylum seekers' names one by one. From the crates, the officers unwound several pairs of handcuffs and waist chains. Each migrant was cuffed at the wrists, the waist, and the ankles, then told to stand on the side and wait.

Putting on the manacles, donning the orange jumpsuit, it was impossible for Razak not to assume an air of guilt. Even the way he stood, silent, hands and legs bound, said it all, the assumption of some grave human mistake, of an unspoken criminality. Certainly these men had done something wrong, certainly something must be wrong with them to end up in a facility bound like this.

For all intents and purposes, the men—some, like Razak, who had journeyed through difficult circumstances to make their plea for asylum legally, many of whom had escaped unjust governments and corrupt justice systems—had themselves been transformed into criminals. The irony of it was too much to bear.

One by one, each was led outside to a long white prison bus. A man from Nigeria, who had been separated from his wife and children by border agents, began to shout. He cried out as he was being put on board, "Where are my wife and my kids? Where are they? Where are you taking me?"

Once inside the bus, an inner metal door was locked in place while armed agents surveyed the men. Razak felt deeply disturbed, recalling a Denzel Washington movie where the actor had been imprisoned—given a uniform and shackled—and then found a way to escape from a bus. He began to consider: *Who am I? Am I criminal? Why are they treating us this way?*

The bus made its way to an airport and pulled into a large hangar. Until midnight, the men waited in their seats, chained. Finally a large Department of Homeland Security plane arrived, its size announcing its importance. Before he boarded, Razak underwent another forced search. Using a small flashlight, ICE agents checked his mouth and his eyes, then escorted him onboard the plane.

The plane, the fourth Razak had taken in his life, was already partially filled with other undocumented migrants who had been taken into immigration custody in other states. All of them were restrained, all had the same look of incredulity and fear as Razak was led up the aisle. Later the men were offered water.

One of the men argued, "You're giving us water but we haven't eaten all day."

The officer shouted, "Shut up! Either take the water or not."

Out of principle, Razak refused the water. ICE officers reviewed the safety precautions for the flight—using the oxygen mask, finding the emergency exits. One of the detainees, a man from Mexico, began to laugh.

"If something happens, how are we going to get out? We're handcuffed. This is fucked."

Razak turned toward him and watched as an ICE officer quickly approached. But the young man would not be quiet.

"You can't do anything to me! You're sending me back to my country! If you're going to kill me, kill me."

Two officers stood around the young man until the flight landed in Texas, where some of the detainees were led off the plane. Razak no longer had any idea what time it was.

From Texas the plane continued through the night, circling back to Arizona. Apparently there were so many asylum seekers, so many migrants awaiting their day in court, that detention facilities had been built in cities and states all over the country, some makeshift, some permanent. DHS planes like these moved groups of individuals from state to state as if they were objects, items of human commerce. By the time the plane landed in Arizona sometime after midnight, there were nearly seventy-five men onboard. Before he was led from the plane in chains, Razak felt as if something had been lost, some unseen part of himself had gone missing along the way.

Eloy Detention Center is a privately owned prison in Eloy, Arizona, fifty miles northwest of Tucson, some sixty-five miles southeast of Phoenix. The city itself is small with less than 17,000 people, many of whom are employed by CoreCivic, the corporation contracted by the U.S. Immigration and Customs Enforcement to maintain a number of the country's private prisons. The Eloy Detention Center is the oldest of these facilities, first opened in 1994. It was followed by Red Rock Correctional Center, the Saguaro Correctional Center, and La Palma Correctional Center.

A faded green highway marker announces ENTERING ELOY. ELEVATION 1565, FOUNDED 1902, as if those meager statistics can somehow give order to the barren, dusty roads, infinite scrubland, somnolent mountains rising in the distance, boarded-up desert homes, tattered truck stop signs—the words themselves inscrutable, the feeling of limbic desolation, biblical in its proportions, stretching out in all directions, interrupted by the shape of one private prison facility after another. These monstrous-looking buildings, perfectly square, perfectly white, appear in stark contrast to the irregularity of the landscape with its scrub brush, cacti, and far-flung rocks. Fences rising high, topped with loops of razor wire, two-story structures lined up less like a prison and more like a military barracks, each surrounding a common yard, with a comical, single cactus standing beside the white and red sign out front. From outside, the facility appears to be well-maintained, efficient, completely obscuring the human complications and miseries contained within.

Although it may appear otherwise, the detention center at Eloy is a commercial enterprise first and foremost. It is not a public prison or military installation. Its employees are not subject to the same guidelines and training procedures that CBP and ICE officers must face. Since opening in 1994, the Eloy facility has generated hundreds of millions of dollars in profit and will continue to do so for the foreseeable future. Its existence, and the rapid development of many other private prisons and detention facilities over the past few decades, call into question the ethics of an industry that benefits from an inefficient immigration system. The more migrants who are detained, the longer the length of their detainment, the more these businesses have to gain. At any one time, nearly 40,000 asylum seekers are held in ICE facilities, with more than 70 percent of these individuals being imprisoned in privately run detention centers throughout the country.

While other First World nations have responded to the ongoing international immigration crisis by hiring more immigration judges and lawyers, the U.S. has confronted the problem by offering billion-dollar contacts to build and maintain more private detention facilities. In some cases, these facilities are the only place an asylum seeker may ever reside in while awaiting their court appearance in the United States. It is all they will ever experience of the country where they are making their appeal. In this way, these facilities become more than mere building or symbol: they are, in fact, their own lopsided vision of the United States.

No moon, no sky. Only a dull black night, seeming to stretch to infinity, marred by the horizon.

In the dark, in the back of the humid prison bus, Razak glanced out the barred window but was unable to see anything but the passing highway lights. Other men slept, but he kept trying to catch sight of something that would give him some clue as to where he was.

Once, in the same dark, they made a stop at some other detention facility to drop off a number of detainees, though Razak was unable to see what it was called. The sight, the fact that there was more than one detention center for asylum seekers, gave him pause.

The bus approached the Eloy Detention Center at 6:00 a.m. on August 13, 2013. The sun began to break beyond the hills to the east. Not having slept or eaten, Razak stared out the bus window at the octagonal view of the scrubland and shadowy mountains in absolute confusion, unable to accept the gravity of his circumstances. The truth that some unknown government could bind him in chains and carry him to some other place, all within a few hours, was terrifying, awe-inspiring.

After arriving at the detention center, Razak and the other men sat on the bus for the next two hours, still in restraints. By then his wrists and ankles had become painfully chafed. Correctional officers eventually boarded the bus and gave an overview of the detention facility. Razak found it difficult to listen. He had never imagined this, had not been prepared to be treated like a criminal in the United States, having been found guilty of doing nothing but legally presenting himself at the border. This dissonance, this lack of fairness, seemed to block out the reality of the events that were now occurring. The words spoken by the officers meant nothing to him. Through the fence he could see a large soccer pitch and basketball court, though the sun blazing overhead seemed to make everything seem smaller.

Once he was led from the bus, Razak felt the intense heat, the unbearable reality of mass, systematized isolation hanging in the air. A silence and a lack of hope pervaded the extensive compound.

"Put up your hands," a correctional officer said, and finally unlocked his handcuffs.

The remaining detainees were led into an air-conditioned room where they would be processed. Benches offered the refugees a place to sit. IDs for each detainee were created with their prison number, account number, and agency number. Officers also explained to the men their case level, which designated where they were in the asylum process.

"You're all level one," the officer said. "You've not been convicted of any crime. You're just here while you go through the asylum process."

Faded green jumpsuits were then distributed, meant to distinguish the asylum seekers from other detainees at the facility.

Razak collected his two green uniforms and a pair of sneakers, a tube of toothpaste and a toothbrush, a blanket and a pillow, and three pairs of underwear. The underwear he was given seemed to have been used by someone else beforehand. Once they collected these items, the detainees were then encouraged to call their family. Corrections officers stood by while the detainees attempted to reach their family members in the United States.

Razak called his uncle in New York, but unfortunately no one answered. He assumed his uncle must be at work and was given permission to try again. He had not spoken to his uncle since before he had appeared at the border. Once again there was no answer.

Later Razak was brought to the Alpha unit of the detention center, while some of the other African detainees he had met over the last few days were sent to Bravo or Delta or Echo units. Each unit held 100 to 150 men and was broken up into several small cells, each of which housed two inmates. The cells contained a narrow, blue metal frame bunk bed, a chair, possibly a desk, and a long rectangular window bisected by two metal lines. Once assigned to his unit, Razak marveled to once again find himself in the company of Fred, the Ghanaian he had met in Honduras, who was also being detained in the Alpha section of the facility.

With Fred, Razak approached some of the other detainees in their unit, migrants from mostly Central American countries, who asked where he was from.

"Ghana."

"Ghana? You don't need to worry. You'll be out soon."

Razak asked how long they had all been detained for. A man in a khaki jumpsuit answered, "I've been here almost two years."

Razak felt his limbs go stiff. "Two years? How's that possible?"

"I was living in the States for a while. I got involved with dealing drugs and they caught me and now they're going to send me home."

"But you've been here two years?"

"You're going to be out of here soon. It'll take probably three months at the most. You never committed any crime, right?"

Razak nodded but he now had no idea what to expect. In his cell that evening, he knelt down to pray, asking God for the patience to face the trials ahead. No one knew where he was—not Cynthia or his mother or his uncle Malik. Other than the alien number he had been assigned, there was no proof he was in the United States, no way to claim he existed anywhere at all.

21

In Eloy, Razak ghosted through the monotony of daily life at the detention facility—wake at 6:00 a.m., first meal, then the aimlessness of American television on three different screens—one in Spanish, one playing sports, one playing the news. Razak preferred the one with the news. Other detainees frequently argued about what to watch. After that, there was time in the common yard, lunch, dinner, then lights out. It was unlike the detention facility in Tapachula where you could wear your own clothes, go to the commissary, start your own business, move about with an illusion of freedom.

Every two hours you were locked down for count. Detainees had to wait in their cells for the next shift of correctional officers to arrive.

In Eloy, you had very little freedom of choice, from what you did to what you ate. Whoever, whatever you had been before entering the facility had been thoroughly and systematically removed—or at the very least put on hold for an indefinite amount of time.

In Eloy, Razak had no way to call anyone—Cynthia, his mother, his uncle. In order to make a phone call he needed a calling card, but he had no money in his commissary account, which had to be contributed to by family members and friends from the outside

world. Razak had been told by other Ghanaians he had met—
Munil and Basit, companions in asylum—that the six-dollar
phone card available at the commissary took more than three
minutes to process calls to Ghana, leaving only two minutes to
speak, so that the cards themselves were basically useless.

The commissary sold junk food—chips, candy—at an exorbitant markup, profiting off detainees, who, under UN conventions,
had done nothing illegal, nothing criminal, other than presenting
themselves for asylum at the border without documents.

In Eloy, Razak began to fill out his asylum application, USCIS
Form I-589, without legal help, asking the other migrants' advice
when he could.

Eloy did not allow you to sell cigarettes or calling cards to make
money. No money ever changed hands between detainees. All financial transactions were handled by the commissary and benefited the private institution, not the individuals held there.

Eloy correctional officers could greet you kindly or act as if you
were subhuman, depending on the day, the weather, their mood.
All of them had been trained to work with criminals; none of
them had been trained to work with migrants, and so the asylum
seekers were not treated any differently than the murderers, the
drug dealers, the felons who were also housed there.

Once during count—when the detainees were forced to wait
in their cells to be visually inspected by one of the correctional
officers—Razak knelt down to pray. An officer peered through
the glass of the cell door and told him to stand. In the midst of his
prayers, Razak did not immediately respond. The officer barked at
him, warning that he was going to write Razak up for an infrac-
tion. Razak apologized, asking why it was necessary for him to

stand for count, why it was necessary for the guard to see his face? But the guard only glowered at him and moved on.

At Eloy, the recreational yard was an unending wave of desert heat. It was seldom used for any kind of recreation, other than staring out at the mirages that sometimes appeared.

At Eloy, there were several detainees who seemed to suffer from severe mental illness. One day, Razak and some of the other migrants were gathered in the common room watching TV when one of the detainees—a Rwandan—began shouting and threw a bottle of water at the television. The Rwandan balled his fist and then started punching the TV, breaking the screen. Correctional officers panicked and called for a lockdown, handcuffing the man and dragging him away.

At any moment, it felt as if something could go wrong, as if anyone might break.

At Eloy, you could not sleep through the night. Every few hours a corrections officer would knock on the cell door to make sure you were alive, still breathing, still moving.

At Eloy, men wore different-colored jumpsuits—khaki for new detainees, green for migrants who had been previously processed, red for those convicted of a crime. Almost all of the men Razak knew wore khaki. According to ICE's own data, 51 percent of incarcerated immigrants were "non-criminal" and "posed no threat," while 23 percent had nonviolent convictions. Only 15 percent were categorized as high-level threats, numbers that clearly disputed the argument that migrants were somehow more dangerous than the general American population.

It was not the other men that were frightening but the

institution itself, the way time refused to pass. The corners where the walls met always seemed to be closing in.

There were also the rumors about those who had died at Eloy. Some detainees said five, some said ten, some said more than a dozen. The truth was that at least fifteen men died at Eloy between 2003 and 2016, including five suicides.

In 2012, ICE's internal Office of Detention Oversight investigated the death of Eloy detainee Manuel Cota-Domingo. While in his cell, Domingo had trouble breathing. Domingo's cellmate banged on the cell door for several hours before corrections officers transferred Domingo to the medical unit. There the medical staff failed to take his temperature, order an EKG, or assess his cardiopulmonary health. He died later at a nearby hospital from complications due to a common diabetic condition.

Others died by their own hand. The listlessness, the hours spent staring, the physical pain of being separated from the people you loved. It was not hard to sometimes imagine simply ending things.

Unlike other migrants applying for asylum in other First World nations, including the United Kingdom and Canada—both of which worked to integrate migrants into their countries with free housing, language classes, and legal counsel—the detainees at Eloy had been severed from all meaningful contact with their countries of origin and from the rest of the United States. Instead of issuing work permits and giving these individuals the opportunity to become acclimated to American life, the men at Eloy were inconspicuously isolated with little access to emotional or psychological support. Some of these men—having been separated from their wives and children with no end in sight, stripped of their personal and cultural identities, placed in a high-stress detention facility, housed with other individuals under the same degree of stress, confronting an all-or-nothing judicial system without the barest legal guidance—simply gave up. It was remarkable that the occurrence of suicide within the detention center was not drastically higher.

Gossip of these men's deaths drifted down the hall like phantoms. At any moment you might lift your head and see a smudge of light, hear someone cry out, then find no one was there.

At meals, Razak sat with a number of other African asylum seekers. Together they complained about the food and how they were treated. What none of them would say was the one thing many of them felt: that they had been lied to; that the United States they had seen in television shows, in films, in comic books, did not exist; that this facility and the asylum process itself was essentially unfair; that life might not have been better where they were born but at the very least it was familiar; that all of them, every man to the last in Eloy, had been foolish enough to believe a dream that was not real; that each of them had made a monumental error in judgment, a mistake that would somehow cost them more than their lives.

Eloy—with its idle hours, long days, the desert sun always obscured through the blurry prison windows. Eloy did not, for one moment, allow you to forget where you were, what you were.

Days, weeks went by, but no time actually passed.

It was two weeks before an asylum prescreening officer called Razak for an interview.

Before an asylum interview could be arranged, a CBP officer noted Razak had requested a translator during his initial processing, so he was forced to wait while USCIS arranged for someone who could speak Hausa to come to the Arizona facility. No one ever came. Other migrants he knew at Eloy had met for their first interviews while Razak continued to linger with no sense of how much longer he would have to patiently abide.

Finally, on August 27, 2013, after weeks of uncertainty, an asylum officer brought a number of documents for Razak to sign. He sat in the tiny room across the officer and read through the papers.

"What is this? I still haven't had my interview."

The officer explained that USCIS had reviewed Razak's initial interview at the border with CBP and determined his case evidenced credible fear. "You're being allowed to continue in the process. See. It says you've got credible fear."

Razak had heard the term a few times before with the other migrants and knew that in order to win his asylum plea, he would need to demonstrate to the judge that his life back home was in danger. During his initial interview, he had been able to believably describe the dire circumstances and the attempt on his life back in Accra, and he was now being allowed to continue in the asylum process. Other less fortunate migrants who were unsuccessful in establishing the life-or-death nature of their pleas during their interviews and who were unable to afford an immigration lawyer had already been denied, and would soon be deported back to their countries of origin once their travel documentation was processed.

But even though Razak felt overjoyed, his mind was flooded with questions. When would he be able to speak to an immigration lawyer? When would he be allowed to appear before a judge? What would he be expected to say? He began to consult the other men in the Alpha unit, getting as much information as he could.

It was another several months before he was assigned a hearing with an immigration judge—a judge who, unlike other federal judges, was not appointed but was an employee of the U.S. Department of Justice, which many critics view as a distinct blurring of the line of separation between executive and judicial functions. Immigration judges work for the executive branch and are, unfortunately, vulnerable to the whims and prejudices of both the president and the U.S. attorney general. Many of these judges are expected to oversee as many as six hundred, sometimes up to seven hundred immigration hearings a year and are evaluated not by the fairness or justness of their decisions but by the number of cases they are able to clear. Unlike a criminal or civil case, one person—the immigration judge—is entirely responsible for overseeing the proceedings and for rendering a final verdict in the case. There is no jury, and because the vast majority of detainees cannot afford immigration lawyers to represent them, the ethical considerations and legal ramifications of these proceedings are largely the outcome of the personality, experience, and political leanings of the immigration judges themselves. There is very little balance or oversight of their immense power in these hearings. Evidence bears this imbalance out: immigration judges in northern cities like New York and Chicago are much more likely to grant an asylum request then those in Texas and Arizona. As much as location can be an indicator of cultural and political beliefs, a detainee's plea—their life—often depends more on where they are detained than on the merits of their case. Razak spent the next month trying to prepare for his hearing, reviewing books and articles in the library, speaking with other detainees.

In November 2013, Razak was finally called before an immigration judge. Within the Eloy detention facility there were four different judges with four different courtrooms. In a long, dark room, the judge sat behind a desk, studying a computer, while a court typist made notes on their computer. Behind the judge stood a flag. Across the aisle was a lawyer representing DHS and the United States. Razak stood penitently before the judge, Richard A. Phillips, an older man with a balding hairline and large glasses, and answered his questions as best he could.

"Mr. Iyal—your name is Mr. Iyal?"

"Yes."

"You are from Ghana?"

"Yes."

"You came into the United States on August 6, 2013?"

"Yes."

"You came into the port of entry at San Ysidro, California?"

"Yes."

"But you did not have any documentation at the time, no visa, no passport?"

"No."

"You didn't have any right to enter the United States without a visa, without documentation, so you are guilty?"

Razak stood completely confused with no idea how to respond. The judge looked up and asked again, "So do you accept that you are guilty?"

"When I came to ask for asylum, I didn't have any visa because I was robbed. I know you don't know that, but I was robbed. My birth certificate, my passport, everything was stolen."

"I understand, but you came into the country illegally because you had no documentation."

"I didn't come illegally. I presented myself at the border, at the port of entry."

The courtroom was silent then. Razak looked around, thought for a while, and then, understanding there was only one answer the judge wanted to hear, said, "I'm guilty. Yes."

The judge nodded and said, "I see you have established credible fear in your initial interview. So we'll schedule another hearing. You have a right to a lawyer to represent you." He then offered

Razak a list of lawyers who might be willing to take his case, pro bono.

Razak looked up from the list and asked, "How long am I going to be here?"

"I don't know. It's up to your asylum officer. The asylum officers decide when your hearing will be."

The judge dismissed Razak from the court and he was brought back to the Alpha unit. In his cell, he sat on his bed and considered the word *guilty* again and again. He had believed by entering the port of entry and presenting himself to the immigration officer he had done everything legally. But now he had accepted complicity in committing an act he did not even know was a crime. In his mind, he continued the conversation with the judge.

I didn't jump a wall. You have my fingerprints, my photograph, all of my personal information. You have my everything. But here you are telling me I'm guilty. And I've accepted that I'm guilty but what does that mean? Am I guilty because of where I came from? Who I am? Because I decided to come here?

The bare walls held no answers.

22

Other months beat down on Razak like a closed fist. On February 11, 2014, after six more months of detainment, the same judge assigned to Razak's case held a custody determination hearing and ruled that he was eligible for bond, which would cost him $7,500.

Razak spoke up. "Can you please reduce this bond? I can't afford seventy-five hundred dollars."

The judge looked away. "I'm sorry, but I'm not going to reduce anything."

Razak walked from the courtroom once again, feeling hopeless.

One of the other detainees, another Muslim named Ali, who Razak often spoke with at dinnertime, had an immigration lawyer from Pakistan.

"Look, I have this guy. He's a Muslim. When I meet with him, I can ask him to come talk to you."

A few weeks later Razak was called for a visitation. He had forgotten about the mention of his friend's lawyer. He approached the detention officer and asked who it was. "An attorney visitation," the officer replied. Razak gathered up all his documentation and followed the officer.

The lawyer, a thin, man in a gray suit, greeted him by saying, *As-salamu alaikum.*

Wa-alaikum assalaam.

"Razak, I see your name and I know you're a Muslim."

Razak nodded.

"I'm also a Muslim. I was born in Pakistan, but I was raised in the U.S. Your friend passed on your agency number and I thought the two of us could talk."

Razak felt a swell of hope.

"Do you have your asylum form?" the other man asked.

Razak handed over the form. The lawyer studied it for a few moments and asked, "Who helped you fill this out?"

"I filled it out myself. Some of the guys here helped me."

The lawyer nodded. "There a number of errors here on the form. You sent it on to immigration?"

Razak nodded.

"Okay. No problem. You have the right to make changes to the form, even after you've sent it in. Let me see if I can help you. Why don't you start at the beginning?"

Razak spent the next hour going over the details of his case.

"Did you ever have an interview with an asylum officer?"

"No."

The lawyer nodded. "They're supposed to give you an asylum interview. During your initial interview with Customs and Border officers, you might be nervous, you might forget something, so they're supposed to grant you an interview with an actual asylum officer. That's the interview the judge is supposed to evaluate."

"But they're already given me my first hearing."

"They take advantage of people who don't know any better or if you don't have an attorney. The thing is you don't have to talk, you don't have to incriminate yourself or answer questions you don't understand. What did the judge ask you?"

Razak felt angry; he looked up, unable to respond at first. "He asked me if I was guilty."

"What did you say?"

"I said I was."

The lawyer nodded again. "You didn't have to agree to that."

Razak understood then that in order to win his plea, he would need an attorney. "Would you be willing to take my case?"

"I can help you, but if you have a family member who can help you with some money . . . If you want me to represent you now, I'm going to need two thousand dollars as a retainer fee, and after that, you can pay five hundred a month."

Razak blinked, shaking his head, all hope crashing down again. "I don't have any money."

"Do you have any family in the States?"

"I have my uncle, but I haven't even spoken with him. When they brought me here, I was unable to reach him."

"Okay, why don't you give me your uncle's number and I'll contact him for you? And if he's willing to get involved, I can come back and see you."

Razak gave the lawyer his uncle's information but felt doubtful. He had no idea what his uncle might do or say. In the meantime, he spoke with other detainees and found out his odds of receiving asylum would be greatly increased if he had legal counsel.

One week later, the lawyer returned, having reached out to Razak's uncle, who explained he was unable to intervene financially. He had a wife and five children that he was working to support. Razak nodded, saying, "This is the way it is."

"I'm sorry. I want to help you. But I have to be paid for my services some way. I've listened to your story and it touched my heart. The one thing I can do is correct the errors on your asylum form so you can resubmit it."

Razak nodded, gratefully.

"Do you have any money so you can buy something from the commissary?"

"No, I don't."

"I want to give you a hundred dollars as a gift. I can't hand it to you because that's not allowed but I'll send it through your account."

Razak smiled. "I appreciate that. But I don't need any money here. What I need is to talk to my fiancée, to see how she's doing."

"What if I send the money to your fiancée back in Ghana?"

"You'd be willing to do that?"

"Sure. Give me her name and telephone number."

Razak happily complied and thanked the lawyer for his generosity. It was almost shocking, this mercy, at that particular time, in that particular place.

The truth was that Razak had been unable to speak with Cynthia since his arrival at the detention facility because he could not afford to buy a calling card. But he decided he couldn't wait any longer. After more than six months at Eloy, Razak approached one of the detention officers and inquired about getting a job at the facility.

"I can get you a job collecting trash from the units for one dollar a day."

"What about the kitchen?" he asked.

"I can give them a call and see if they need anybody."

Razak was placed on the line in the kitchen to serve food to other detainees. Almost all of the kitchen staff were detainees who worked for one dollar a day. The position allowed Razak the opportunity to eat more than the meager amount of food usually offered. Three times a day, Razak donned plastic gloves and an apron and portioned out formless mounds of food onto other migrants' plates.

Only a few days after being hired, a female kitchen supervisor took Razak aside and told him to serve less food per detainee.

"Just put a little on their trays," she said.

Seeing what the staff in charge of the kitchen did with the leftovers—tossing everything into the garbage—made Razak furious, as it was a waste of food and a waste of the government's money. The detainees he knew frequently complained about the insignificant portions in the cafeteria. Some of the men even believed it was a way to increase sales at the commissary.

"I can't just put a little on their trays when the men here are starving and you're throwing the rest in the garbage."

"If you don't want to do it the way I say, then leave."

"I can't do this. Some of the men don't have money for food at the commissary."

"If you can't follow my instructions, then you need to go."

The staffer called a correctional officer and complained Razak was not following her instructions. He was removed from the line and installed at the dishwashing station.

Razak muttered, "It's better this way. I can't stand seeing people starving."

For the next several months Razak cleaned dishes three times a day, seven days a week, scrubbing cooking implements, hotel pans, and pots for one dollar a day. With the money he made, he would buy a calling card or a soda or some cookies or soup. When he was not in the kitchen, he would help the other detainees read letters from home and then write responses for them in English. In exchange, these men would give him a soda or sometimes a calling card. Over his lengthy detainment, Razak became a well-known figure around the facility, sometimes even going so far as to call a migrant's family back home to explain their predicament.

In the end, as the months passed, he realized he had been taken out of the world. He no longer had any association with what was going on outside of the detainment facility. It was as if he had died, had not woken up after the attack back in Ghana two years before, as if his spirit was trapped and could no longer pass on. Days, nights, everything outside the windows became the same colorless gash of gray.

By that time Munil, one of the other Ghanaians he had met at Eloy, had been released on bond and went to New York to live with his sister. When he was able to afford it, Razak called Munil in New York to get news from Accra. Munil soon became acquainted with Razak's mother, aunts, grandmother, and Cynthia, and would relay messages back and forth from Razak to his loved ones, as it was cheaper to call New York than Accra.

One day, during one of their calls, Munil sounded different. *There is something I want to tell you, Razak. You're going to be upset but please, I need to tell you.*

What's going on?

The line became silent for a moment.

It's very difficult but your grandma . . . I'm sorry. She passed away.

Razak did not know what to say. He thanked Munil and hung up the phone. *Kaka.* The name, the word, felt empty on his tongue.

After he returned to his cell, he thought about what his grandma had told him growing up. *Be a good person. Respect your elders. Take your education seriously. Don't give up on your religion.*

Now he had lost her, too.

There were so many of them, the people he had left behind back in Accra, people who helped him, who supported him, who helped him escape. His mother, his aunts, Cynthia. Would he ever see anyone he loved again?

In detention, Razak sometimes watched the American news in one of the common areas. There was some controversy in Missouri, a riot of some kind. A black man, a young person named Michael Brown, had been shot by police. Razak stared at the screen intently and remembered what his neighbor back in Accra had said when he was boy about African Americans living in the States, how happy they were, how privileged. He thought, *So this is how the world is. Back in Ghana, we don't have a problem between people of different colors. We have a problem between ourselves. Whoever has money has a voice. Whoever has money has power. Whoever has money has justice.*

23

Eight months after arriving at Eloy, Razak stood at his third hearing before the same judge who, having reviewed Razak's documents, stated he needed to see evidence of the threats against Razak's life before he was able to make a ruling. "Please prepare any and all evidence that you have," the judge ordered.

Razak felt despondent and decided to speak directly to the judge in English. "I can't make long-distance calls back home. The calling cards only give you two minutes. I can't use the internet. What am I supposed to do? How am I supposed to get evidence?"

"I understand your concerns but I need proof that what you claim in these documents actually happened. If you get me the proof, then we can figure out how to proceed. You have one month to show me some kind of evidence."

After the hearing, Razak tried to contact the immigration lawyer he had spoken with but got no response. He spoke with other detainees; all of them were facing the same impossibility. None of them had any answer on how to attain evidence while being held inside a detainment facility.

Because there was no newspaper article or specific police report documenting Razak's assault, because he could not materialize demonstrable proof of the corruption of the local police and the involvement of the member of parliament in his family's inheritance, he had no way to proceed. If he had been given access to the internet, there would have been a trove of newspaper articles about Mustapha's predilection for corruption, and criticism by members of his own political party.

If he had been allowed long-distance phone calls back to Africa, he could have gathered testimonies from witnesses—his mother and aunt and Cynthia or the local Islamic elders. He could have asked for their help in gathering documentation from Accra, such as his hospital records.

But without any basic privileges and lacking the support of an attorney, Razak could see no way to supply evidence for his claim.

By then he had only two weeks left before meeting with the judge again. He called his uncle Malik in New York and explained the situation.

"Would you be willing to write a letter on my behalf?"

As it turned out, Malik had gone back to Ghana in 2014 and spent three weeks there. During that time Malik learned what had occurred between Razak and his half-siblings.

His uncle agreed to write a letter explaining the complications of Razak's case, arguing that if Razak was sent back to Ghana his life would be in danger. He then had it notarized and mailed it on to Razak in Arizona. Razak had the letter sent to the judge. In the meantime, Razak's uncle had contacted Razak's mother, who wrote a letter of her own, describing what happened, which was sent to the judge as well.

During his fifth and final hearing on August 1, 2014, nearly one year after arriving in the United States, Razak stood before the immigration judge and was deeply disturbed to hear his asylum had been denied.

"You have failed to produce any necessary evidence."

"But my uncle sent a letter explaining everything."

"All you'd been able to show are letters from your relatives. We need actual evidence to decide your case. I'm sorry, but there's just not enough evidence to continue. You don't have an attorney, so we're going to have to deny your case."

One year after presenting himself at the border, after one year of being incarcerated, the judge formally denied Razak's asylum plea. Razak was furious.

"How can you keep me here for one year and then deny my case? You want to send me back home? Why didn't you send me back home from the beginning? You let me waste my life here for one year!"

The judge slowly removed his glasses and looked over at him. "Would you like to appeal my decision?"

"How long does the appeal take?"

"It's nine months before a decision is reached. But you'd have to stay here during that time."

Razak did not need to think about it for a single second. "No."

"If you say no, then you will be deported back to Ghana. The deportation order will be final."

Razak lowered his head and with a deep sense of grief and frustration, said, "I understand."

The judge put his glasses back on and said, "We will send all the necessary documents on to your deportation officer."

Razak was led back to his unit, where the walls themselves seem to crumble beneath the wave of anger he was feeling.

One week later, Razak's asylum officer appeared with a number of documents for him to sign. Razak looked over the paperwork and said, "I'm not going to sign anything."

"If you don't sign, they're going to keep you here a long time. You better sign it, then we can go from there."

"If I don't sign, how long will I be here?"

"I don't know. A long time."

Razak eventually conceded and signed the papers, accepting the ruling of the immigration judge, giving up his right for appeal. His bond was also immediately canceled.

"We're going to send all of these documents to the Ghanaian consulate in D.C. It'll take a few weeks. We'll see what the consulate says."

One month later, at the beginning of September 2014, Razak was called in by ICE officers for an interview with his consulate on the phone. On the telephone, a woman at the embassy asked Razak several questions first in English, then in Twi, an Akan dialect spoken in Ghana.

How are they treating you over there?

I'm doing okay.

Did you get an attorney?

No.

What did you have when you came into the United States? Your birth certificate? Your passport? Your ID from Ghana?

No, all of that was stolen from me in Mexico.

What do you have to prove you're from Ghana?

I was born in Rich hospital in Accra.

Anybody can say that.

I grew up in Ghana, I went to school at Kanda Estate.

Okay, I can check on that. You'll hear from us. Can I please talk to the officer?

Razak handed the phone back to the ICE officer and listened carefully to the officer's responses. The Ghanaian embassy needed to verify Razak's identity in order to issue travel documents. Without the travel documents, the U.S. could not deport him. But Razak had no faith in either institution. From the officer's expressions, there was no way to know how much longer he would be detained.

Another two months crept by—a second November had passed since Razak was confined at Eloy. By then other asylum seekers he had met had come, been processed, and then deported, over and over and over again. Razak wandered the halls like one of the spirits the other men told stories about.

By then something had shifted. Razak's frustration at having lost his asylum case turned to a disquieting sense of disbelief. Although his plea had been denied months before, he was still unable to be released. His dream of staying in the U.S. was now superseded by the much more pressing reality of needing to escape the detention facility, of returning to some version of life, even if it meant facing a grave, mortal threat from his siblings and the unfair political system back home.

But there was no end in sight, no sign of reprieve, only more days, pacing the halls at Eloy.

One day Razak spoke with his asylum officer who—also frustrated by the lack of response from the Ghanaian embassy in Washington D.C.—asked Razak to write a letter to the Ghanian consulates in D.C., New York City, and Houston, in order to verify his identity so that he could be released. Razak wrote three letters, knowing that by doing so, he would be deported and returned to a corrupt political system and the certain danger he had already faced back home.

In his cell, Razak came to the conclusion that he let everyone down, his fiancée, his mother, his family, that he had been removed from them for so long. He had been unable to start a new life in a new country, could not find a way to support them, or even hear their voice. It would be better to face whatever he had to face in Ghana than to go on, separated from them, detained at Eloy for another year, another month, another day.

One of his back teeth began to hurt a few weeks later. A medical staffer inspected Razak's tooth and decided it would have to be pulled. In order to receive proper dental care, he would have to be sent out of the detention facility to a county hospital nearby.

In the morning an ICE officer called his name and brought him to a separate room, where they instructed him to put on an orange jumpsuit—the uniform convicted criminals wore in the facility.

"Why do I have to put this on?"

"We're taking you out of the prison."

"But I already have my green uniform."

"Listen, I'm just doing my job. Just do what I ask you to do."

"I'm not going to wear that."

"If you don't put it on, you're not going to the hospital."

Razak stared at the jumpsuit again and said, "Then I'm not going." The ICE officer nodded grimly and then brought Razak back to his unit.

Later that same day, another ICE officer found Razak and told him the van had arrived to take him to the medical facility.

"The van is here. You need to put on that uniform."

"Why are you making me wear that uniform? Why do you want people to look at me like I'm some kind of criminal?"

"No, you're going right to the hospital. You're not walking around the city."

The pain in his tooth was unrelenting. He looked at the uniform and, against his better judgment, put it on. Once he was dressed, the officers bound him in chains, handcuffing his wrists to his waist and putting manacles on his ankles.

•

It was worse than he had imagined. It took three officers to lead
Razak into the modest county hospital. Two of the officers carried
rifles. Razak entered the waiting room, having difficulty walking
with the chains about his ankles. Everyone looked up and began
to gawk—adults, children, the elderly—while some moved away,
a look of pure terror crossing their face. Deeply ashamed, Razak
lowered his head, afraid to make eye contact with anyone.

In the dentist's examination room, Razak was led to a re-
clining seat. The officers waited uncomfortably in chairs like exhausted parents. Finally the dentist appeared, looked at Razak,
and asked, "Who are you?"

"I'm from Ghana. I'm here for asylum."

"And how are you finding our country?"

Razak frowned and the officers gave the dentist a look of
discouragement. Even here, in this small, unseen place, in this
most common and mundane of human moments, he would not
be allowed to be treated like a person, to engage in a basic, civil
conversation. The dentist began his examination and eventually
concurred that Razak's tooth would need to be removed.

The dentist turned to one of the officers and asked, "I need to
remove this man's tooth. Can you unlock his handcuffs please?"

The officer glanced at his partner and then shook his head.
"I'm sorry. That's against protocol."

"Really?" the dentist asked.

"I'm sorry," the officer responded.

Razak shook his head.

The tooth would have to come out with Razak bound in the
chair like a victim of some outdated torture.

Later, after the procedure, Razak asked to use the bathroom. One
of the ICE officers escorted him to the lavatory. Decked in the

orange jumpsuit and handcuffed at the waist, Razak could not unzip the jumpsuit in order to urinate.

"Can you please unzip my jumpsuit?" he asked the officer.

The officer quickly looked away. "I can't do that."

"Please. I need to go. How can I manage?"

"Whatever you're going to do, you need to do. I'm not going to unzip you."

Furious, Razak began to yell, cursing, becoming—for a few moments at least—exactly what the officers and everyone in the medical facility had assumed him to be. A criminal, a trouble-maker. He raged against the indecency of his situation, calling forth all the anger that had accumulated over the last several months. When he finished shouting, he attempted to urinate, but his hands—still handcuffed—were shaking too hard. It was the lowest he had felt in years.

Once he was finished, he could not forget the feeling of painful embarrassment, of allowing himself to become something he was not. When he was back in the van, one of the officers said he was going to file a grievance against him for his behavior at the facility.

"Look, you do whatever you want to do. You have the power. You can keep me here as long as you like," Razak said.

The next day, the case manager of the unit called Razak in to discuss the incident. The ICE officer had indeed filed a grievance. Sitting in the case manager's office, he calmly studied the other man's face, his belongings. He asked, "How would you feel if you were hands were chained, if you needed to do the most basic, hu-man thing, and you weren't even allowed to do that? How would you feel?"

The case manager was silent for a while and then looked down. "These men, these people are just doing their job."

"They're doing their job, but what about me? How would you feel, to not to be able to use the bathroom on your own?"

The case manager could not answer. He looked down at the paper on his desk and said, "One of the officers wrote a grievance against you. You need to sign here and here."

Razak stared at him and said, "I'm not going to sign anything."

"You have to sign it."

"I'm not signing it."

The case manager frowned and then dismissed Razak with a nod of his head.

One day later, the warden called Razak into his office. Razak had never been in the warden's office before; he tried to stay out of trouble, to be known as a conscientious detainee. The warden gave him a sad look.

"Razak, I know you've been here a long time. What's going on with you?"

Razak did not know how to answer.

"Let's try to fix this. I can talk to the case manager and the officers. Can you just sign this grievance, please? Everyone that works here, they're just trying to do their job."

Razak stared at the other man's face for a long time and then picked up the pen and signed it.

"Okay. You have a strike against you. You're going to work for eight hours with no pay. Every day, you'll work two hours for free until your time is paid off."

Razak was led from the warden's office in a daze of deepening disappointment and doubt.

Months passed and there was still no response from any of the Ghanaian embassies. Razak showed copies of the letters he had written to the ICE officer and said, "Look. I'm trying. I'm trying to go back. It's not like I want to stay here."

"Razak, we can't take you back home without your travel

documents. If you can work with your embassy to get your documents together, we can take you as soon as possible."

"What else do you want me to do? I feel like I'm not part of the world. Nobody knows what's going on with me. I don't know what's going on with them. What do you want me to do?"

The powerful absurdity, the notion that an asylum seeker—having been incarcerated for more a year and a half, having been denied a future in the U.S.—would have to plead to be sent back to the country where his life had first been put in peril filled Razak was an unadulterated numbness, the feeling that there was no rule of law, no sense of fairness anywhere.

One day at the library, Razak met another asylum seeker who asked how long he had been detained.

"For more than a year and a half."

"You're here for asylum?"

"Yes."

The other man studied him for a moment and said, "You know, there's an organization called the Florence Project. They help refugees get released."

"How can I talk to them?"

"I have a number and address. I can give them to you."

The man opened his bag and gave the phone number and an address with a name. *Benjamin Harville.* "Write to Benjamin or call him. Here." Reaching into his bag again, the other man produced a stamp—which at the moment seemed like a small, magical thing—and handed it to Razak.

Razak wrote furiously, explaining his case and how he had been in detention for more than a year. He sent it to the Florence Project, a not-for-profit agency that provided legal aid and social services for detained migrants throughout Arizona. After a week, he received a response saying someone from the organization was planning to come to visit him on December 15, 2014.

Benjamin Harville, a tall young man in his early thirties who was a staff attorney for the Florence Project, arrived with a legal assistant and asked to look over Razak's documents. Benjamin went through his asylum application, looked over his other paperwork, and then asked, "Do you know that they've violated your rights?"

"No."

"The Department of Homeland Security has violated your rights."

"How did they do that?"

"If you lose your asylum case, they have three months to coordinate with your embassy to deport you. If they are unable to produce the necessary documents, they have another three months to comply or they have to release you. But they're still keeping you here."

Razak sat at the table, stunned. He felt a jolt of shock and relief overcome him.

"You know what, Razak? We're going to write a letter to the District Court of Arizona. We're going to send a copy to you. We're going to send one to the warden, and we're going to send a copy to your deportation officer. These people are violating your rights. Do you understand?"

Razak nodded.

"It might take a week or two, but we're going to file these documents and send it to you."

"No problem. I can wait."

"Usually you have to pay to submit these documents to the court, but we're going to pay it for you. We'll send you the receipt that it's been paid."

•

One year and nine months after first being detained at Eloy, Razak received a receipt saying the letter had been received by the District Court of Arizona, along with a copy of the petition. The petition challenged Jon Gurule, the warden of the Eloy facility, for Razak's immediate release based on the U.S. Supreme Court case *Zadvydas v. Davis*, 533 U.S. 678 (2001), which successfully argued that aliens with a final order of removal could not be detained beyond a 180-day period unless the alien's removal was significantly likely to occur in the foreseeable future.

One week after that, the court replied, asking Razak's asylum officer why he was still being detained, and giving ICE twenty days to comply with his release.

The asylum officer approached Razak in his cell, asking, "What are you trying to do? Are you trying to mess with my job?"

"Why are you keeping me here?"

"You should have talked to me before you went to them," the officer complained.

"Why do I have to talk to you? I did everything you asked me to do. Now I'm doing everything I can to get out of here."

The warden of Eloy invited Razak into his office. Uneasily, Razak he sat down across from the desk as the warden announced, "The court has already issued its response, so you have to be patient. They're working to get you released."

"I want to go back. I'd rather go back to Ghana then be here any longer."

Days later Razak found out that Fred, who was also from Ghana and who had also lost his asylum plea, had written to the District Court of Arizona and had successfully petitioned for his release. In April 2015, Razak and the other men in his unit were in the recreation yard when a correctional officer announced that Fred had a visitor.

After the Alpha unit was forced to return to their quarters, Fred appeared and began shouting, *I'm free. I'm free. The court ruled in my favor. They can't keep me here any longer.*

Razak approached Fred, who hugged him and exclaimed, *I'm being released!*

That's good. That's good for you, Razak said.

I'm praying for you, too.

Before Fred left Eloy the next day, he asked Razak, *What are you going to say to Cynthia?* They came up with a plan: Razak gave him Cynthia's number and asked him to explain what happened and asking her to please pray for him.

While still in detention in late April 2015, Razak and Fred coordinated a conference call with Cynthia back in Accra. Razak telephoned Fred, who then contacted Cynthia, and connected them over the line.

It was the first time they had spoken in nearly two years. He almost did not know how to begin. It was like they were strangers once again, everything timid and awkward.

How are you doing? he asked.

Cynthia's voice was ecstatic, quavering with joy. *I am okay, my husband. I prayed every day that you were alive.*

He felt a rush of relief at the sound of her voice, at the shape of the word *husband*. A pain erupted in his chest. It felt as if he were in two different worlds at the same time, pulled between two unfamiliar universes. He took a breath and asked:

How is my mother?

She is okay but she's been very worried about you. She's worried about when you're going to be released.

Before he could finish his next question, the line cut out. The entire conversation lasted less than a minute. Later he found out that Fred had explained what had happened to Razak, how he had traveled north from Mexico, and why had been detained for so long. Both Cynthia and Fred were Ga, a Ghanaian ethnicity, and spoke the same language.

A few weeks later, Razak was sitting in the common room watching the news when a correction officer named Peterson told him he had a visitor.

"It's someone from USCIS. Good luck."

"Thank you."

Razak was led to a small conference room and immediately saw a different asylum officer. A tall African American man sat across from him and smiled. "Razak. You're going to be released."

"Released to where? Am I being sent back home or somewhere else?"

"You're going to New York."

Tears welled up in Razak's eyes and creased his cheeks.

"I'm sorry. I know you've been here a long time, but it was part of the process."

Razak was too stunned to speak.

"You know where I'm from?" the officer asked. "I'm from New York. I see your uncle's address here. He's close to Yankee Stadium. That's where I grew up. When you get there, there's a lot of bad guys, troublemakers, make sure you don't get mixed up with them."

On the way back to the unit, a female correctional officer who worked near the visitation area stopped him to say, "I know you're a good guy. You've never gotten in trouble with anybody. They kept you here a long time. I'm so sorry for that."

Razak stopped, nodded, then kept walking.

Although he had lost his asylum plea, the Department of Homeland Security was legally obligated to release Razak while the U.S. government continued its deportation proceedings. It was a complicated victory, knowing he would be freed from Eloy but could be sent back to Ghana at any moment.

•

Immigration officers contacted Razak's uncle in New York, asking if he would provide money for a bus ticket across the country. Malik had no idea his nephew was still in the United States: he thought he had already been deported.

"Can I talk to him, please?" his uncle asked the immigration officer.

Razak took the phone and listened.

"Razak, is that really you? I thought they had deported you. I haven't heard from you. Is it really you?"

"It's me. They released me today. They want to know if you'd be willing to buy me a bus ticket to New York. I'm so sorry to call you like this."

"Of course, don't be sorry," his uncle said. "Ask them what I need to do."

The ICE officer helped Razak's uncle send a wire through Western Union for the bus ticket.

Razak's uncle also spoke with Razak's friend from Ghana, Munil, who then contacted Cynthia back in Accra and gave her the news.

On May 6, 2015, Razak was freed from the Eloy detention facility. Before his release, he signed an Order of Supervision, agreeing to report in person to the DHS/ICE field office in New York City. He also agreed that he would assist ICE in obtaining any necessary travel documents and that he would not leave New York for more than forty-eight hours without first contacting ICE. Once he had signed his release papers, once he was finally able to remove the khaki jumpsuit, he told himself he would not allow anyone to put him through anything like that again. No imprisonment, no shackles. Never.

It would be a two-and-a-half-day bus ride from Phoenix to

New York. ICE officers returned Razak's meager belongings to him, some clothes, his diary, and his portable Koran, but he had no other documents, nothing but his asylum applications and release papers. Officers brought Razak along with a few other men who had been released to the bus station. He took his seat in the middle of the bus and waited for the sound of the door closing. He could not believe he was finally free. A cold sense of disquiet set in. Once the bus pulled away, he stared out at the passing terrain, feeling as uncertain and as lost as ever.

24

Something had been broken.

By the beginning of the second decade of the twenty-first century, a quiet explosion of asylum seekers had begun to affect nearly every part of the world. What had been a steady escalation of individuals leaving their countries of origin starting in 2009 became one of the world's greatest humanitarian crises by the end of 2014. Asylum applications that year reached as high as an estimated 121,200 in the United States, which at the time remained the world's largest recipient of asylum requests.

At the beginning of the crisis, the Obama administration did what it could to respond to the worsening disaster, leading the world in support of refugees as the top resettlement country. In 2016, the U.S. resettled nearly 85,000 individuals, dramatically raising the number of allowable refugees. That same year the U.S. also granted asylum to more than 25,000 seekers who presented themselves at U.S. ports of entry or made claims from inside the country.

During this time, the Republican-led Congress failed to respond with any kind of meaningful immigration legislation. Years earlier, in 2012, the Obama administration had created the Deferred Action for Childhood Arrivals program, or DACA, through an executive order that gave "Dreamers"—2 million young people brought here by their parents—a renewable two-year amnesty from deportation. Frustrated by Congress's inaction and aware of the growing crisis, President Obama expanded DACA to cover additional undocumented immigrants— men and women who had lived in the U.S. since 2010 and who had children who were American citizens or permanent residents—on November 20, 2014.

At the same time, the Obama administration deported a large number of undocumented migrants, many from South and Central America. By the end of his presidency, Barack Obama oversaw the repatriation of more than 2 million individuals, more than any other U.S. president in history, a policy that further complicated his administration's position on immigration.

The nearly unfathomable numbers of refugee claims, asylum applications, Dreamers, and migrants who were deported each year continued to grow, completely overwhelming the resources of the Department of Homeland Security. Men and women, working to do their best to enforce federal laws, were unable to cope with the bureaucratic onslaught from a legally paralyzed system.

All legislative attempts by the Republican-led U.S. Congress to pass legislation that directly responded to the ongoing humanitarian crisis or to reimagine the hopelessly out-of-date system were either ignored or not allowed to come up for vote in either the Senate or the House of Representatives. Instead, senators and representatives reacted only nominally during this period by requesting additional funds and opening emergency detention facilities. Unlike other Western democracies such as the United Kingdom or Canada, which offered free accommodations to asylum seekers, pro bono legal aid, free healthcare, and a monthly stipend to provide for necessities while asylum seekers awaited their legal decisions, the United States continued its woeful practice of lengthy detainment in privately run prisons without any kind of legal support.

Instead of hope, instead of safety, what many asylum seekers coming to the U.S. found was a country seized by fear and an inability to act, a nation crippled by its own bureaucracy and partisan infighting, with a citizenry largely ignorant of the human catastrophe taking shape all around them.

Objects, discarded or taken by CBP officers at the border, began to tell the story of the lives of migrants and what they were seeking in the U.S.

Bibles, thousands and thousands, in all colors and sizes. Hairbrushes in every conceivable shape and configuration. Gloves piled in human-size mounds. Photographs—faces, families, compositions. Cans of tuna, thousands upon thousands. Toothbrushes. Toothpaste. Billfolds and wallets. Condoms. Contraceptive pills. Cell phones. Dried fish. Virgin Mary statues. Toilet paper. Pairs of reading glasses. Paperback books. Scissors. Shaving razors. Watches of all kinds. Cans of Coca-Cola. Caffeine pills. Perfume. Cologne. Matches. Makeup. Batteries. Baseball caps. Backpacks. Socks. Belts. Documents. Flip-flops. Toy cars. Human remnants of the past, fragments of an imagined future, all put in limbo, all confiscated.

25

Seidu presented himself to the immigration officer at the San Ysidro Port of Entry on May 17, 2015. After waiting in line for several hours, he was briefly interviewed and then told to wait in a separate area. Ten hours later, having watched other travelers and migrants being attended to by Customs and Border Protection officers, Seidu and a group of other undocumented immigrants were separated by gender for in-depth interrogations with individual CBP officers. Officers processed him—getting his information and fingerprints—and led him to a holding room filled with other men seeking asylum.

The holding facility was industrial, bare, frightfully inhuman-feeling. Each of the men—Africans, Ecuadorians, Mexicans—were given two gray blankets, though the temperature of the room was frigid. There were no mattresses, no bunks, only a few benches to sit on.

Some of the immigrants complained about the temperature and were yelled at, told to be quiet. The fluorescent lights overhead blinked unforgivingly, which to Seidu somehow made the room feel even colder.

The men were not given anything to drink but were offered cold Taco Bell tacos. When some of the men argued, the officers said, "This is it. Either eat it or starve."

Seidu studied the shape and size of the room, heard how the officers spoke. *Is this the United States?* he thought. *Is this how they're treating people here?*

For a week and a half, he was not allowed to shower or brush his teeth. On the floor, there was nowhere to stretch your legs, no way to sleep.

At any one time between fifty and a hundred men sat behind the tall wire walls, waiting to be processed.

An asylum officer arrived for Seidu's first formal interview a week and a half later. Given the opportunity to tell his story of who he was and why he had come to the U.S. to request asylum, Seidu found he was unable to put into words the reasons he fled Brazil. After years of keeping his sexual identity hidden, he was afraid to admit to a foreign government official he had been with another man of his own volition. He did not know if he could trust the U.S. legal system, as the courts back home were both corrupt and dangerously hostile to LGBT individuals. Knowing nothing about the asylum process in the U.S., he was certain he would be sent back to Ghana if he could not persuade the officer that his life was in immediate danger. He was also concerned that if the U.S. government found out he had come from Brazil, that he might be deported back to South America. Perhaps, too, he was worried about how a confession regarding his sexuality might affect his future job prospects, and how any record of such a confession might be used against him.

Having spoken with a number of other detainees while he was waiting to be processed, and lacking any legitimate legal support, Seidu made the decision to devise a story as to why he could not go back to Ghana. He borrowed from several incidents, both real and imagined, and told the asylum officer that one of his uncles back in Ghana had offered him money in exchange for sex and that he and his uncle had been caught in the act by other family members and then beaten. After the incident he claimed he fled the country, fearing for his life.

In his statement Seidu also mentioned his brother and sister-in-law in Florida and his hope of finding a job to support his mother and family back home. After reviewing this information, the asylum officer granted him credible fear status, allowing him to proceed in the process. Once the interview was concluded, Seidu was returned to the holding facility.

Three days later an ICE officer called his name off a list. Seidu stood, certain the officers were going to release him, or at the very least, bring him before a judge. Instead they presented him with documents stating their intention to transfer him to a detention center somewhere else in California while he awaited his asylum proceedings. No one explained anything more than that. Seidu and a number of the other men were then placed in handcuffs, while ICE officers attached waist and leg chains.

Put on a bus, he could barely see the hills of California, with its dispassionate wilderness, going by.

At a second holding facility, the men were allowed to shower and brush their teeth and were given green jumpsuits to wear. For three days the asylum seekers waited, having no thought as to where they might end up.

In their own languages, in their conversations together, the men tried to express the feeling of doubt, of disbelief hanging over them.

Once more Seidu and a number of other migrants were hand-cuffed, put in manacles, and transferred in the middle of the night in a small white van to Adelanto Detention Center, a privately run federal prison located in Adelanto, San Bernardino County,

California. The detention center is owned by the GEO Group, the largest private prison company in the U.S., which maintains billions of dollars in federal contracts each year. GEO purchased the prison from the city in 2010, then built and expanded the facility to accommodate 2,000 additional prisoners.

In 2011, GEO contracted with U.S. Immigrations and Customs Enforcement to house immigration detainees, making it the largest ICE facility in California. Since then it has been the site of a number of protests and controversies.

Located sixty miles northeast of Los Angeles in the Victor Valley area of the Mojave, Adelanto is a series of white and beige buildings surrounded by scrubland and high desert. Its elevation is 2,800 feet above sea level, making it breezy though irrepressibly hot. Beige suburban-looking homes dot what would otherwise be empty lots of sand and dirt. A sign, visible upon entering town, announces WELCOME, CITY OF ADELANTO, THE CITY WITH UNLIMITED POSSIBILITIES, which stands along the side of a vacant road without the faintest trace of irony. Framed by enormous cactus and the rising slopes of the mountains in the east, there are very few trees that cast any shadows. A terminal vacancy consumes the small city. Orchards of deciduous fruit trees once dotted the land, bringing with them the sweetness of nectar and a sense of manifold prosperity. The orchards were later replaced by chicken farms. Progress soon halted. When the George Air Force Base closed in 1992, the city—the smallest in San Bernardino County—fell into economic difficulties. Several prisons opened in the area soon after but failed to contribute much to the city's economic outlook.

By the time Seidu arrived on May 26, 2015, the city was not much more than a site for prisons and their prisoners. Adelanto had seen a marked increase in detained migrants and had been expanding its facilities to accommodate a much larger inmate population.

Seidu arrived at Adelanto at four in the morning and saw the gigantic wire fence, the beige walls, the narrow, vertical windows, and immediately recognized the building for what it was: a prison. It had never occurred to him that he would be sent to jail for legally presenting himself at the border. He had no idea how this had happened.

Once inside, Seidu asked for water. A correctional officer immediately told him to shut up.

For several hours the men waited in a holding room. Finally several corrections officers arrived and told them to take off their clothes, handing out jumpsuits based on the men's legal status. Seidu was given a pair of blue coveralls; others were given orange jumpsuits, in light of their previous deportations. Officers then handed the migrants boxes to collect their personal belongings. Seidu was also given underwear, socks, and shoes and led to the living unit where he was to be detained, which the officers referred to as "pods," each holding eighty men in just twelve cells.

The cells featured two bunk beds, a toilet, a rack for towels and shower items, and several plastic crates for storage. Sterile, institutional—the cell was a beige room reeking with a profound sense of grief and hopelessness. Seidu sat on the edge of the bed he had been assigned, some ten months after leaving Brazil, facing the reality of imprisonment for an indeterminate length of time.

Someone down the hall began shouting.

26

Seidu soon became aware of the differences between being detained in the U.S. and being detained in other countries like Panama or Mexico. Adelanto was a constructed world, entirely false; it was nothing like real life. The air was recirculated, the sunlight came through opaque, barred windows, even the shadows seemed unreal. Regardless of how much money you had when you entered the institution, the detainment facility used an electronic currency system and so there was no bartering. You could not trade food or phone cards. In order to make calls to the U.S. or beyond, you needed to purchase a phone card directly from the commissary. There was no way to make money on your own.

Everything within the institution was highly regulated, happened at some preordained time, and made the daily flow of life feel like surviving under military rule—the hour you woke up, ate, went outside, went to sleep—these were all beyond your own choice or determination. It was as if you had been pulled violently out of life and set down in the middle of some kind of nonexistent place, built by rule after rule. There was nothing uncertain, untidy, or human.

Seidu was given the opportunity to call his brother Kamal once he arrived, but did not know what to tell him. He had no idea how long he would be detained in California, how long it would be before he could make a plea before a judge. Kamal added fifty dollars to his brother's commissary account and told him he would help however he could.

The food at Adelanto was caustic. On maroon plastic trays, it seemed to appear as if manufactured by machines. Waxy mashed potatoes, a slurry of peas, slices of raw onion, a gloppy pile of turd-like beans. The meat tasted rancid. Two pieces of dry bread, an orange for dessert.

Then again, the same food for dinner.

Then again and again, day after day.

Seidu would sometimes sneak a slice of bread back to his cell, hiding it under his uniform. On the way out of the cafeteria, correctional officers would search the men and sometimes uncovered such items, but the risk was worth it—to be able to eat something alone, to have ownership over a single moment, small as it might be.

The desert heat was unbearable. It radiated along the halls, the floors, the ceiling, hung about the air, making each day torpid, longer than it should have been.

Seidu and the other men in his pod were sent outside for an hour each day. There he played soccer and then rested in the shade, sharing brief conversations with the other detainees before their recreation ended.

On the way back inside the facility, Seidu glanced over his shoulder at the edge of the world, the mountains, the desert, remembering his childhood roaming Nima, chasing a soccer ball down a narrow street. Then the powerful metal gates would lock behind him and he would be forced to stay indoors for another twenty-four hours, the outside world becoming like a figment, a daydream.

Most of the correctional officers seemed young and appeared to be of Mexican or Central American descent. Some were friendly and professional, though others seemed to hate where they were, what they were doing, the men with whom they were forced to interact.

After a few days Seidu was surprised to find a number of other Ghanaians detained in his pod. Some had been in the facility for several months awaiting their immigration court hearings. Some recognized Seidu as a local soccer player; others Seidu recognized as soccer fans from Accra. All the men spoke Hausa, and Seidu was once again relieved to be among his countrymen.

The other Ghanaians showed Seidu how to navigate the institution, bought food for him at the commissary, prayed with him as fellow Muslims. For the first time in many months, it felt as if he was part of a community. As they gathered before and after prayers and at meals, he asked the other men how long they had been there.

Four months, replied one man.

Six months, replied another.

Why does it take so long? Seidu asked.

It takes a long time. There's a lot of us here.

One of the men added with an air of regret, *I'm still waiting for my bond hearing.*

Eventually Seidu asked some of the Ghanaians to help complete his asylum application. During this process Seidu told a number of the men that he was seeking asylum in the States because he was bisexual. It was a perilous moment, revealing his sexual identity to his fellow Ghanaian detainees. He was not sure how these other men would react once they found out the truth. But it soon became clear, within the walls of the detention facility, that the other asylum seekers did not care. Some of the Ghanaians detained at Adelanto were gay or bisexual themselves, had escaped dire family situations, or were avoiding governmental or personal recriminations because of their sexual preference.

Seidu shared the truth of his escape from Brazil with each of his fellow Ghanaians, carefully, one at a time. The other men did the same. Within the facility, strangely enough, it was one of the first times he could actually be who he was among people from his own country.

Even with the support of his fellow Ghanaians, Seidu found Adelanto increasingly difficult. As days and then weeks and then months passed, Seidu became more and more concerned, fearing he had made a tragic mistake fleeing Brazil and traveling to the U.S. The more time passed, the more inhumane the facility seemed to be. If he wanted to call his mother back home, if he wanted to hear the voice of his sister, he couldn't. He had to wait for his preappointed calling time, and even then—with a six-dollar phone card—there was almost no possibility of getting his mother on the telephone and actually speaking to her within the few short minutes he was allowed to make phone calls. The food the institution served was making him sick, he was sure of it. He vomited frequently. When he filled out a medical services request, signing his alien number, he had to wait a week before a member of the medical staff came to inquire about his condition. All the medical staff offered him was a tiny blue pill, telling him, "Take this and you'll feel better."

He felt as if he could die and it would mean nothing to any of them. Far from Accra, he realized he was only an A-number now, no longer any kind of person at all.

27

On June 25, 2015, Seidu appeared at the Adelanto Immigration Court for his first hearing, presided over by Judge Elizabeth Mc-Grail. It was strange to go to court in the same building where he was being detained. Typically, hearings were supposed to be set within days or weeks of the beginning of a detainee's confinement, but due to the enormous backlog of cases and the lack of federally appointed judges to oversee the proceedings, an entire month had passed since Seidu entered the U.S. before he was able to formally begin the asylum process.

In his application, Seidu had mentioned his ability to speak Hausa and English, though he had requested a translator, fearful of what would happen if he misunderstood something during his initial interview or the court proceedings. That day, the appointed translator stood beside Seidu at the hearing. Like most detainees, Seidu had no lawyer to represent him. A prosecutor from the Department of Homeland Security waited with a sheaf of papers. The judge took notes as Seidu's translator offered details of the case. It felt like a burden, not being able to speak for himself, but Seidu kept quiet and listened intently to the judge's questions, responding to the translator directly when asked.

At the end of the proceedings, the judge presented Seidu a list of lawyers that he could try to retain in order to support his case.

She also mentioned that she would schedule a hearing within a few weeks to determine if he was eligible for bond. Before the session ended, the judge warned Seidu that in order to be granted asylum, he would need to present evidence on his behalf, something he had not previously considered.

Seidu called each lawyer on the list, but every one of them required payment of some kind—$3,000, $4,000, $5,000—before they would even consider his case.

On his own, he contacted his brother in Florida and his boyfriend back in Ghana to try to help him document the threat against his life.

It was difficult to produce any direct evidence, as no one other than his manager had made any such direct claim. Other than submitting a copy of Ghanaian law, which called for homosexuals to be imprisoned for a minimum of three years, and writing a statement about witnessing the persecution of other queer people back home, he did not know the best way to prepare a strategy. How do you prove your life is in danger for being bisexual when being bisexual would only lead you to being terrorized in the first place?

It was several weeks later, on July 15, 2015—more than a month after Seidu arrived at Adelanto—before he was given a hearing with the same judge to negotiate his immediate release on bond. Although Seidu had no prior convictions and there was no evidence of any violence in his past or that he posed an extraordinary flight risk, the judge set his bond at $28,000.

"But I don't have that kind of money," Seidu complained in English.

"I can't do anything," the judge replied. "You can appeal the bond decision, which usually takes about three months."

"I don't want to be here that long."

The judge seemed impassive and quickly moved to end the proceedings.

Seidu again called his brother Kamal in Florida and explained the situation.

"I don't know. I don't know if I can get that much money," Kamal confessed.

Kamal sat down with his wife, Maria, and went over their options. Eventually the couple decided they would take out a loan and work with a bond company if and when Seidu's asylum plea was denied.

Although the threat Seidu perceived to his life and liberty was incredibly real, he was unaware how tenuous his plea actually was. Without an immigration lawyer to help him negotiate the process, Seidu relied solely on the advice of other detainees at Adelanto. Some of this information was useful, while other recommendations were misinformed about the complicated specifics of immigration law.

Like a number of asylum seekers asking for protection based on their sexual orientation or identity, Seidu had little evidence to support his claims of persecution. He also had not yet decided whether or not he would reveal his sexual identity in court. If he publicly stated that he was bisexual, he could claim that he was part of a particular threatened social group in Ghana. Other successful asylum cases, including the landmark *Matter of Acosta* in 1985, gave LGBT applicants the opportunity to seek asylum based on being part of a particular social group in which a "common characteristic of the group either cannot change or should not be required to change because it is fundamental to their individual identities or consciences," which helped to establish sexual orientation as grounds for asylum.

But a Board of Immigration Appeals decision in 2002 made the matter even more complex. Applicants claiming membership in such a social group had to also demonstrate their social visibility, meaning the government from which they were fleeing had to recognize the social group to which they belonged. For many LGBT asylum seekers, this was a burden that almost none of them could satisfy. The most oppressive governments—like those in Ghana—refused to recognize gay, lesbians, bisexuals, or transgender individuals as social groups in the same way an opposing political party might be recognized. Seidu, like other LGBT asylum applicants, would also have difficulty proving he belonged to a particular social group if he was not publicly known to be a member. In Seidu's case, being bisexual in Ghana but doing so in secret meant he was not socially visible.

To win his asylum plea, he would need to establish that the public back in Ghana recognized him as bisexual and that his life was now in danger as a consequence.

His final court appearance was set for November 25, 2015. He had four months to build his case. Seidu continued to ask his brother and friends back in Ghana for help in gathering evidence for his upcoming court date. His boyfriend Jamal initially agreed to write a declaration explaining his and Seidu's relationship, but eventually declined, claiming he was unable to afford to send the document through express mail. Things started looking bleak. The only evidence Seidu was able to obtain was a generalized newspaper article about LGBT persecution in Ghana. Seidu's friend sent the newspaper report to Adelanto, where Seidu presented it to his asylum officer.

"I want to send this to the judge."

His officer agreed to pass it on.

As the court date drew closer, Seidu, in the solitude of his cell, was unsure if he would be able to come out to the world and tell his story.

28

Is it my mother laughing? It was the day Seidu's father brought home a television. Almost no one in Nima owned a television. Somehow his father got his hands on one before his parents separated. It was hard to remember how old he was then. A boy. Seven? Eight? The TV was used but expensive. It did not come with an antenna, which it turned out was even more expensive than the television itself because it had to be installed.

More than his mother's face, he remembered the sound of her laugh.

Sometime later, his parents got a DVD player and a variety of videodiscs. Always enterprising, his mother brought the television outside, in front of the rooms they rented, then dragged out chairs or borrowed some, and put on a movie. It was *Commando*, the Arnold Schwarzenegger action movie from the 1980s. Everyone would come to sit and watch. Seidu's mother would make his favorite drink, ice kenkey, a delicious milkshake of fermented corn. Whoever wanted to watch the movie had to buy a drink.

In the heat of the evening, Seidu would lean back and watch. On-screen, the action star pummeled several bad guys. In America, the good guys always won, the buildings were tall, cars and buildings and houses looked new. One day he hoped to visit. He turned from the television set and looked around.

It was now growing dark. He watched his mother move among the crowd, selling her drinks. On the television screen, something exploded and the audience around him applauded. He looked over at her and smiled.

I am here.

The air around me, the sky, the streetlights, my mother's laugh.

What can hurt me?

When he was awoken by the sound of the guards each morning, his dream would disperse. He would find himself facing the same pale wall, the same unmoving shadows. Adelanto became more and more unbearable each day. Two months after arriving, each daily task seemed to become more and more difficult, fraught with tension. One day, a correctional officer approached Seidu in the common area and asked, "What are you in here for?"

"What do you mean?"

"What crime did you commit?"

Seidu had no way to explain that he'd done nothing wrong. He'd met a man in Brazil, then ran from the terror of his previous life. His documents were stolen while crossing the jungle. He presented himself at the U.S. port of entry with the best of intentions, to become a productive part of a society that claimed to value freedom and individuality. The fact that the guard even asked made Seidu realize no one knew what was happening to the asylum seekers behind the private prison walls. Why was he being detained with common criminals, drugs dealers, and murderers? He came to believe it was because it was an industry, a profitable one, and that industry was capitalizing on the ignorance and the lack of awareness of the American people. There was no other way to explain it.

Even praying each day became a problem. Seidu noticed that some of the correctional officers and some of the other detainees did not like Muslims praying in public. They would yell and jeer, while others would purposefully cross and walk past wherever the Ghanaians happened to be kneeling.

One day several ICE officers assigned to the facility approached Seidu and the other Ghanaians in the middle of their prayers and told them to stop. Seidu looked up. One of the officers remarked, "That's not the right way to pray." Some of the officers forced the men to their feet and said, "You don't have the right to pray like that here."

Seidu immediately became furious. "We're Muslims. We have the right to pray anywhere we are."

The ICE officers attempted to disperse the group, but the encounter soon became tense with shouting and physical taunting. Correctional officers from the facility attempted to control the situation by handcuffing the detainees and carrying them bodily to a large detention room until the conflict abated.

Seidu also noticed that while priests were allowed to visit Christian detainees and lead them in religious services, no cleric was allowed to come pray with the Muslim men.

Days before the Muslim holy day of Eid in the middle of July 2015, the men requested permission to go outside and pray in the courtyard, following their religious tradition. There was a large Islamic contingent at the detention facility, from many African, Middle Eastern, and Asian countries. But the correctional officers refused to let the men out. They told the detainees that they needed to send a letter to the facility's chaplain in order to get approval.

"We're Muslims, we're not Christians," Seidu said. "Why do we need a priest to approve whether we can pray or not?"

Further arguments between the Muslim detainees continued until finally the officers relented. On the day of Eid, the men were hurriedly led outside where they began praying before they were forced back in a few minutes later, unable to complete their prayers.

It never happened to him before coming to America, this feeling of having his religious rights violated, of being persecuted as a Muslim for a particular set of beliefs.

A month later, one of Seidu's friends decided to begin a hunger strike to protest the conditions of the asylum seekers. A number of the men, including Seidu, were being held indefinitely and without any sign of release, and so together they decided to refrain from eating anything for two weeks, hoping to gain attention from the Department of Justice or the media.

But no one seemed to take notice. One of the fasting detainees grew so weak that he had to be taken out of the facility by ambulance. As they were carrying him out, Seidu watched the corrections officers remove his blue coveralls and replace them with orange ones. Even in the middle of a medical emergency, the system insisted on unfairly identifying him as some kind of a criminal.

The ongoing incidents forced Seidu and the others to speak up, to challenge their own fear of the officers at the facility and the authority of the facility in general. For the first time in his life, Seidu considered the role he had to play, and how he might put his beliefs into action. He was finding out what it meant to be part of a community and was challenging himself to no longer be silent.

29

The court date before the immigration judge finally arrived. At eight in the morning on November 25, 2015, Seidu had his final hearing before the same judge, with an interpreter at this side and legal counsel representing DHS. Stepping into the courtroom, he found he could barely stand. He had never before in his life been so nervous. His hands shook uncontrollably at his sides.

When it was his time to testify, a silence filled the courtroom. Seidu once again followed the advice of his fellow detainees and repeated the story he told the CBP and later his asylum officers—that his uncle had coerced him into having sex for money and that he and his uncle were caught and beaten; how he then fled to the United States, fearing for his life. Seidu spoke through the translator, answering the judge's questions as best as he could.

"Do you fear the government of Ghana for any reason?" the judge asked.

"I'm scared of the police because they can lock you up for three years if you're gay."

"But you're not gay? So why are you afraid of the police?"

Seidu paused, not knowing how best to answer. "The police know a lot about gay people. Most of the time they lock you up and don't give you a chance to talk."

"But why would they associate you with anyone who is gay?"

Again, Seidu became quiet for several seconds. It was the moment he had been hoping to avoid. Everything slowed to an appreciable silence. Under the intensity of the courtroom lights, knowing his life was now hanging in the balance, he found he was still unable to admit who he was or what had actually happened to him. After years of hiding, now facing the scrutiny of a foreign legal system, having never said those particular words out loud in public before, he found he was too afraid tell the truth.

Instead the young man lowered his head and murmured, "They will lock me up. That's why I'm scared of them. Because they will never consider what I say."

After another half hour of testimony during which the judge and the DHS lawyer continued to explore some of the conflicting elements of his story, Judge McGrail finally rendered her verdict.

"Sir, your story is not consistent and you failed to present any evidence. So I can't possibly grant you asylum based on what I have."

Seidu barely considered the judge's decision as it hung in the air. How, after seven months in detention, had he failed to explain who he was, what he was facing? If he had told the truth, would things have gone differently?

The hearing ended—Seidu could be released on bond or wait in custody while the government began its deportations proceedings.

Afterward, Seidu was asked by an asylum officer to sign a deportation letter. He refused.

"I'm going to appeal the case," he said.

He immediately called Kamal in Florida and discussed the outcome of his hearing.

His brother's support was unwavering. *Okay*, he said. *I know what we have to do.*

Within a week, Kamal was able to secure a loan, which he and

Maria used to pay a bond company, who then put up the majority of the bond. Kamal explained each step of the process to Seidu through a series of short phone calls. *Someone from the bond company will be in touch with you. Don't worry. You'll be out of there soon.*

On December 14, 2015, Seidu was sitting in his cell when a correctional officer appeared with news of his release.

A bond company employee arrived at the facility and took Seidu to a nearby restaurant where he signed several documents, agreeing not to leave the country. Later the bondsman attached an electronic monitor to his ankle to track his movements and then bought him a bus ticket to travel to Kamal's house in Florida. It would take two days to reach the small town of Heaven, Florida.

Having spent nearly eight months in detention, Seidu was gratified to see the glimmer of flashing lights as the bus passed through desert towns and the occasional city. As he got closer to Florida, his anticipation grew, although he was well aware that without a final decision in his asylum case, his legal status was unclear, which would make transitioning into American life that much more difficult.

Seidu immediately spotted his brother in the bus station. It had been almost eleven years since they last saw each other. Seidu was overcome with joy, hugging his older brother. He turned and introduced himself to Maria, whom he had never met in person.

Maria began crying, embracing her brother-in-law, and together the couple took the young man back to their home. Seidu happily took a long shower, enjoying the privacy, the freedom of being allowed to bathe alone.

It was only five days before Christmas and the town of Heaven was decorated accordingly. Kamal and Maria took Seidu shopping and bought him American clothes and a new pair of shoes. Having never experienced Christmas before, Seidu stared at the ornaments—trees, lights, ribbons, glass animals—with wonder. It truly seemed like something out of a book of fairy tales.

Back at their home, Kamal and Maria put up a Christmas tree, something Seidu had never seen in person before. A tree in the middle of the room, adorned with objects and lights. It seemed like now, here, anything might be possible.

Kamal had a job restocking at Walmart at night, while Maria—who struggled with severe back problems and was temporarily unable to work—helped Seidu apply for a work permit while he waited for his asylum appeal to be processed. Although his work permit was denied, he was able to apply for a Florida state ID, which he received. Staring at it, for the first time in many months, Seidu started to imagine a future for himself in the United States. It was almost too much, this homecoming, this feeling of unabashed love and support.

30

Beginning on January 13, 2016, Seidu was required to check in with an ICE officer in Tampa, Florida, as part of his bond agreement. The ICE facility was a one-story beige building, flanked by windswept trees. Inside the benign tan and blue office, Seidu sat across from his case officer, who seemed unfriendly and generally unsupportive.

"You need to get your documents from your embassy," the officer barked at him.

"But my case is still being appealed."

"I know it's being appealed, but you still need to get your documents in order."

In reality, Seidu had tried to contact the Ghanaian embassy several times to obtain copies of his birth certificate and passport but was told that without his birth certificate, they could not give him a replacement passport. It was absurd Ghanaian inefficiency and bureaucracy at its worst. No one at the embassy ever responded to his letters or phone calls.

Every two weeks after that, Seidu met with the officer to argue about his lack of progress. In between visits, the officer would call, demanding Seidu find some other way to produce the documents.

Once again, Seidu tried calling the embassy in Washington, D.C., but received the same response. Without a valid birth certificate, there was no way for him to prove he was born in Ghana.

Two weeks later, the ICE officer assigned to Seidu's case phoned the embassy himself and was told the same thing. Still, the officer continued to call Kamal's cell phone, demanding that Seidu somehow produce the documents he himself had been unable to.

Each month Kamal had to pay four hundred and fifty dollars to the bond company for the use of the ankle monitor. The bills incurred by Seidu's legal problems were quickly adding up.

Without a work permit, Seidu was unable to gain employment and help pay his legal costs or contribute to the household. He felt ashamed to have to depend on the generosity of his brother and sister-in-law without any end in sight.

In February 2016, Kamal was transferred to a Walmart facility in Youngstown, Ohio. When offered the position, the family hoped a move to Ohio would allow Seidu to apply for a new work permit.

In Youngstown, Seidu felt ill at ease at first. The city was like a dream deferred, with crumbling midcentury buildings and long-shuttered factories amid old homes and desolate-looking apartments. The people seemed to be struggling, seemed to be as desperate as the ones he had passed throughout much of the Third World. To him, the city did not feel safe. Drug dealers huddled on the corners and graffiti marred public buildings. It was not the America he had imagined or seen portrayed in films or on television.

Once they were settled in Youngstown, Maria helped Seidu apply for an Ohio work permit, but once again, his application was denied.

•

In Ohio, Seidu was required to report to his immigration officer for an in-person interview only every three months. The climate and atmosphere of the state seemed much more restrained, reasonable, more hospitable to migrants, though he could not understand why. Seidu would travel an hour from Youngstown to Cleveland to meet with the new ICE officer assigned to his case. Cleveland itself was beautiful—with modern skyscrapers, the sprawling lake, a city full of parks and trees. The officer in Cleveland was more supportive and did not question him about the outstanding documents from Ghana. After their initial visit, Seidu was allowed to call in once a month and did not have to return to Cleveland for an in-person visit for another three months. Seidu started to feel more comfortable, believing in Ohio he finally had a chance to make a life for himself.

One day in early spring 2016, Seidu took a knife and began to inspect the ankle monitor. He found several hooks keeping it in place and was able to remove it easily. He began to wear it less and less, not wanting to be judged or scrutinized when he went out in public. The people in Youngstown were almost all white, but for some reason they seemed willing to accept him.

Seidu and Kamal often played soccer together at a nearby park. They were playing one day when a white man named Steve approached Seidu and asked if he would coach his kid's soccer team.

"They're all twelve to fifteen years old. They do a tournament every summer. Is that something you'd be interested in?"

Seidu happily accepted, offering to do it for free. Admittedly, it was difficult at first, as Seidu had never actually coached before. He started with the basics of passing, how to make a touch on the ball, how to shift the ball. He often had to remember he was working with kids who played only a few months each year. Twice a week he had the children doing drills, scrimmaging, and working on conditioning their bodies. Even though all the kids were white, he felt they treated him with a profound respect. He realized he loved coaching as much as playing and considered finding a job doing it permanently at some nearby school or park.

A group of adults on an amateur soccer team also asked Seidu to join their team. They'd never won a tournament before, but after Seidu accepted and they began playing together, they secured their first tournament win. Everyone else on the team had been born in the U.S., but Seidu felt comfortable enough to tell his teammates about his immigration status and how he had come to be in Ohio. His teammates were incredibly supportive. Steve had gotten Seidu a tryout with the Columbus Crew, a major league soccer team based in nearby Columbus.

Seidu filled out the paperwork and went for a one-day tryout in October 2016, bringing his best cleats and shin guards. Sixty other young men were all trying out and Seidu was put in the midfield, even though he preferred to be on defense. He pushed himself as hard as he could, knowing he might not ever have an opportunity like this again.

When the tryouts were finished, the coaches said the prospective players would be contacted via email.

Days later, Seidu—aware his immigration status could certainly be an issue—waited for any kind of response. None came.

In his thoughts, in his heart, Seidu hoped life in America would be better. He had an idea of the U.S. as a place where migrants were accepted and given the chance to start over. But without a work permit, without a job, everything continued to feel tenuous.

By late October, the 2016 presidential campaign had taken over the media—television, radio, Facebook, the entire internet. It had become inescapable. The charged words of Republican candidate Donald Trump seemed to zero in on Seidu's greatest fears. Almost everything Trump talked about at rallies and in interviews had to do with immigration. He said he wanted to build a wall to keep out immigrants. He claimed migrants from Mexico were criminals and rapists. He even blamed these same migrants for the economic downturn in manufacturing and coal production in Midwestern states. Parts of the nation seemed gripped by a spirit of anger and intolerance, even though the economy was performing strongly and unemployment was the lowest it had been in years. Candidate Donald Trump seemed to be somehow capitalizing on this dissonance.

Before the election in November 2016, a Facebook friend sent Seidu a post about eighty-seven Ghanaians who had been deported back to Ghana by the U.S. Department of Homeland Security. Reading the story online, Seidu began to fear his situation in America could quickly turn.

He began to mention his growing frustration to Kamal.

I don't know if I want to be here anymore. I'm tired of waiting. I'm tired of this country. What can I do? Where can I go?

The appeal in his asylum case had not come; might never come, it seemed.

Kamal told him to be patient, but Seidu was growing increasingly anxious. He was having trouble sleeping, felt unsafe leaving the house. The walls, the world seemed to be closing in.

The election of Donald Trump only affirmed what he knew to be true.

One day during the second week of November, Maria handed Seidu a large envelope and together they began to read the brief, formal letter that stated Seidu's appeal for asylum had been denied. There was no legal recourse, no other opportunity for a second appeal. Both of them stared at the piece of paper without speaking.

Maria later admitted she had found the letter in the mailbox three days before, had read it but didn't want to say anything, didn't know how to break the news.

All Seidu knew was that he could not go back to Ghana. He was certain that if he was deported, he would be tortured, sent to prison, or worse. He sat down with Kamal again to explain his thoughts.

Where can I go? How can I leave this country?

Kamal was silent for a long time. *I don't know.*

I could go to New York. I don't think anyone will be able to find me there.

No, they can find you in New York. Then, after some time, Kamal offered, *What about Canada?*

On December 1, 2016, Immigration and Customs Enforcement issued Seidu a final order for his removal and deportation back to Ghana.

Days after that, the phone began to ring. Seidu was sure it was his immigration officer trying to get a hold of him. Everyone was afraid to answer it, staring at the device as if it were a ticking bomb waiting to explode.

Taking his brother's laptop, Seidu searched the shape of the country, looking at the various border crossings between the U.S. and Canada. There was one by New York and another by a town in the upper Midwest near a Canadian town called Emerson. The Emerson crossing appeared to be closer. He discussed what he found with Kamal later that evening. Everything became startlingly clear all of a sudden, his entire life quickly becoming settled. He began to put things in his backpack, thinking of the objects he should bring, the clothes he would need. The ankle monitor lay blinking uselessly on the bedside table. He began to consider how—after so many months of being a person, of having a name and a home and somewhere to sleep—he would have to once again become a no one, a nothing, something nameless, hiding alone in the dark.

31

Colors were different at night. After nearly two years in detention, Razak had forgotten how the night looked. The moon seemed far off; the cars with their headlights passing were beautiful and incongruent. Once again, Razak was on a bus crossing an unknown country, staring out the scratched windows at a foreign land, fleeing the past, on his way from Arizona to New York City. All these cities, all these buildings, each a different size, a different shape. Every skyline the bus passed had tall skyscrapers, modern homes, parking lots, formations of pavement and concrete, all of it aglow with thousands of rectangles of light. Sometimes he could see people moving, attending to their lives, lit from behind, in the windows of their houses, having no idea who he was, where he was going. The distance between things seemed discouraging. When it was time to change buses, he stood and looked around, hoping to find something recognizable. But there was nothing.

If there was light, he would read from the pocket-size Koran and pray.

When he stepped out of the bus station in Times Square in New York that night, all he had were the clothes he was wearing and the documents given to him by Immigration and Customs Enforcement. The city itself was a collision of light, all corners, all intersecting streets, all of it alive, electric, overwhelming, the stop-lights blinking, people hurrying by in every direction, entranced by their cell phone screens. Billboards and signs were chaotic, advertising products he had never heard of. It was May 8, 2015. There was no end to the motion, the voices, the languages. Razak was overcome by the strange sounds, the unending variety of human faces. He made his way over to a taxi and knocked on the window. The driver looked up and then rolled down his window. He appeared to be a fellow African. Razak said, "Good evening. I am going to the Bronx but I don't know the address."

"Do you have a phone number?"

"Yes."

"Where you from?" the cabbie asked.

"Ghana."

"I'm from Gambia," the driver said, nodding.

Razak gave the cabbie his friend Munil's phone number. The cabbie spoke to Munil, who gave him an address on Burnside.

On the way, the cabbie said, "I have a lot of friends here from Ghana who drive cabs. There are lots of opportunities. You can make a better life here."

Razak realized the cabdriver had no idea that over the past two years, he had already come to a complex understanding of the United States. He decided not to say anything to correct him.

Munil was standing outside an apartment building, waiting to give Razak a fierce hug. That evening Razak slept on a couch at Munil's sister's apartment. Munil's sister worked long shifts at a retirement home and was often gone for several days in a row. Though they had never met in person, Razak had spoken to her on the phone one time while at Eloy.

Once Razak awoke, Munil's sister asked him about his family, his journey, where he had grown up. She had come to the States with a visa fourteen years ago. She also asked about Razak's uncle and mentioned knowing several of his extended family in New York. *You have a big family here*, she told him.

I didn't even know about my uncle until I came here.

I know your mother, from the market in Nima. I remember she used to sell food. And your uncle, he used to tease me when I was little. You also have an aunt. She's lived here for thirty years.

An aunt? I had no idea!

You can talk to her later. She has a store and sells things from Africa.

Munil's sister prepared a Ghanaian breakfast—rice balls and soup.

I know it's been a long time since you've had food like this. When Munil was released I made this. He ate like someone who hadn't eaten in a year. He told me about being detained. I'm sorry for what you've been through.

For the first time in months, years really, Razak was surrounded by familiar sounds, smells, by goodwill. It was almost indescribable, this feeling, being in a physical place where—for a moment—he felt he belonged.

Later the next day he traveled to his uncle's apartment in Yonkers. Malik and his wife had five children, from the ages of twelve to twenty-five, but somehow still had room on a sofa for Razak to sleep. Razak was unsure what business his uncle was involved in, but assumed it must be financially sound if he could afford an apartment, support his family, and take him in. He did not feel it was his place to ask.

At the apartment, Razak explained the difficult circumstances of the last two years of his life. When he finished talking, Razak's uncle—a skinny man in his midfifties—smiled and said, *Do you know the year I left Ghana? It was right after you were born in 1982. It's been almost fifteen years since I spoke to your mother.*

When she called me and said you were coming, I knew something was wrong. She had never asked me for anything. So I knew I had to do something.

To have left Ghana, to have fled because of his half-siblings, only to travel to the other side of the world and discover a family, and then to be welcomed by them, to be given room in their busy lives, it was joyful, almost too much to accept.

After his cousins returned to their busy lives, talk between Razak and his uncle quickly turned to politics in Ghana. Malik had been involved with the NDC party, which supported Mustafa, the MP who Razak believed was involved with his half-siblings in their dispute over his father's land and on the attempt on his life. His uncle admitted, *Even we didn't like Mustafa. He doesn't help us as a party. But he was elected by his own people.*

Whenever there are elections, he gives people money. So he always wins.

Malik nodded knowingly. Razak looked at him and then glanced away.

You know that your government is very corrupt, don't you, Uncle?

No, that's just politics.

No, you haven't been there in fifteen years. The system doesn't work. It's not fair, how they treat their own people.

Malik conceded the point. *Both parties are not doing right. But that's how it is in any country.*

Razak did not answer, as he did not want to force a confrontation. Instead he discussed his plans for the future. How he needed a Social Security number and a work permit. How he would try to locate his birth certificate. The possibility of finding work.

Back in Ghana, Razak's mother went to the Accra police to report Razak's missing birth certificate and was able to get a replacement.

The document arrived two weeks later through FedEx. In his uncle's apartment, Razak stared at the paper and wondered why it was possible for his mother to get a copy in a matter of days while the Ghanaian embassy had been unable to locate it for almost two years. It seemed both dubious and a miracle. He was coming to understand how agencies, entire departments, systems, even the U.S. government—when faced with the complexity of a single individual's life—completely broke down.

Using the birth certificate and a form ICE had provided prior to his release, he applied for a Social Security number and a work permit. It cost three hundred and eighty dollars. Razak's aunt in New York—whom he had never met before, had never even known about—loaned him the money, which he changed into a money order and sent in with his application.

On May 26, 2015, Razak reported to the U.S. Immigration and Customs Enforcement field office at 26 Federal Plaza in Manhattan. The officer assigned to his case was a considerate African American man. He asked Razak, "Are you still complying with your embassy to try to get your travel documents together?"

"Yes."

But no one from the embassy had been in touch since Razak had sent three letters to each of the Ghanaian consulates. Any time he had tried to contact them, he had been forced to leave a voice mail, which no one ever replied to.

"Okay. Make sure you keep complying with your embassy. If they ask you for anything, make sure you get it to them. Just try to stay out of trouble."

Razak agreed that he would. It frightened him slightly—the fact that his mother had obtained a copy of his birth certificate so quickly—and that at any time, the Ghanaian embassy might respond to the ICE's outstanding requests. All he could do was try to build a life here, in the midst of so much uncertainty. Two weeks later—at the beginning of June—an envelope with his work permit arrived. It would be valid for one year.

Razak's first job in New York was at the Dream Hotel in Manhattan, beginning in the middle of June. During his interview, a manager asked Razak about his experience working in a kitchen.

"In Arizona, at the detention facility, I was a dishwasher."

The manager smiled, saying, "The workers we have doing the dishes now are usually pretty slow. We get to a point sometimes where we run out of dishes. We need someone who's willing to work hard in that position."

Razak told him he could. He handed the manager his work permit and his uncle's cell number. The manager helped Razak set up direct deposit for his checks at Bank of America, where he had recently opened an account.

Five days a week, Razak cleaned and scraped the dishes of the elite, the wealthy, urbane Manhattanites, sophisticated tourists, and well-to-do foreigners alike, toiling through his version of the American dream in grueling twelve-hour shifts. When he was done, he would take the train home and collapse on his uncle's couch, or speak to Cynthia on Facebook.

On December 26, 2015, after a nearly ten-year engagement, Razak and Cynthia were married. Following Islamic tradition, a ceremony was held in Accra at the mosque, followed by a reception at his family's house with Razak's and Cynthia's families. Razak's close friend Alidoo stood in for him during the ceremony. His half-siblings did not attend but also did not attempt to interrupt the celebration.

In the middle of the night, back in New York, Razak received a phone call from Alidoo saying the ceremony had gone well and congratulating him on becoming a married man. Razak thanked his friend for his support and for helping him to marry the person he loved. Cynthia—after the attempt on Razak's life, his journey through Central and North America, and his almost two years in detention—was overjoyed.

Weeks later, Cynthia sent him a bottle of his favorite cologne from Accra. He held the package, realizing how much it had cost her to send it. Opening the bottle, he was transported, for a brief moment, to the past, to his room back in Nima, to all the plans they had once made. In their own unpredictable way, these plans were slowly coming true.

The four-hour time difference between Ghana and New York and thousands of miles between them did little to interfere with the couple's relationship. Razak and Cynthia spoke as often as they could on the phone or on Facebook. Sometimes Cynthia complained about the economic conditions back in Ghana. Razak could hear the desperation in her voice, the weariness.

The price of milk keeps going up, she said. *I can't afford it anymore. The government is useless. No one is helping. It's like living in hell.*

Please don't say that.

When they finished a conversation, Razak would sit on the sofa, staring at his cell phone. He could not understand why nothing in Ghana ever got better, no matter how long he was away. The country and the people did not seem ready to change. Each phone call or message only reminded him of what his family back home continued to face, no matter how hard he worked or how much money he made. It was then, staring down at the phone, that the past, the entire nation of Ghana, felt like a boulder or some other formless object hanging over his head.

You didn't have to be invisible in New York. Although he was still an outsider in the city, he began to notice others like him on the buses, on the subway, in restaurants, stores, moving on the street. The city was a city of immigrants, after all, first from Denmark, then England and other parts of Europe, Asia, Africa, Haiti, Jamaica, the Dominican Republic, Russia, Poland, the Middle East, all with different kinds of food and clothes and music, their posters, graffiti, shop signs in a glorious explosion of languages and culture. No one owned the city because the entire metropolis was forced to constantly reinvent itself. Fifteen months after he been released from Eloy, he was beginning to see people like him every day—asylum seekers, migrants, refugees, men and women and children without countries—all trying to build something new out of the remains of their previous lives, all struggling to find their place.

After a few months of living in New York, Razak also saw how the West seemed to benefit from the uncertainty that surrounded these same migrants. Beyond living under a constant threat of deportation, the undocumented took difficult, backbreaking jobs that others refused to fill—in agriculture, hospitality, and construction. Even though they added to the local economies by buying goods, paying taxes, and often starting their own businesses, the undocumented did so without legal protection.

Contrary to the perception that they were criminals who took advantage of welfare benefits, the vast majority of undocumented workers were law-abiding individuals, contributing to federal programs like Social Security and Medicare and paying state taxes, without ever being able to draw from these programs themselves. Business owners, right-wing politicians, and lobbyists were aware of how much the U.S. depended on this undocumented labor force, all while ramping up fallacious rhetoric and calling for tougher enforcement against them. But the truth was that without undocumented workers, the entire system would come crashing down.

In Arizona and Alabama, two states that had passed strict

laws at curbing undocumented immigration, the total number of jobs and the total gross domestic product both decreased dramatically, due to the loss of possible consumers and the fact that U.S. citizens and migrant workers often have different education and skill levels. There simply weren't enough workers, taxpayers, or business owners to keep the economic system going.

It was a foul arrangement, a shadow economy built from the blood and desperation of millions of people each year. To take part in it meant to give something up, to accept that you were no longer a person, that you were a no one, an object. It was connected to an even more powerful structure that benefited the wealthiest while preying on the least empowered, and there appeared to be very little momentum to change it. It was the same system Razak had seen employed over and over again back home. It was terrifying to see the shape it had taken in the U.S. and how people avoided confronting the reality of it at all costs. The election of Donald Trump only seemed to reinforce this purposeful obfuscation.

One day Razak got a message on his cell telling him that he needed to report to his deportation officer on the afternoon of November 15, 2016. It was during a time he had been scheduled to work at the hotel. After worrying about it for several hours, Razak called his manager and told him he had to go to Federal Plaza to report, fearful he would lose his job for having to miss work. It was the first time he had been forced to discuss his immigration status.

"Do you mind me asking what's your immigration status?" the manager asked.

"I came here as an asylum seeker but I lost my plea."

"Are you on deportation?"

"I am."

"I'm sorry to hear that. There's some other guys in the kitchen who're also going through the same thing. I know everything is going to be okay for you. Go to your reporting and we'll cover your shift."

Razak reported to his deportation officer at 26 Federal Plaza in downtown Manhattan the next day. The officer that had been previously assigned to his case was no longer on site. Instead another ICE officer, who was particularly aggressive, began yelling at him.

"You need to comply with your embassy. You need to get your passport so you can be returned to your country. You need to go back home."

"I would like to try to reopen my case."

"Don't waste your time or your money. You're going to get sent back either way."

At the end of the conversation, the officer told Razak he would not need to report again until February 15, 2017.

One week later, the same Immigration and Customs Enforcement officer called his uncle's cell phone. His uncle answered cautiously.

"Hello, I'm trying to get a hold of Razak," the officer said.

"He's working. You can try him there."

"We need him to come in. His documents are ready."

Razak's uncle paused, becoming immediately aware of the gravity of what the officer had just said. He told the officer he would relay the message and then quickly hung up.

When Razak returned from work that evening, his uncle told him the deportation officer had called again.

I don't understand. I just reported. Why are they asking me to come in again?

His uncle looked at him and frowned. *He said your documents are ready.*

Razak was speechless. It did not seem possible. It did not seem fair. It had taken years and yet it all had come too soon. His uncle learned forward.

What are you going to do?

Razak felt the enormity of the moment, the sense he had been caught up, trampled by something historical, inhuman.

I don't know.

What's your plan?

I don't know.

Are you going to go back to Mexico?

I can't go back. It's been two and half years. When I was there, they gave me twenty days to leave the country. They won't let me go back.

You have to do something.

That night, even though he was exhausted from work, he could not sleep. He was worried ICE officers might show up at his uncle's apartment at any moment and physically remove him from the country.

Instead he decided to go to Munil's sister's apartment in the Bronx. He thanked his uncle and took the train across town. When he arrived he explained to Munil what happened. Munil only stared at him and asked, *Why can't you go to Canada?*

I don't have a visa.

A lot of people from Somalia go to Minneapolis, then head up to Canada. All you have to do is get to Minneapolis. After that you can ask someone and find your way.

Panic soon began to set in. On Facebook, Razak tried to call his friend Jabba, one of the men he had traveled through Central America with, to learn more about crossing into Canada, but he did not get a response. He was afraid to leave the apartment, afraid to go to work.

Soon his supervisor from the hotel began to call, asking where he was. Terrified to even answer the phone, he felt hunted. He called his uncle to let him know he was okay, but did not tell him where he was staying or where he was going to go.

Looking at his bank account, he realized he had only a few hundred dollars, which would not be enough to cross the border into Canada and start over. So Munil got him a job at a Korean beauty and cosmetics supply store. The owners preferred to hire migrants without papers. Beginning November 17, Razak worked in a basement warehouse, stocking and restocking items, trying to put in as many hours as possible, to save up money for another journey, this time even further north.

By then winter had set in and the city had become inhospitably cold. It was a place he no longer recognized, no longer a city of dreams. One day he collected his wages from the cosmetics store and withdrew all of his money from his bank account.

On December 22, 2016, Razak went to the Greyhound bus station downtown and bought a ticket. He had not done any research, had not looked into how to get from Minneapolis to Canada, preferring instead to believe his friend Munil who had suggested that once he arrived in Minneapolis, he would some-how be able to find his way.

Ask the Somalis, ask the Africans, they will help you.

Once aboard the bus, he recognized everything he had built over the last year and a half was gone, the city itself no longer existing for him.

Whenever the bus stopped, Razak would go to the restroom and wash his hands and face to make his ablutions for prayer. He then returned to his seat, folded his arms, and began to pray.

You are the truth and Your promise is true. And the meeting with You is true.

And Your words are true.
And paradise is true. And hell is true.
And the prophets are true. And Mohammed is true.
And the hour is true.

On December 23, 2016, after two days of traveling on the bus, he arrived at the Minneapolis Greyhound station. Unsure what to do, Razak wandered around for a while, looking for someone to ask for help, but among the bleary faces, he found no one. Tired from his travels, he decided to sit down and wait. He glanced around— the only other black person was an African American security guard, who did not seem willing to assist.

Hours later, a young man approached.

"Nada ka?"

Where are you going?

The words familiar, the sound, a fragment of Ghana, hanging momentarily in the air. He marveled at the small joy of being able to talk in his native tongue after several days of not speaking to anyone. Soon they had exchanged names, parts of their stories, a few of their misfortunes, and quickly came up with a plan. Together they gathered up their belongings and then headed out into the evening's cold.

Outside the black taxicab was waiting.

Part Four

Home

32

Night became a coffin, a container, a see-through box. From within the rectangular confines of the cab, both men faced the long drive, speaking and then not speaking, until the vehicle finally pulled to the side of Highway 29 several hours later. There was the startling openness of the upper Midwest, the falling snow, the surrounding fields—all of it uncomfortably white. For two and a half hours they walked, then their hope quickly turning to panic. There was the rough, ice-covered fields, the searchlight, both men having to lie in the snow as the determined beam swung over their bodies, and then, finally, they climbed over the fence into Canada. Once they passed the border into yet another country, they came to find their hands and their fingers were no longer working. Their cognition, their brains, and other major organs all slowed to a halt as hypothermia set in.

On the side of the highway, Seidu tried to retrieve his cell phone from his backpack. He had waited to use his phone until he had crossed into Canada, afraid that somehow he might be tracked by his phone signal, but—fingers having gone numb—he found he could not get his digits to work the zipper. Razak's cell phone was in his pocket, but because his hands were also frozen, he could not turn it on. Having lost any sort of physical coordination after more than four hours in the subzero weather, Razak tore his jacket off with his teeth, removing a sleeveless coat he had been wearing under his topmost layer, then managed to dress himself again. He used the sleeveless coat as something to wrap his fingers in, then turned to Seidu, who had his own hands folded under his jacket. They had planned on phoning someone for help, to find shelter, but there was no one. It was now five thirty in the morning and the sun was a far-off wound.

All they could do was carry forward, marking their way beside each other through the unapologetic darkness.

A sign up ahead stated the name of the highway, which Razak stopped to read.

We're in Canada, he announced.

Blinded by the snow, Seidu trusted that it had to be true.

Continuing beside one another, the two men made their way forward through the cold. Each of them walked, each of them struggled to breathe, feeling their bodies beginning to give way. Shape of breath. Wordless fog. What cannot be said or named.

The fear, the past, history drifting away.

Bodies failing them now. Each footprint a struggle, another small victory. One foot in front of the other.

Blood gone cold in their skin. Hair on the surface rising, trying to heat itself. Muscle fibers shortening. Ninety-five degrees Fahrenheit.

Line of footprints going on, going nowhere.

Ice forming in the corner of their eyes, blurring their sight. A dazzling, futile brilliance. Cold, silent, like the end of time.

One man's, then the other man's shadow, one struggling, the other continuing to fight, both moving on.

As hypothermia set in, their body temperatures dropped, hearts and brains slowing, blood becoming absent from hands and feet and toes. Thoughts going quiet. The urge to give in, to fall to your knees, to sleep.

No longer shivering, the cold having struck bone.

Muscle and tendon beginning to freeze.

No one was leading, both of them stumbling, the world at a standstill.

Finally there was a sign announcing the town of Emerson in both English and French. The men walked past it, seeing several trains stopped along the side of the road. By then they could no longer feel their extremities, boots, shoes, feet, hands—all deadened by the cold. At some point they were simply unable to keep walking.

On the side of the road they huddled together and waited, giving themselves over to fate. Every twenty minutes, every half hour, an eighteen-wheeler bolted by. The men waved their arms and shouted but none of the vehicles slowed down or pulled over. Ten hours had passed since they had left the taxicab. It was as if—feet numb, legs frozen, bodies given over to exhaustion—they were much farther from their destination than they had ever been. Razak felt his heart beating too hard. He could feel it pounding in his throat, hear it in his ears. He tried to slow his breathing, but his pulse continued to thrum violently.

Eventually, standing there in the snow, unable to take another step forward, he turned to Seidu and murmured, *We made it. We at least tried to make it. But if something happens here, we did our best. If we die here, it's the will of God.*

Seidu nodded and then began crying, the tears mixing with the ice stuck to his face. Another vehicle hurried by.

Razak looked at the road and said, *I don't blame them. I don't blame them. They're not stopping because they don't know who we are. Everything that happened here is between us and God.*

Quiet then.

Only silence.

Both men, staggered by the cold, continued to wait. Soon Razak, too, began to cry, quietly speaking to God.

If I have done something wrong, please forgive me. Please help us get to where we are going safely. Please.

On the side of the road, both men could no longer stand and fell to their knees, like supplicants, kneeling before the infinite, the highway becoming a church, a temple, a mosque.

33

Before completely giving themselves over to the ice and cold, both men looked out at the highway and the surrounding desolate fields, praying to God for an end to their suffering. Neither man had any idea what time it was, only that it continued to be dark. Sometime in the dwindling afternoon, another eighteen-wheeler approached. The sound of its brakes whining and its tires slowing echoed across the empty road.

Both men raised their arms as the truck paused before them and weakly shouted for help. The truck's headlights momentarily fell upon their faces and then blinked once before hurtling past. Neither man thought they had the strength to stand but somehow managed to help each other to their feet. Their clothes were weighed down with so much ice and snow that Razak, unable to use his hands, could not keep an extra pair of pants he was wearing up around his waist.

He asked Seidu for help, but Seidu, too, could not bend his fingers.

I'm sorry. I can't. I can't move my hands.

Even this, after so many hours in the cold, this small act of dignity, of keeping himself clothed, seemed like it too had been taken from him.

When they turned and faced north, both men were amazed to

see the lights of the black truck parked some fifty yards away. It was idling along the side of the road.

It stopped . . . Razak murmured, trying to hurry, dragging his feet along. *It stopped.* The world fell away as they tried to run, their limbs unwilling, unable to respond.

Finally they could hear the truck's engine humming noisily as they approached, the vehicle's taillights illuminating the distance between it and the two men.

Seidu, through frozen eyes, could barely see the shape of the vehicle on the side of the road. Razak stumbled and decided to kick the outer layer of his pants off in order to move more quickly. It would be hours later before he realized that his remaining money and the Koran he had carried with him for ten years had been left behind in the pocket of his second pair of pants, one of the many things he had lost along the way.

By then the driver had come out of the truck and was helping them up into the passenger side of the eighteen-wheeler's cab. He was short and skinny with gray hair, somewhere in his fifties, a white man. He was wearing a sleeveless jacket and looked confused to see the two men standing before him out in the cold, in the middle of nowhere.

"Where did you come from?" the man asked. He had an accent of some kind, from Europe or Russia, and Razak was worried about trying to communicate with him in English.

Razak carefully asked, "Where are we?"

"You're in Canada. You're safe."

Razak nodded. The man looked at them. "Where did you come from?"

"The States."

The driver gawked, taking in the desperate sight of them, and said, "I've never seen anything like this before in all my life. You're frozen to death. Come in, come in."

•

The unknown driver—who out of fear of losing his job never gave them his name—helped the strangers climb into the passenger side of the cab, Razak up front, Seidu in the back. He gave each man water from a plastic bottle and took paper towels to wipe the ice from Seidu's eyes, who, by now, was no longer able to speak. The younger man was sitting on a small bed in the back of the cab, shaking and crying from the frostbite on his hands and face. Unable to drink the water, he spat it out. The unknown driver continued to wipe the ice from Seidu's face with a paper towel and water.

"Where are you guys going?" the driver asked.

"We're just trying to get to Canada."

"You made it. You're here."

The man took his cell phone and dialed 9-1-1 and put it on speaker.

The emergency switchboard operator asked, "What's your emergency?"

The unknown driver leaned forward and spoke. "I need some help. Two people are almost frozen to death over on Highway 75, near Letellier. I'm in a truck."

"Okay. Someone will be there in ten minutes."

By then it was past 4:00 p.m. on the afternoon of December 24. The unknown driver drove slowly, watching his rearview mirrors for the approach of the emergency vehicles. Along the other side of the highway median, the three men saw the approach of colored lights. The driver flashed the truck's lights in response. An ambulance followed by a police car turned around, blocking the traffic on the other side of the highway.

The emergency workers did not ask any questions; only opened the cab door and put Seidu—who was by then in critical condition—on a stretcher and brought him into the back of the ambulance. Razak carefully followed.

Inside the emergency vehicle, a paramedic put blankets and warming gel-packs along Seidu's extremities as the driver piloted the vehicle toward the emergency room. Razak watched with deep concern as a medic asked Seidu his name and saw he was unable to answer.

After a few moments, Razak told them it was Seidu Mohammed.

The medic asked Seidu his age and the young man replied weakly, "Twenty-four."

The paramedic turned to Razak and asked, "Is he your brother?"

Razak frowned, and after a moment, was able to murmur, "No, he's my friend. We just met."

On the way to the hospital, they passed a few seemingly unincorporated houses and farms. Tiny homes, open lots, narrow streets with green signs. Glancing out the window of the ambulance, Razak saw faint, glimmering lights along the buildings in odd colors—red, blue, white, green. Parts of the same buildings seemed aglow, and at first he did not understand. Then he remembered it was the day before Christmas. Outside the window, the world appeared both terrifying and wondrous.

The hospital was only fifteen minutes away, a facility suited to the small rural town of Morris. The men were brought into the emergency room around 4:30 p.m. Their primary diagnosis was hypothermia, along with frostbite. The ER staff performed several basic, necessary life-saving measures—they warmed the men's limbs with blankets, then attempted to slow the necrotizing effect of the frostbite through rehydration. One of the nurses examined Seidu's hands—saw the ice crystallized between the fingers—and remarked that she had never seen anything like it before. Staff members struggled to remove the men's clothes and shoes, which had frozen directly to their bodies and skin.

The pain Seidu felt was unlike anything he had ever faced before, even worse than the stomach pains that had plagued him when he was thirteen. After ingesting several rounds of pain medication, the ER doctors added morphine to his IV drip, at which point he finally fell asleep.

Seidu awoke thirty minutes later, rocked by growing intense pain in his hands and feet, a burning, sharp sensation he could not make sense of. He cried out for help. A nurse came into the room and attached a second morphine drip. He was unable to be officially admitted into the hospital until hours later, around 7:00 p.m., because he had not been able to speak. Over the course of the next twelve hours, nurses resupplied the morphine drip or injected it directly into Seidu's body. He could not see properly, could not feel his limbs, and the sensation he had was one of falling. At that moment, he was certain he was going to die.

Around two in the morning, Seidu awoke and found himself alone in a hospital room and immediately looked at his hands, which had yet to be bandaged. *What is this?* His fingers were unrecognizable, blackened, gigantic, and swollen. Some of the digits he could move, others he could not, but there was no feeling in any part of them. Alone, he began to cry. He climbed from the hospital bed and saw that some parts of his face and one part of his ear had also gone black. Some of his toes were swollen and it also hurt to walk, to stand.

Doctors later drained the fluid from his hands, and then bandaged his extremities. Nurses changed the bandages every few hours after that.

Pain continued to haunt his fingers and toes. He couldn't sleep. Hours passed. Eventually Seidu blacked out from exhaustion.

In the emergency room, Razak confronted the ongoing pain and discomfort in much the same way he had faced his two years in U.S. detention, with an intense stoicism and a rising anger. Nurses and doctors had to chip away the ice that had formed between his fingers. The pain appeared in ever increasing waves. Soon he was given a number of medications to help fight off the discomfort, including Advil and morphine. From the corner of the ER, he watched as medical staff attended to Seidu, who was having difficulty communicating.

Some time later Razak lay in a hospital bed. He had been given an IV drip to help him rehydrate, which also allowed nurses to inject medication intravenously. Both his hands had been drained of fluid and were bandaged and covered with white mesh gloves. He held up his wounded appendages and stared, shocked that a part of his own body could cause him so much agony.

Within a day, the hospital moved the men into a shared room. Both of their medical prognoses looked dire. Under heavy medication, they lay beside each other, fighting to recuperate.

When Seidu felt overwhelmed with pain, he would ask Razak to press the call button to ask for more medication, as the younger man was still unable to use his hands to do anything. Moments later, a nurse arrived to tend to his friend. Razak wondered how being injured would affect their attempts to apply for asylum. The hospital's ventilation, the air itself, hummed like some unanswerable question.

34

Hands carry the history of humankind. There are four fingers, one thumb, twenty-seven bones, and thousands of years of triumphs and failures represented by eight carpal and five metacarpal bones. The palm, used for conveying secrets, for whispering, can become a cup, a bowl, a map, a device for holding on to that which is small, indefinite, something that can be used to cover the ears, the eyes, to shut out the world entirely.

The opisthenar, the back of the hand. A blank page. A wall. A weapon.

The heel. The source of power, an anvil, a rock that quietly supports all others.

Thumb, parallel to the arm, the appendage of advantage, the one thing that makes someone human. Index finger, pointer finger, ring finger, pinky, each with their own customs, each with their own histories, an entire species bound up in the making, the fighting, the use of its hands, borne in blood, bone, and gristle. The fingers, which contain some of the densest collection of nerve endings in the body; what we know of the world to be true, what we can feel, all coming through the fingertips themselves.

The birthplace of all unspoken language.

Your mother's, your father's, your friend's, your lover's hands as recognizable as the face. All the power, the glory, paintings, poems made plain by the fingers, the thumbs, civilization built upon civilization, who we are because of these things we did, these elegant machines. The story of every person the world over, hands reaching out of the darkness for something, anything to grasp on to.

Neither man's hands were healing from the cold. Their fingers had become something else, something foreign.

Even two days later, Seidu woke in the middle of the night overcome with an unresolvable pain coursing throughout his hands and body. It was December 27, 2016. A nurse came in and asked what was wrong. "I need help. Please. I need help with this pain." She injected him with a dose of fentanyl and he began to cry, certain the fierce discomfort in his body would never go away. Nothing seemed to slow the incessant agony and ache.

The next morning, several doctors inspected his bandaged hands and saw that the situation had not improved: the digits themselves were corrupt, blackened. There was the possibility of gangrene setting in, the death of tissue caused by the loss of blood flow.

"It's one of the most severe cases of frostbite I've ever seen," one of the doctors commented.

Seidu had never heard the word before. He asked, "What is frostbite?"

Another doctor explained what happened to the extremities during prolonged exposure to subzero weather, then added, "There is a possibility you may lose all your fingers." There was also the danger that if the wounds became infected, Seidu would become septic, that he might lose his life if the staff did not intervene further. Doctors decided to schedule a consultation for him with plastic surgeons at the Health Sciences Centre in Winnipeg for a possible amputation.

After the doctors left, Seidu asked the attending nurse, "Am I really going to lose my fingers?"

She said she was not sure and that she didn't want him to worry about it at the moment. That evening, and during several nights that followed, he was unable to sleep, tortured by pain and the possibility of loss.

During those first three days the medical staff helped both men eat, change their clothes, use the bathroom, and bathe, as their hands continued to be useless.

A hospital social worker asked Seidu, "Do you have a relationship with anybody here in Manitoba so that we can contact them?"

"I have a friend from Ghana who lives in Winnipeg. But I haven't been able to get a hold of him."

The social worker contacted Seidu's acquaintance, another young man who in turn reached out to other members of the Ghanaian community. Seidu and Razak later spoke on the telephone with several people from the Ghana Union of Manitoba, who offered them both encouragement and hope. It seemed strange to hear the familiar dialect, the inflection of kindness, so far from home.

After four days at the Morris hospital, Seidu was sent one hour north to HSC in Winnipeg, the largest medical facility in Manitoba, to consult with a plastic surgery specialist on the abrasions caused by frostbite on his ears and his hands. Seidu watched as the medical vehicle approached the midsize city of Winnipeg, its surrounding fields, forests, suburbs, and finally midcentury buildings, a western Canadian town, comforting in its modest simplicity and pleasing lack of opulence. He was then sent back to Morris to await the results of the consultation. It was December 28, 2016.

His bandages were frequently changed, his blisters were drained, but Seidu continued to have no sensation in his hands. He developed clear signs of gangrene and was sent back to Winnipeg, where he was admitted to the burn unit of HSC on December 30.

Once admitted, a nurse at HSC unwrapped the bandages that guarded Seidu's deeply wounded fingers. She seemed shocked by what she saw, the disfigured digits, the swollen, blackened flesh.

Seidu asked her directly, "Will I lose my fingers?"

"I can't answer that. You'll have to ask the doctor when he comes in."

Moments later, a burn specialist, a short, balding doctor, seemed equally upset as he examined Seidu's hands.

Once again, Seidu put forward the otherwise imponderable question. "Am I going to lose my fingers? I want to know."

The doctor drew in a sharp breath and at first did not answer. Then he said, "We can't be sure yet. We want to give you some more time to heal." But Seidu felt the staff did not want to upset him by telling him the truth. At the same time he also felt hopeful, believing there was still some chance to keep his fingers, to salvage a part of what had been taken from him.

Soon representatives from the Ghana Union of Manitoba and other refugee organizations appeared at HSC to offer Seidu their support. Maggie Yeboah, president of the Ghana Union, prepared traditional food and helped him eat, dress, and communicate with his family and friends back home.

Not long after, news of Seidu's arrival at the hospital spread to journalists throughout Winnipeg, beginning with Carol Sanders at the *Winnipeg Free Press*. Sanders interviewed Seidu on January 4, 2017. The young man was eager to share the story of how he and Razak had crossed the border, fearing for their freedom and their lives. Photographs captured the dramatic images of Seidu at HSC—his hands covered in bandaged gloves, his face surprisingly full of joy—and soon these images proliferated throughout the Canadian media.

Bashir Khan, a thirty-eight-year-old immigration lawyer living in Winnipeg, read the news of Seidu's arrival at HSC on the front page of the *Winnipeg Free Press* on January 5. In a photograph accompanying the news story, he recognized several of his current clients who were in the process of applying for refugee status or who had recently obtained it. He then called Welcome Place, the government-run refugee facility, and a staffer there explained they were overwhelmed with recent asylum seekers and had no staff available that day to go to HSC to interview Seidu to begin the asylum process.

Khan, overcome with emotion from what he had read in the story, decided to go straight to the burn unit at HSC to offer his support.

With his closely shaven head and narrow glasses, Khan was also a Muslim and an immigrant to Canada. He had moved with his family from Pakistan to Toronto at the age of eleven. Khan had been raised as an Ahmadi, a group of Muslims who follow the tenets of Islam but do not believe Mohammed is the final prophet. By strength of personality or force of will, he had become deeply connected to his adoptive country. As a teen, he was part of the Royal Canadian Army Cadets, and later, after law school in Australia, he joined the Manitoba Historical Society in Winnipeg, where he offered lectures and reenactments for the benefit of newly arrived migrants interested in learning more about Canadian history and culture.

Typically, Khan only ever met with asylum seekers after they had been interviewed by a staff member from Welcome Place and started the refugee process through a series of applications and written claims. If their claims were justified, asylum seekers would then be offered free legal aid. Immigration lawyers like Khan were often assigned twenty-five or thirty immigration cases per year, and were paid a nominal fee by the province of Manitoba. Over the past several months, however, the number of cases had quickly increased.

When Khan arrived at the HSC facility, he found Seidu in a hospital bed, his hands bandaged, part of his face badly frostbitten from the cold. He was surrounded by well-wishers from the local Ghanaian and African communities. Khan introduced himself and took the young man's statement.

It was a moment, several brief seconds, where Seidu was once again surprised to find himself being treated like a human.

Separated from the remnants of his previous life and with nothing left to lose, Seidu decided to tell the truth of his sexual orientation and how it had led to him fleeing Brazil. It was the first time he admitted he was bisexual to a lawyer or public official of any kind—a tremendous turning point in the young man's life. The incident at the border, the possible loss of his hands, and the ongoing trauma he was still facing had finally forced him to accept a part of himself he had kept hidden for years.

35

Beyond the calls of support and condolence, Razak knew nothing was changing going into the second week of his stay at the Morris hospital. His hands still throbbed and ached, and although he had recovered feeling in his right thumb, being able to move one thumb was not enough; his other digits were not responding to treatment. Doctors at Morris tried everything they could to save Razak's hands, but the situation grew more desperate each day. Gangrene had set in. The thirty-four-year-old was sent to HSC in Winnipeg on January 3, 2017, for a consultation with a plastic surgeon. As he rode in the back of the ambulance, he recognized he was once more being taken to some unknown facility, some unknown place, completely beyond his control.

Upon his arrival, a specialist at the center examined Razak's fingers and said, "You have severe frostbite. I'm sorry to tell you this but there's a good chance you're going to lose all your fingers. There's a strong possibility we're going to have to amputate, but we'll have wait and see."

Razak did not want to believe it could happen, that the loss of his fingers was even a possibility. After the doctors left, he cried in the hospital bed, questioning everything that had happened to him. All the suffering he faced was because of his siblings, because of greed and corruption, because of a systemic failure of government power and justice. *How can I explain this to my family back home? How can I explain this to anyone? In just one night my life changed. Just one night.* Every job he had ever done—as a barber, an electronics repairman, a dishwasher, even his ability to pray—all involved the use of his hands.

He cried all day and remembered a phrase from back home, *A man never cries*, but found he was unable to stop.

When he returned to the Morris hospital, when the lights had gone out that night, something came into his mind: *Only God knows why this happened. I don't blame anyone. I don't blame myself. I don't blame the Americans. I don't blame the system. I blame Ghana. I blame the government there. Because of injustice, this is the consequence. If I had been protected in my country, I would still be in my own country.*

The possible loss of his fingers resolved Razak's urgent need for equal rights, for justice. But first he would need to confront the difficult truth of his situation. He phoned his Uncle Malik in New York, who passed the hospital's phone number on to Cynthia, back in Ghana. One afternoon she called and a nurse placed the phone between Razak's ear and his shoulder. He was ecstatic hearing her voice once again, his eyes brimming with tears.

My husband. What happened? Are you all right?

We made it. We made it to Canada.

I've been praying for you.

After a few moments of incandescent joy at hearing her voice, he explained what had happened on their journey and that there was now a good chance he was going to lose his fingers.

Look. We made it but unfortunately this is what happened. We're still waiting for the results but I need you to know I might lose my fingers.

Cynthia cried out. The receiver felt hollow against his ear. The sound of her crying became abstract, distant, an emptiness that filled the room.

Razak was transferred to HSC in Winnipeg on January 5, 2017. Days after Razak's arrival, officers from the Canada Border Services Agency conducted brief interviews with both Razak and Seidu, then took their photographs. Both men remarked how surprised they were to be treated with so much courtesy. The next day, the same officers returned with temporary identification cards, which would allow Razak and Seidu to apply for medical support, a work permit, income assistance, and housing. At first, Razak believed it was because he had been injured that he was being treated so well, but he later found, in his discussions with other migrants, that all asylum seekers were given the same opportunities. It was so unlike his experiences at the San Ysidro port of entry, where Customs and Border Patrol officers shouted "This is America!" and put him in handcuffs. Looking at the temporary identification card, Razak felt a sense of relief.

Maggie Yeboah and others members of the Ghana Union of Manitoba visited frequently, bringing home-cooked meals and messages of support from the migrant community in Winnipeg. Razak was pleased to be surrounded by so much kindness and laughter. Both men would refer to Yeboah as Auntie Maggie and come to think of her family.

During the second week of January, Razak met Bashir Khan, who offered to support him legally. Razak was relieved to find out Khan represented some of the other Ghanaians he had met in Winnipeg. "I'm sorry for what happened to you on your hegira," Khan said, referring to the prophet Mohammed's migration from Mecca to Medina.

"Thank you," Razak said, moved by the lawyer's words.

That day Khan helped Razak with his application for refugee status.

After being officially assigned to both of their cases, Khan assessed the strength of each asylum plea. He considered that because Seidu identified as bisexual and was a member of a persecuted, socially visible group, he could argue for asylum under the UN Refugee Convention. He also recognized that although he had represented similar cases in the past, on average, fewer than half of such asylum seekers were ever granted asylum.

Razak's case would be an even more difficult argument to make. Torture claims were often overruled unless the physical evidence was overwhelming in favor of the victim. The members of the Immigration and Refugee Board—political appointees and civil servants who ruled on such cases—were known to argue that such individuals could return to their nations of origin and take up residence in other parts of the country. The percentage of torture cases Khan had successfully argued was low. In his modest office on Broadway Avenue, Khan assembled the facts of the case, all too aware of the difficult legal process they were about to face. He had no illusions that their asylum claims would be accepted.

There were also the ongoing complexities of their medical concerns and possible surgeries, and the multiple statements they had given under the influence of powerful opiates, which all had to be considered.

The growing media attention surrounding the two men further complicated their cases. Khan frantically wrote to the CBSA—the Canada Border Services Agency—and requested an extension to submit their refugee paperwork so that they could recover from their injuries and face their prospective surgeries before completing their applications.

•

The unknown truck driver came to HSC to visit both men while they were recuperating. During their brief conversation, the man told Seidu and Razak that he was from Poland, that he was a Catholic, and that he was far from his family. He was driving to Mass on Christmas Eve when he saw the two men struggling on the side of the road and decided he had to pull over. He said something had told him he would have the opportunity to help someone that day. It was just a feeling, he said.

36

Confined for weeks within his hospital room, Seidu struggled to stay positive, to ignore the unending pulse of pain that filled his body. But the shadows in the corners became stronger and stronger, while the light through the windows was uneven and diffuse.

One afternoon, while Seidu spoke to well-wishers—other recent immigrants from Ghana and parts of Africa, including a few men he had met while in detention in California—the pain became so unbearable that a nurse offered him a powerful narcotic. She said it was the strongest pain reliever they had and warned it might cause him to hallucinate. After the medicine was injected into his IV drip, Seidu began to feel dizzy. Eventually the pain started to subside. Animals appeared in his hospital room. Shadow elephants. Monkeys. Lions. He was unable to see, his vision going blurry, and found he could no longer speak. The visitors tried to talk to him. He could hear their voices but he could no longer make out their faces.

My eyes are open but I can't see you, he murmured.

He felt as if he were falling down, then drifted off into unconsciousness.

Each morning, the medical staff at HSC—both the doctors and nurses—inspected his hands, changed the bandages, and gave him several injections of strong opiates and other pain relievers in-cluding gabapentin, hydromorphone, and Elavil. He could move two fingers on each hand, though he had not recovered any sensa-tion in his fingertips.

After two weeks, specialists in the burn and trauma wards at HSC once again inspected Seidu's hands and reviewed his file. The doctors sat before him with blank faces and then announced their bleak prognosis.

"You're going to lose your fingers. If we don't operate soon, it could eventually lead to death."

Seidu began to cry. "If I lose my fingers, how am I going to work? How can I take care of myself and my family?"

Since he had first considered crossing into Canada, he had been hoping to bring his mother over as well. Without his hands, without the ability to find gainful employment, he recognized the futility of such a dream.

One of the nurses tried to encourage him. "It'll be okay. You can still work. You can still do a lot of things."

"How?"

"There are a lot of resources here to help you. You shouldn't worry about that now."

But Seidu felt as if his life was over, as if he were being pun-ished. For the entire week following the conversation, he cried, unable to sleep.

Seidu was finally able to call his mother on Facebook. It had been weeks since they had spoken. His family back in Ghana helped set up the connection. None of his relatives except his brother Kamal had any idea what had happened to him, that he had crossed into Canada, that he was going to lose the use of his hands.

Mom, he began. *I'm in Canada.*

How did you get there?

He could hear the shock, the consternation in her reply. He took a deep breath and went on, *I walked. I'm in the hospital now.*

Why are you in the hospital?

There was a sudden note of panic in her voice, a tone he had not heard since he was a child. How could he tell her? As clearly as he could, he explained the series of events that led him to crossing the border into Canada.

I'm here now, he said. *I'm okay. I crossed with a friend.*

Then—for the first time—he told his mother the truth of who he was, who he had been his entire life.

I'm bisexual. I've been this way for as long as I can remember. I can't come back home. I can't come back to Ghana.

His mother did not sound shocked or disappointed. There seemed to be a tenuous indication of relief in her voice. *I understand,* she said. *I understand this is who you are.*

Then, taking another breath, Seidu added, *Okay. I have something else to tell you. I was caught in the snow on my journey here. I was out in the cold a long time. My hands were frozen and I'm going to lose my fingers.*

Over the flat tone of the internet connection, Seidu could hear his mother crying. The sound of her weeping made him do the same.

I'm asking for you to please pray for me, he said.

There was a pause and then she said, *Okay. I will. I will pray for you very hard. But you need to stop crying. Everything that happens, happens for a reason. You should put faith in God and pray, too. I will be praying for you every day and every night.*

Seidu's brother Kamal called from Ohio and simply asked, *How? How did this happen?*

We got frozen.

Both of you?
Both of us.

In the hospital, days later, Seidu happened to come across a magazine article about a Canadian athlete and activist named Rick Hansen. At the age of fifteen, Hansen had been in a pickup truck accident that severely injured his spinal cord. Afterward he became an outspoken critic for accessibility and equitability for people with disabilities. In 1985, inspired by fellow Canadian athlete Terry Fox, Hansen began his Man in Motion World Tour, traveling thirty-four countries and four continents in his wheelchair over a period of two years. Seidu had never heard of Hansen before and began to feel some degree of hope that, even in the midst of so much tragedy, he might find some purpose.

37

Out of time, Razak had no choice but to confront the truth. Although bandaged and covered in white mesh gloves for the moment, his hands would soon be lost, his fingers amputated. He called Cynthia one week later and told her the surgery was inevitable.

Cynthia cried again and asked, *How can you work?*

I don't know. I need to focus on how I'm going to recover for now.

I'm so sorry, she said. *I'm sorry not to be by your side when you need me the most.*

Razak later talked with his mother and asked her to please try to avoid the attention his case was drawing. He feared for her safety as media coverage increased. Papers and websites all over Ghana were covering the events, and some reports falsely claimed that Razak, along with Seidu, was also gay or bisexual.

One day that same week, Razak walked down to Seidu's room and took a seat across from his bed. He told Seidu about the doctor's prognosis.

I'm going to lose my fingers. All of them. All except part of my thumb.

Seidu did not answer at first, then remarked how distraught he was, too, how worried, how the doctors had given him a similar prognosis. Razak stared at the other man for a long time and said,

You know what? We need to give everything over to God. I don't know why this happened, but it happened. It happened. It was an accident and only God knows why this happened. We have to give everything over to Him.

Both men listened to the hum of the hospital's ventilation system, allowing for this silent agreement.

Before either amputation surgery could be scheduled, Seidu and Razak were subjected to several tests, including a painful biopsy: skin was removed from their thighs and tested for its viability for a graft after the amputations. After the biopsies, both men were laid up in their hospital beds for a week.

Hours prior to his surgery, Auntie Maggie and others from the Ghana Union came to pray. Razak felt grateful for their ongoing support while his loved ones were so far away. These individuals standing at his bedside, who only weeks before were complete strangers, had become everything, the only people he knew in Canada who cared about his immediate well-being.

On January 18, 2017, Razak had amputation surgery, which included the removal of eight fingers, his entire left thumb, and the top part of his right thumb. The surgery lasted three hours, during which skin from his thighs was grafted onto the open wounds of his hands.

Although he was unconscious, Razak recalled feeling an intense pain even through the anesthetic.

After the surgery, Razak came to in a recovery room and found a number of other refugees by his beside. Some of them were crying, taking in the results of the operation. Razak looked at them and said, *You need to stop crying. You have to be strong.*

Later, right in the middle of speaking to them, he felt the effects of the anesthetic and promptly fell back asleep.

•

On January 20, surgeons at HSC amputated all of Seidu's fingers and both of his thumbs, grafting the skin from his thighs and stapling it onto his hands.

By then Seidu had accepted his fate and faced the surgery with both patience and faith. *This is what it is. I can't change it. These people are trying to help me. I want to survive.*

The surgery was eight hours long. As Seidu awoke from the anesthetic in the recovery room, he saw that his fingers were gone and began to cry. Pain suffused what remained of his hands. A nurse came in and injected an opiate into his IV and he once again fell unconscious.

That evening, he was returned to his room in the trauma ward. Still suffering the effects of the anesthetic, he was forced to urinate and defecate using a bedpan for a week before he was allowed to leave the bed. During this time his hands, his legs, his frostbitten ear, all of it continued to hum with pain.

All at once, everything had become difficult. It was frustrating to try to eat. It was hard to pick anything up, to get dressed. The life both men had known before, for all practical purposes, was over. It was sudden, totally irrecoverable, and the weight of it seemed to inform every part of their daily lives. To scratch an itch, to pick something up, to touch their own faces.

A physical therapist gave them exercises to develop their mobility and flexibility by rotating and flexing their wrists. An occupational therapist started teaching them how to survive without the use of fingers. Both men learned how to attach Velcro bands to their wrists, using their palms and teeth to pull the device into place. Hidden within the bands were a number of implements and tools, including a spoon used to practice eating. One of the wristbands contained a pen, another a stylus, another a powerful magnet.

Within a few days each man had begun feeding himself.

From there Seidu started dressing himself, using the bathroom, going for a walk. Weeks after the amputations, he told medical staff that he wanted some independence, to see how far he could go on his own.

On his walks—which were encouraged by the surgeons to help his thighs heal—he moved steadily down the hallway, and once, when one of his friends came to visit, he even ventured outside. It was the first time he'd been out on his own since arriving in Canada.

The snow made even the bleakest parts of the city sparkle. People he saw, strangers on the street, seemed friendly. It was late January and there was a sense of order, of safety, of kindness in the way he was treated. But there was also the grim recognition of what the cold had taken from him, and what—in such a short time—he had lost. All of his thoughts, all of his ongoing fears, became visible, became fog, took to the air with each and every breath.

38

The immigration debate in the United States seemed to reach a stultifying conclusion. In the first few weeks of his term in January 2017, President Donald Trump drastically cut the number of allowable refugees from 100,000 to 50,000, the lowest it had been in decades, at a particularly fraught moment when the rest of the Western world was struggling to accommodate the ongoing tide of individuals seeking a better life abroad.

The administration also issued an executive order to expand ICE's list of priorities for deportation, going so far as to include any noncitizen who was suspected of committing a criminal act. ICE agents began a series of public and highly dramatic arrests and deportations, going into churches and hospitals and other places previous administrations had deemed as non-enforceable sanctuaries. The message being sent was obvious, as blunt as any of the president's numerous rancorous tweets.

Within weeks, the number of migrants fleeing the United States and crossing into Canada dramatically increased and would continue to do so for the foreseeable future, rising from 300 people in January 2017 to 5,712 by August of the same year.

Approximately ten days after their surgeries, Seidu and Razak were both discharged from the hospital and transferred to Lennox

Bell, a rehabilitation facility, across the grounds from HSC. Bashir Khan met with them and offered a proposal for submitting their refugee protection applications.

As Khan was able to interview them only one at a time, he asked if they would be comfortable settling the issue by flipping a coin to see who whose claim would be prepared first. Perhaps it seemed strange, after everything that had happened, that their lives would once again be decided by such an oblique, random action, but Khan insisted on being fair. Both men agreed.

The coin went up, hung in the air for a moment, then came back down, landing in Khan's hand. Seidu would be interviewed first, then Razak.

Over the course of eight hours for each man, Khan interviewed Seidu and Razak on February 11 and 12, 2017, to complete their Basis of Claim forms. The hours Khan spent went above and beyond the amount of time he was legally required to devote to each plea, but because he felt their cases were so clearly unprecedented, he was motivated by a genuine sense of wanting to help. On February 16, Khan submitted Seidu's and Razak's applications for refugee protection in Canada.

By the middle of February 2017, news coverage from local media outlets had attracted national and international interest from the Canadian Broadcasting Corporation, CNN, *The New York Times*, and *Vice*, which offered Seidu and Razak the opportunity to share their experiences and the devastating results of their journey. As the U.S. continued to struggle with the results of the presidential election and the Trump administration's unconventional policies, news of Seidu and Razak's grim odyssey seemed to capture the dire mood of the country.

In interview after interview, both men searched for answers for what had happened, placing much of the blame on Ghana instead of condemning the United States. In a conversation with CBC radio, conducted while he was still in the hospital, Razak recounted the corruption in Ghana and his struggle for justice that led to his years in the U.S. detention facility in Arizona. In a separate interview, Seidu also criticized Ghana's unethical laws regarding the treatment of LGBT members back home.

Almost all the ongoing media coverage was picked up overseas, played and replayed over social media and the internet as far away as Japan, and was then featured back home in Ghanaian newspapers and on several news sites throughout the month.

Khan recognized a unique opportunity and formulated a plan for Seidu's and Razak's upcoming refugee hearings: because they had been so vocal in criticizing the Ghanaian government and had done so with such openness and with such a high degree of publicity, it was reasonable to argue *sur place* on their behalf. *Sur place* refers to activities that a refugee claimant engaged in that might place their life in danger after leaving their homeland. Because their faces and story were now so well known, there was nowhere in Ghana where either man could be safe. Khan could now use these various media appearances as evidence for a *sur place* claim for both men.

After completing all the documents and mailing them to the board, Khan was still not sure that either Seidu or Razak had a strong enough case to win their claim. Seidu's case was eerily similar to other pleas based on sexual identity that Khan had argued, many of which had been rejected by the board. Razak's attempted murder and corruption claims seemed just as difficult, if not more so. He put the likelihood of each men receiving asylum at somewhere between 5 and 8 percent.

By the end of February, both Seidu and Razak felt as if they were retraining their brains, finding a new way to live without fingers.

One day Seidu could button his shirt, another day he figured out how to throw a ball. Both men volunteered at the Canadian Muslim Women's Institute. There Razak practiced picking up and sorting clothes. In the midst of those simple, repetitive movements he discovered something resembling hope.

Whenever either was interviewed, they continued to shed light on the corruption, cronyism, and lack of legal rights for the LGBT community back home. Within two months of their arrival in Canada, they had become outspoken critics of the Ghanaian government and the face of the ongoing immigration crisis in Canada and the West.

At the beginning of March 2017, Seidu and Razak left Lennox Bell and moved into Hospitality House Refugee Ministry, a nonprofit institution responsible for sponsoring refugees. The CBC covered the event on television. Homecare nurses assisted each man with bathing and preparing meals. Karin Gordon, the head of the organization, was instrumental in helping them acclimatize to their new living situation. Thousands of dollars of renovations were made to the facility to accommodate both men—doorknobs to levers, toilets to bidets—which were paid for by local churches and private donations.

At the same time, Khan came to the house to help them prepare for their upcoming appearances before the Immigration and Refugee Board of Canada. Similar to the United States, the application process for asylum was overseen by a single person, in this case the Immigration and Refugee Board of Canada Member. The Board Member could be a judge, a lawyer, a political appointee, or a civil servant. The power the Board Member wielded, regardless of their legal or professional background, was considerable.

With Khan's guidance, Seidu was able to reach out to his community back in Accra for letters of support. His sister Ayisha described how the team manager came to their house and told Seidu's family he had found Seidu with another man and how Seidu's father was shocked and disappointed and threatened to disown him. In another letter, Jamal, Seidu's boyfriend, explained in detail the specifics of their relationship, again repeating the claim that Seidu's father had disowned him, and affirming the threats that appeared on social media. Seidu even managed to get a letter from Mohammed Aminu Lenient Dauda, the president of the Nima Lenient International Football Club, his former team, who swore in writing that Seidu's claims were true.

Days before the hearing, on March 15, 2017, activist and athlete Rick Hansen, whom Seidu had read about before his surgeries, came to visit Seidu in Winnipeg. The two men embraced, and Hansen later remarked, "His attitude is powerful and strong, positive, seeing not disability but ability."

On March 23, during a four-hour hearing, Seidu presented his claim to the Immigration and Refugee Board of Canada alongside Khan, explaining his story and answering questions from the Immigration and Refugee Board Member. The hearing was somewhat surreal as the Member oversaw the proceedings through a teleconference monitor from Calgary. The Member began by saying she was sorry for what had happened to Seidu. He thanked her, then went through the events that led him to apply for asylum in Canada. The Board Member repeatedly questioned Seidu's nationality, claiming he sounded more Nigerian than Ghanaian even though he had already sent in his birth certificate. During a break in the proceedings, Khan tried to reassure Seidu that the hearing was going all right, but the young man felt uncertain. After the break, the Board Member requested Seidu produce photo documentation—a government ID or some other kind of supporting evidence—to prove he'd been born in Ghana.

At the end of the proceedings, the Member refrained from

issuing an immediate decision. Seidu felt confident he had answered every question truthfully and that he and Khan presented as much evidence as possible. Bashir told him not to read too deeply into the Board Member's interest in further deliberation, as about half of the cases he handled ended without any formal decision after the initial hearing.

Seidu called home in the days following the hearing and asked his mother to please send any documentation she could find. The only identification she still had in her possession was his National Health Insurance card. Seidu paid $100 Canadian to have the card sent express mail to Winnipeg. Within two weeks the ID arrived. In the photo on the identification card, a much younger man in a blue soccer uniform stares proudly at the camera, unaware of the tumult ahead of him, already a lost fragment of some previous life.

Several weeks later, on May 12, 2017, Bashir received a copy of the Immigration and Refugee Board's decision in the mail and immediately telephoned Seidu, asking him to come to his office. He was unwilling to say anything more, wanting to share the news in person. Seidu got a ride from a friend to Bashir's office, unsure of what the results were. There, on a single sheet of paper, in the starkness of black and white letters, he read:

> *The Refugee Protection Division determines that the claimant* **is a Convention refugee.** *Therefore, the* **Refugee Protection Division accepts the claim.**

Seidu gave Bashir a powerful hug. Already news of the decision was appearing on local websites, adding to the odd sensation that somehow he was in a dream, that other people had learned his fate before he did. The entire asylum process had taken less than four months, a fraction of the time he had spent in United States detention without any legal counsel.

For almost all of his life he had kept his sexual identity a secret. In the United States he had been placed in detention for close to nine months. During his asylum hearing in California, he had not been ready to share the truth of who he was. Now, hours after news of the Immigration Board's decision was released, emails and phone calls poured in with congratulations and invitations for interviews from major media outlets like CNN and Al Jazeera. Having been silent for so many years, Seidu finally began to tell his story.

39

At the Muslim Women's Institute, the other volunteers would challenge Razak to see what he could do—move boxes or pick up coins using a Velcro strap attached to the remainder of his hand. For him, holding a coin in his palm was now nothing short of a miracle.

On March 27, 2017, four days after Seidu's hearing, Razak planned to appear before the Immigration and Refugee Board alongside Bashir Khan to explain the details of his case. But the hearing was unexpectedly postponed because of administrative delays, suggesting that the Board Member overseeing the claim was unavailable or that the Board needed additional time to complete a background check.

As a response to the increased number of border crossings and refugee claims, such delays in court proceedings were becoming more and more common. Razak accepted the news with humility and patience and used the extra time to compile as much evidence from Ghana as possible.

Razak collected signed testimonies from his uncle, mother, and Cynthia, all of whom had directly witnessed the intensifying struggle between Razak and his half-siblings—as well as Alidoo, who stood up for Razak at his wedding. Alidoo was able to collect a number of documents in Accra, including sworn testimonies from the imams from the Muslim community in Nima, who all supported Razak's claims. In the States, communicating with such authorities back in Ghana had been impossible, but here, within weeks, he was able to assemble a substantial case. Razak passed every piece of evidence on to Bashir and the Immigration and Refugee Board.

During their discussions, Bashir cautioned that even with strong evidence, his case did not neatly fit into one of the five categories laid out by the UN Conventions. Razak looked at Bashir calmly and said, "I know I can prove myself."

The refugee hearing was rescheduled for June 13, 2017, almost six months from the day he and Seidu had arrived in the country. During this time he and Seidu were staying at Hospitality House Refugee Ministry's residence and continued to volunteer at the Canadian Muslim Women's Institute, while still learning to survive without their fingers.

As media outlets back in Ghana continued to falsely claim that he was bisexual or gay, Razak now had to contend with social media accusations and physical threats about his sexual identity, in addition to the ongoing danger posed by his half-siblings and the Ghanaian government, which he frequently criticized. Even Cynthia called to ask if there were any truths to the scurrilous rumors about his sexuality being circulated on Facebook and Ghanaian news websites.

Almost out of hope, Razak resoundingly replied no.

Meanwhile, Razak's half-siblings sent a message through a family member saying he was lucky to be alive.

Bashir submitted these accusations to the Immigration and Refugees Board, along with other compelling evidence, including letters of support from the Islamic community leaders, who attested in writing to the circumstances of Razak's departure from Accra.

It was hard now, so many years later, not to give up, but seeing

Seidu successfully win asylum gave Razak a modicum of hope. Every day there was the ongoing struggle, believing someone would believe his story, and that his story would change something.

On June 13, 2017, Razak appeared before the Immigration and Refugee Board alongside Bashir and answered questions about his plea for asylum. The hearing was held over a teleconference monitor and lasted four hours. The first question the Board Member asked was Razak's age, then date of birth, then where he was born, then about his extended family. There was a question as to how many siblings Razak had, as his father had one child before marrying Razak's mother. In her letter of support, Razak's mother declared that there were seven children, although in local Islamic law, if you had a child outside of marriage, the child was not usually claimed by the father. In his Basis of Claim paperwork, Razak mentioned only six. The judge continued to interrogate Razak about the perceived discrepancy. She also asked why Razak didn't go to some other part of Ghana after his brothers attacked him.

He replied that Ghana was a very small country and that the government officials there were very powerful. He explained they could, with one phone call, end someone's life. "If I move from Accra to Kumasi, they could find me. They would find me and get me."

As the hearing wore on, Razak responded to every question asked by the Board Member. Bashir also asked a number of questions, focusing on why he had reached out to the various press outlets and how the media had become involved in his case.

"I didn't reach out to any of them. They all came to me. I had to share what happened to me."

"You didn't go to the media because you wanted your case to be stronger?"

"No, it never occurred to me."

After returning from a half-hour break, the Board Member announced, "I'm going to give my verdict."

Razak braced himself for the results, standing in the small courtroom.

"Razak, congratulations," the Board Member said, and then went through the reasons for her affirmative decision. Crying, Razak was unable to take in her words. Auntie Maggie and other members of the Ghanaian community, as well as Karin from Hospitality House, were in attendance. They all took turns hugging Razak, who was uncharacteristically overcome with emotion.

The Board Member ended the proceedings by stating, "I'm sorry for what happened to you. I'm sorry what you've been through. But you are safe here. You're now part of the Canadian community. Good luck."

As soon as the hearing was over, Razak took his phone out and called Cynthia. *I made it*, he told her. *I've gotten my refugee status.*

Once again she started crying. *I'm so happy. Your mother's not around. But I'll tell her the good news.*

By the time he arrived back at Hospitality House, the news had already appeared on Facebook. It had been five years since he left Ghana, five years before he finally had his asylum application approved. During those years, he had withstood degradation, persecution, detention, the loss of his hands. In some ways still unknown to him, he was forced to become a completely different person. Every attachment to who he was previously—his relationships to the people he loved back home—had been challenged, questioned, torn apart, or lost. The pain of separation had become physical, and it had left something more than just scars. In the end, it almost broke him. Like other asylum seekers, he had been given an opportunity of freedom, of the possibility of a new life, but it had cost him almost everything in return.

40

Outside Canada, the world, other nations, headlines all carried on, seemingly unaware of the two asylum seekers and their ongoing triumphs and difficulties. By then they had become two men again, like so many others, striving to build a life in a foreign land, although matters from abroad continued to weigh heavily upon them. In the end they had been caught up in something beyond their control—history—and no matter how much time passed, it had marked them; it would always be part of who they were.

In November 2017, the Ghanaian football team failed to qualify for the World Cup—a major upset in the world of soccer, after their three previous consecutive World Cup appearances. Ongoing conflict between the Ghana Football Association and Edwin Nii Lante Vanderpuye, the Minister of Youth and Sport, over the team's budget and players' bonuses called the GFA's transparency into question amid continuing allegations of corruption.

In the United States, on January 10, 2018, the Trump administration moved to rescind temporary protected status for nearly 200,000 El Salvadoran immigrants, even though undocumented immigration had fallen to a historic low. These migrants, who had been allowed to stay and work in the country since two earthquakes devastated their country in 2001, suddenly found their entire lives thrown into chaos after their immigration status was revoked.

One day later, on January 11, 2018, in a closed-door meeting with a bipartisan group of senators, President Trump asked why the United States had to allow entry to immigrants from "shithole" countries like Haiti and a number of African nations.

That same week, the U.S. Justice Department instructed federal immigration judges that they would need to complete 700 cases per year—more than three a day—in order to receive a satisfactory performance review. The Trump administration's focus on undocumented immigration—completely out of proportion to the problem it actually posed—seemed motivated by an imagined fear based on perceived differences in ethnicity and culture. The Department of Homeland Security continued to report precipitous declines in illegal border-crossing and undocumented migrants who appeared at the ports of entry seeking asylum.

In March 2018, the Trump administration and Justice Department changed protections from domestic abuse for asylum seekers, undoing twenty years of legal precedent. Shifting away from a more expansive description of a pattern of emotional and psychological harm, the Trump administration redefined domestic abuse as physical injury only, thus limiting the number of individuals who could claim protection. Nearly 200,000 Central Americans— women and their children—would be affected by this maneuver.

Donald Trump, a billionaire who inherited his wealth from his father's real estate business, seemed to view the nation as a country club, a high-rise, or a fortress that his administration desperately needed to defend. Other Republicans seemed to recognize that the notion of a white majority would soon become a thing of the past, and remained largely complicit in the administration's aggressive tactics when it came to immigration. Some critics argued that by upending the immigration norms that had been in place for decades under previous Republican and Democratic presidential administrations, there was a plot to maintain a white majority at all costs, undermining a more contemporary, complex view of America.

From any other perspective, it was hard to see the necessity of placing such a high emphasis on limiting immigration when the U.S. economy had been consistently strong and continued to add hundreds of thousands of jobs each month, leading to a 4 percent unemployment rate. Ignoring basic facts, the Trump administration persisted in propagating several untrue and deleterious myths about immigration as a way to bolster support among its conservative base. It claimed that immigrants were a burden on public services, that they took jobs from Americans, and that the economy would do better without them, though none of these claims had any basis in reality.

The truth was that all research affirmed the contrary: immigrants added more in taxes than they took from government benefits, based on a 2017 report from the National Academies of Sciences, Engineering, and Medicine, which found immigration was necessary for "the long-run economic growth" of the country. Second-generation immigrants were "among the strongest fiscal and economic contributors in the U.S." and contributed nearly $1,700 per person each year, more than native-born citizens.

Other evidence showed that immigrants were an essential part of the American economy. As birthrates for American women continue to decrease from 3.65 children in 1960 to 1.8 in 2018, immigrants were necessary to offset the shrinking workforce. Government programs such as Social Security relied on immigrants to help pay into the system, and these same immigrants also boosted the demand for goods and services.

In fact, many American businesses dependent on seasonal workers—who were often immigrants with H-2B visas—found themselves struggling to survive as the Trump administration changed the visa system from first-come, first-serve to a lottery system, making it harder for businesses to access skilled foreign workers.

On April 6, 2018, Attorney General Jefferson Beauregard Sessions III, acting on behalf of the Trump administration, enacted a controversial "zero-tolerance policy" on illegal immigration in order to begin prosecuting border crossings. Although undocumented immigration across the southern border continued to plummet, the administration instituted the vile and reprehensible policy of separating children from their parents at the border. As the Justice Department is legally unable to prosecute children alongside their parents, children were then placed separately into Department of Homeland Security custody. No court order or law ever existed calling for these kinds of separations.

In May 2018, a Honduran man, who had fled with his children to the U.S., committed suicide after one month of separation and detainment.

By June 2018, nearly 2,000 children had been separated from their parents. Several hundred adolescents went missing within Department of Homeland Security custody and could not be properly accounted for.

On the other hand, businesses responsible for housing detained children were reported to have earned upward of $458 million. The longer the children were forced to stay, the more money these businesses made. The CEO from Southwest Key, one such business, was reported to have earned $1.5 million in compensation.

On June 9, 2018, Italy turned a ship full of northern African refugees away from its port at Sicily, demanding Malta give it permission to dock. Malta also refused. After days of international dispute, Spain eventually granted the boat entrance.

By June 18, 2018, outcries against the Trump administration's family separation policy—including complaints made by fellow Republican lawmakers—reached a startling pitch. An audio recording obtained by news outlet ProPublica captured children separated from their parents at the border, screaming and crying in a way that can only be described as devastating. Beneath the sobs captured on the recording, a Border Patrol agent jokes, "Well, we have an orchestra here. What's missing is a conductor."

Protests, marches, and a wave of media coverage brought the policy decision to the forefront of American life.

Public opinion—properly focused—forced the administration to quickly revoke the policy. For the first time in decades, citizens across the political spectrum began to engage with the issue of immigration.

Also in June 2018, the U.S. Supreme Court upheld President Trump's travel ban on Muslim nations, granting the administration another deeply problematic victory.

In a lower federal court in September 2018, a judge blocked the Trump administration's attempt to remove protected status for Ecuadorians. The Trump administration immediately announced its plan to appeal the decision in an upper court.

On Sunday, November 25, 2018, U.S. Customs and Border Patrol agents confronted a group of migrants who attempted to rush the border at the San Ysidro Port of Entry by firing tear gas— 2-chlorobenzalmalononitrile—at a group of unarmed civilians. Barefoot mothers and their babies, many in diapers, fled the clouds of chemical gas. An ankle, a hand disappeared momentarily beneath the waves of toxic smoke.

Photographs from that day captured this unprecedented historical moment. Acrid white clouds rising from the ground. The look of terror and confusion mirrored in the faces of a mother and child. Military vehicles occupying an otherwise ordinary public space. For several hours, the U.S. Port of Entry at San Ysidro was closed to all vehicle and foot traffic. No one moved. No one spoke.

Beginning at midnight on December 22, 2018, President Trump shut down the U.S. federal government when he sought to include $5.7 billion for a border wall, refusing to negotiate on modern, more effective forms of border security. Some 800,000 federal employees, many of them from DHS and ICE, were furloughed or forced to work without pay for thirty-five days. It became the longest shutdown in U.S. history.

On January 25, 2019, the Trump administration and the Department of Homeland Security enacted a new policy forcing undocumented asylum seekers to wait in Mexico while their immigration claims were being processed in the United States. "They will not be able to disappear into the U.S.," Department of Homeland Security Secretary Kirstjen Nielsen said in an appearance before Congress. All data suggested that the immigration of undocumented migrants across the southern border continued to be near the lowest point in years.

Critics, journalists, and legal scholars all questioned the legality of the decision. Even the Border Patrol union, a traditionally conservative body, criticized the plan, saying it would discourage individuals from following the law and would "open up a Pandora's box." The policy was introduced at the San Ysidro port of entry, the busiest port in the country. It was unknown if the policy would be extended to other ports of entry or what the actual effects would be.

Months later, Customs and Border Protection reported a dramatic rise in undocumented migration along the southern border.

In retaliation, the Trump administration ended foreign aid to Guatemala, El Salvador, and Honduras in March 2019, cutting off more than $700 million in assistance.

Without desperately needed foreign aid and facing severely limited opportunities for legal immigration, hundreds of thousands of undocumented migrants continued to flood the southern border, enacting what, in the end, had become a completely contrived crisis. Week by week, illegal border crossings skyrocketed, with more than 100,000 individuals taken into custody each month in the spring of 2019. This mass migration completely overwhelmed available CBP and ICE facilities, leading to a humanitarian nightmare with families once again being separated and the bodies of dead migrants washing up on riverbeds. Children, up to a hundred in some places of detention, were forced to sleep on concrete floors, kept in what appeared to be large wire cages, all the direct result of President Trump's regressive immigration policies.

On July 14, 2019, President Trump criticized four U.S. congresswomen on Twitter, asking, "Why don't they go back and help fix the totally broken and crime infested places from which they came?" All four congresswomen were U.S. citizens. Days later at a campaign rally in North Carolina, Trump supporters chanted "send them back" in response to his ill-informed online trolling.

On July 15, 2019, the Trump administration attempted to enact a new interim rule that would severely limit legal migration across the southern border by requiring asylum seekers who passed through another country on their way to the U.S. to apply for asylum in any other nation first. The irony of hundreds of thousands of El Salvadorans, Hondurans, and migrants from abroad applying for refuge in Guatemala, a country already facing economic challenges, corruption, and a crumbling infrastructure, seemed lost on the members of the Trump administration. Weeks after this new announcement, the U.S. Supreme Court upheld the policy's implementation as several legal challenges to the maneuver made their way through the lower courts.

On the morning of August 3, 2019, a young man opened fire at a Walmart in El Paso, Texas, killing twenty-two people. He had posted a manifesto online minutes before, claiming to be a proponent of white nationalism and that the "attack was a response to the Hispanic invasion of Texas," echoing much of the language and many of themes of the president's own anti-immigration rhetoric. It was the fourth racially motivated mass shooting in the U.S. since President Trump had been elected.

Throughout the summer of 2019, asylum seekers continued to gather at the border in Tijuana—many of them women with children, living in tent cities. They did not seem to recognize the many policy changes that had taken place over the past few months. Waiting in line, they could see the same color sky on the other side of the border, unaware of the hundreds of thousands of lives put in question, now hanging in the air. Everything on the other side still appeared to be clear and strange and open.

41

In the summer of 2019, Seidu was once again on the soccer pitch, pushing himself as hard as he could. There seemed to be nothing that could stop him. Months after recovering from his surgeries and having his refugee claim accepted, Seidu had joined a local soccer team composed of recent refugees, the Winnipeg Wasps FC. He played with the Wasps for one season, becoming their captain, scoring several goals, and leading them to a winning record in Manitoba's second highest soccer division. After that, he joined an amateur Winnipeg team in the Manitoba Major Soccer League as a defender.

Although he was not yet being paid to play, he was considering trying out for Canada's new professional soccer league, which was holding its trials for the Winnipeg team in October.

He had moved into his own apartment, was going to school to get his high school equivalency, and had landed his first job in Canada, working as a soccer coach for a team of refugee children at Seven Oaks School. He was also continuing his physical rehabilitation, which involved practicing with a pair of prosthetic hands. He had lived without prosthetics for almost two years and had developed a way of getting through his day, and often marveled at what he was able to do. Four times a month he tried using the prosthetics and—in all honesty—preferred living without them.

When he was not attending school or out on the pitch, he still faced dozens of papers to fill out in order to apply for permanent residence in Canada. The amount of time and money he had spent trying to complete the forms, getting his medical exams, and requesting an FBI background check was overwhelming.

Alone in his apartment, he sometimes missed the noise of his family's house back in Nima. He missed his sister and most of all his mother, the conversations, the arguments, the *tuo zaafi*—a dish made of corn flour and gravy that she used to cook. The spices she used . . . no one—even the other refugees from Ghana living in Winnipeg—could cook like that. Every day they spoke on Facebook, but not being able to see the shape of her face as she laughed in person; it was not the same.

He missed Montreal Football Club, the other players, the familiarity of the pitch where he learned to play.

He missed the Eid festival in Nima, the concerts that took place on the street, his neighbors, friends, the conviviality.

As long as his family was in Ghana, it would always be home.

At the same time, he recognized that something in him had changed. His uncle, his nieces, the people he loved had been threatened because of their relationship to him. He was afraid nothing in Ghana would ever change. He prayed, day after day, that he could bring his family here. As soon as he got his permanent residence, he would do everything he could to help them. It was impossible to move on with them being menaced back home. Just the other day his mother mentioned a distant family member that had threatened her for continuing to support her son's sexual identity.

Be calm, he told her. *Time will tell. You will be here soon.*

He felt comfortable being himself among the Ghanaian community in Winnipeg. There were other gay men and bisexuals and lesbians and trans individuals from Ghana who lived in Winnipeg without fearing for their lives. In July, there was the Pride Parade, which he happily attended.

"Everything here is beautiful," he later remarked after a newspaper reporter asked his opinion about the parade.

In those moments, the city felt like his own. The Ghanaian community, his friends from his soccer team, slowly made the city feel more familiar. He had no interest in returning to Accra but dreamed of Ghana changing its repressive laws, knowing the challenge was great.

In August 2017, Seidu and a number of other LGBT members of the Ghanaian community held a protest at Winnipeg's Folklorama Festival, gathering more than 1,000 signatures from attendees and calling on the Canadian government to use its diplomatic powers to promote human rights in Ghana, as Canada continued to donate millions of dollars in official development assistance to his home country.

Ghana media picked up footage of the protest. Several Ghanaian MPs, including Rev. John Ntim Fordjour, lashed out at the refugees, stating that Ghana should never decriminalize homosexuality because the laws safeguarded the nation's values. During that same time, members of the Canadian House of Commons, who served on the Canada–Africa Parliamentary Association, were visiting Accra, promoting cooperation between the two nations. One of these members, Rob Oliphant, a Liberal MP—an out gay man and a former United Church minister—had a series of meetings with a number of Ghanaian parliamentary and civil groups to discuss human rights concerns, including LGBT issues.

When Oliphant returned from Ghana, he was interviewed by the press and exclaimed that he was interested in meeting with the protesting refugees from Winnipeg. Oliphant came to Winnipeg on September 28, 2017, and met with several refugee claimants, including Seidu, who spoke at length about his experiences.

In the spring of 2018, Seidu began going to school to earn his high school equivalency. Once he received his high school certificate, he would begin looking for a full-time job. He had not dated anyone, had not been in a relationship since he left Ghana in 2014, and although there was a man in his neighborhood, and also a woman he met downtown whom he spoke with a few times, he did not want to rush anything. There would be a time for that after everything was settled.

Almost two years after his arrival, Seidu was invited to testify before the Standing Committee on Citizenship and Immigration at the House of Commons in Ottawa on Tuesday, July 24, 2018. Members had been debating suspending the Safe Third Country Agreement between Canada and the United States in order to send a strong message that Canada was concerned about the rights of refugees around the world in the face of President Trump's decision to limit such protections. Seidu stood before the formidable audience and felt nervous. But once he began to speak, everything fell away.

"As a newcomer to Canada, I would like to begin by recognizing that here in Ottawa I am on the traditional territory of the Algonquin and Anishinaabe people." Seidu then recounted his story. After he finished, the entire chamber was silent. His appearance at Parliament was covered by the media, once again affirming his belief that he had something to contribute and an obligation to speak out, to not remain silent any longer. Even the negative comments he observed online, claiming he was a criminal, a drain on national resources, other words and phrases much harsher than that, would not dissuade him. Over the last few months, the last few years, it had become clear that this was who he was and what he needed to do. For now, he would continue telling his story and see what the future would bring.

42

By the end of the month it had become winter once again. Outside the sky was dark with what appeared to be snow. It was a Saturday, the end of September 2019. Razak awoke and began to get dressed—though it was still difficult to work the buttons on his shirt, the last year and a half living on his own had given him plenty of practice. Once he got his sweatshirt and jacket on, he pulled on his headphones, pulled up his hood, then walked outside to wait at the bus stop nearby. The city was quiet and cold. He studied the clouds for some time until the bus arrived, and when it was his turn, climbed on. The vehicle would bring him to the Muslim Women's Institute, where he continued to volunteer. Other days he went for job training at the Society for Manitobans with Disabilities, which, if everything went well, would place him in a job by December. His goal was to save up money so he could open a business of his own, an electronics repair store or, if and when Cynthia got her visa, a barbershop and hair salon where he and his wife could work, a place where people could come and talk, tell stories, discuss politics. Since he had left Ghana, Cynthia had built a successful jewelry business, which allowed her to pay for her own apartment and gave her the opportunity to sell her jewelry in neighboring countries like Togo. But before she could apply for a visa, Razak needed to be awarded permanent residency in Canada.

Often as he rode the bus, he was caught off guard by some image, some sound that reminded him of Ghana. The colors, the faces, the noises, all the unresolvable remembrances from his years as far back as elementary school. The bus passed several school-children practicing soccer on the way to school. Razak suddenly recalled being a boy, his father giving him a brand-new soccer ball, going out to the field, the other boys wanting to use the ball but saying he could play later and Razak saying, *No. No, if you want to use my ball, you have to let me play.*

Sometimes as he rode the bus, he thought about what had happened over these past eight years, beginning with his father's death. He could recognize that his life had not ended but had changed irrevocably. These thoughts often led to a series of questions: What if he hadn't had to endure his half-siblings' greed? What if he hadn't had to leave Ghana? What if he hadn't lost his fingers? Before everything had gone wrong, what would his life have been like? Going back to those moments, the open, unpredictable feeling of afternoons as a young man. Accra, from behind the handlebars of his motorcycle. The taste of certain fruits. A flag waving. Men kneeling at the central mosque, beggars gathering outside. Back further still, to when he was a boy. All the wonderful, nameless alleys, corners, streets. The children on the soccer field, arguing about what was fair and what wasn't. Perhaps it had been there all along—his need for justice, his desire to make things equal and fair. Perhaps all of it had been inevitable, even then.

In March 2018, Razak appeared at an Amnesty International event in Winnipeg with Seidu and other refugees from a number of countries, including Syria and Sierra Leone, to describe their experiences. They called on the Canadian government to end the Safe Third Party Agreement with the United States, so that refugees who lost their asylum cases in the U.S. could apply for asylum in Canada by presenting themselves at the border instead of crossing illegally. In interviews and in conversations, Razak appealed for common sense and fairness in how governments were allowed to shape people's lives, in both the United States and in Canada.

Every day on Facebook and on WhatsApp, his friends in Ghana sent him stories of ongoing scandals, tales of corruption back home. But Razak did not want to dwell solely on the past. He was beginning to consider what he would leave behind after he was gone. He did not want to only be remembered for crossing the border from the United States, for the tragedy, for the losses he suffered. He wanted to do something bigger, make some difference, to fight for his community in Nima. Even though he was thousands of miles away and slowly adapting to life in a new country, he could not stop thinking about those people back home.

He looked over at a newspaper on an empty seat. He glanced over the headline and saw the latest news from America. Over the past three years, President Trump had singlehandedly revised the immigration policy of the United States. Attempt after attempt to limit legal immigration, to make it harder to apply for asylum. In a country of so much wealth, of so many opportunities, it didn't make any sense.

Climbing down from the bus, he realized he had not talked to Cynthia yet. He smiled briefly, thinking of her face, and decided to call her as soon as he had a chance.

Inside the shelter, Razak once again began to sort the clothes that were piled on tables. It was not long before he and the other men started talking politics.

Every day I read the news from Ghana, he began. *Every blessed day. I see the corruption, the allegations. Being here in Canada, I can see how the political system back home is destroying itself. Unemployment has not changed. The literacy rate seems to be falling. Children here in Canada learn how to use computers, learn how to embrace the future, they're all given public education and access to technology. But boys and girls back in Accra are living in some other century.*

The other migrants nodded as Razak spoke.

Everyone knows that all the wealth back home remains with the same politicians and their children. Look at the current president. He's the son of a former prime minister. Then there were the MPs who were just caught selling visas. Then the scandal with the Ghana Football Association. Everyone might think Ghana's a democratic country because every four years they have elections. But how can you treat your people like that? There's no sanitation. People are sick, get diseases, have to go to the hospital. They don't want anyone to talk about it. Everywhere there's more and more corruption. Just look at the power people have and how they are using it.

The other men nodded. Razak continued.

Even in the United States. There are a lot of things going on there. Look at the way people are being treated, asylum seekers, refugees. We ran from trouble, only to find more trouble. Why should this happen? I was coming to get a better life, to find safety. How can you put me in a place like a criminal for two years? Mentally, how do you expect me to feel, with chains on my hands and feet? How do you want me to be part of society? There are a lot of people who went through what I went through, even worse. But they didn't have the kind of opportunity I have to speak. I know I'm safe now. I know if I was in Ghana and speaking like this, I'd no longer be alive. So I have to let the world know. To get people to see, this is what's going on. This is what's happening to other people. Who will stand up on their behalf? Who's going to say something?

The other men worked beside him, sorting, stacking, and soon their talk became a quiet hum, their hands and faces in constant motion. Before him on the table was another pile of unfolded clothes—a shirt, a dress, pair of child-sized pajamas—a fragment of what one day would become a life. Others would be coming. Over and over, he carefully folded the garments and then put them to the side. By the end, there was a pile of ten, fifty, a hundred, all waiting to be put to use, all waiting to begin again.

Acknowledgments

For their trust, friendship, and uncompromising courage: Seidu Mohammed and Razak Iyal.

For their encouragement, support, and conversations: Koren Zelek, Lucia Meno, Nico Meno, Sami Tesfazghi, Ian Dimerman, Dan Lerner, Shawn Vaughn, Jon Resh.

For finding a way to get Seidu and Razak's story out to the wider world: Erin Hosier, Dan Smetanka, Dan Lopez, and everyone at Counterpoint.

Thanks also to my colleagues in the English and Creative Writing Department at Columbia College Chicago.

Grateful acknowledgment is also made to the following articles, essays, and resources, without which this book would not have been possible, beginning with Carol Sanders at the *Winnipeg Free Press* who first covered Seidu and Razak's incredible journey. Her reportage introduced their struggle to the world.

Other articles and resources are listed below.

Adedeji, John. L, "The Legacy of J. J. Rawlings in Ghanaian Politics, 1979–2000." *African Studies Quarterly*, Volume 5, Issue 2, Summer 2001.

Moore, John, "An immigrant's dream, detained." *The New York Times.* November 25, 2013.

Motlagh, Jason. "A terrifying journey through the world's most dangerous jungle." *Outside Magazine.* July 19, 2016.

Porter, Catherine, "After a harrowing flight from U.S., Refugees Find Asylum in Canada." *The New York Times*, July 16, 2017.

"Asylum in the United States." Center for Immigration Studies. March 26, 2014. cis.org/Report/Asylum-United-States

"Asylum in the United States." American Immigration Council. May 14, 2018. www.americanimmigrationcouncil.org/research /asylum-united-states

"Frequently Requested Statistics on Immigrants and Immigration in the United States." Migration Policy Institute. March 14, 2019. www.migrationpolicy.org/article/frequently-requested-statistics-immigrants-and-immigration-united-states#Numbers

"Applying for asylum in the US takes, on average, 6 months . . ." CNN.com. May 1, 2018. www.cnn.com/2018/05/01/world/asylum-process-refugee-migrant-immigration-trnd/index.html

"Refugees and Aslyees in the United States." Migration Policy Institute. June 13, 2019. www.migrationpolicy.org/article /refugees-and-asylees-united-states

"Undocumented Immigrants." *New American Economy.* www .newamericaneconomy.org/issues/undocumented-immigrants/

"Profile of the Unauthorized Population: United States." Migration Policy Institute. www.migrationpolicy.org/data/unauthorized-immigrant-population/state/US

"Corruption claims and rows tarnish Accra's record." *Africa Confidential*, Vol. 50, No. 21, October 23, 2009. www.africa confidential.com/article/id/3290/Corruption-claims-and-rows-tarnish-Accra's-record

"Police to quiz Rawlings." *Ghana Web*. January 20, 2009. www .ghanaweb.com/ghanahomepage/newsarchive/artikle.php?ID+ 97923

"Why Hon. Dr. Mustapha Failed to Consolidate his Mugabeship in Ayawaso North." *Modernghana.com*. February 12, 2015. www .modernghana.com/news/659337/why-hon-dr-mustapha-ahmed-failed-to-consolidate-his-mugabe.html

"Human evolution may have amped up our Fight-or-Flight urges," *Psychology Today*. April 23, 2018. www.psychologytoday .com/us/blog/the-athletes-way/201804/human-evolution-may-have-amped-our-fight-or-flight-urges

"Migrants flowing through is like Cost'a Rica's new normal." *The Tico Times*. June 10, 2016. ticotimes.net/2016/06/10/europes-crackdown-on-migrants-costa-rica

"Record $120 billion sent home to 3 top nations flooding US with illegal immigrants." *Washington Examiner*. March 20, 2019. www.washingtonexaminer.com/washington-secrets/record-120-billion-sent-home-to-3-top-nations-flooding-us-with-illegal-immigrants

"Most Dangerous Journey." Amnesty USA. www.amnestyusa
.org/most-dangerous-journey-what-central-american-migrants-
face-when-they-try-to-cross-the-border/

"Migrant deaths and disappearances." Migration Data Portal. September 23, 2019. migrationdataportal.org/themes/migrant-deaths-
and-disappearances

"Five ways Immigration System Changed After 9/11." ABC News.
September 11, 2012. abcnews.go.com/ABC_Univision/News/ways-
immigration-system-changed-911/story?id=17231590

"Through the Prism of National Security: Major Immigration
Policy and Program Changes in the Decade since 9/11." Migration
Policy Institute. August 2011. www.migrationpolicy.org/research
/post-9-11-immigration-policy-program-changes

"9/11 and the Transformation of U.S. Immigration Law and Policy." American Bar Association. January 1, 2011. www.american-
bar.org/groups/crsj/publications/human_rights_magazine_home
/human_rights_vol38_2011/human_rights_winter2011/9-11_trans-
formation_of_us_immigration_law_policy/

"Medical care in Eloy detention center criticized." *Tucson.com.* July 7,
2016. tucson.com/news/local/medical-care-in-eloy-detention-cen-
ter-criticized/article_fbca130e-23fa-5a3c-bb9c-8cfe3448b5cf.html

"Migrant detention centers in the U.S. are under fire for their 'horri-
fying conditions' . . ." *Business Insider.* July 5, 2019. www.businessin-
sider.com/ice-immigrant-families-dhs-detention-centers-2018-6

"A surprise inspection of an ICE Detention Center reveals horrific

conditions." *Mother Jones*. October 2, 2018. www.motherjones.com
/politics/2018/10/ice-adelanto-detention-facility-inspector-report/

"Living in the Shadows: Detention center deaths raise immigrants
rights questions." *Radio bilingue*. February 10, 2014. radiobilingue
.org/en/features/vivir-en-las-sombras-faltan-mejoras-de-
atencion-medica-en-centros-de-detencion/

"Inside Adelanto, California's largest immigration detention
center." KCRW. June 7, 2017. www.kcrw.com/news/articles
/inside-adelanto-californias-largest-immigration-detention-facility

"Social visibility, asylum law, and LGBT asylum seekers." *Twin
Cities Daily Planet*. October 7, 2013. www.tcdailyplanet.net/social-
visibility-asylum-law-and-lgbt-asylum-seekers/

"Two charts demolish the notion that immigrants here illegally
commit more crime," *The Washington Post*. June 19, 2018. www
.washingtonpost.com/news/wonk/wp/2018/06/19/two-charts-
demolish-the-notion-that-immigrants-here-illegally-commit-
more-crime/?noredirect=on

"What claimants receive from the government." CBC News. August 18, 2017. www.cbc.ca/news/canada/montreal/asylum-seekers-
support-housing-1.4252114

"Canada rejecting more refugee claims amid border-crossing increase under Trump." *The Guardian*. May 23, 2018. www
.theguardian.com/world/2018/may/23/canada-rejecting-more-
refugee-claims-amid-border-crossing-influx-under-trump

"Illegal border crossings from U.S. increase by nearly 23 per cent."

The Globe and Mail. August 14, 2018. www.theglobeandmail.com /politics/article-illegal-border-crossings-from-us-increase-by-nearly-23-per-cent-from/

"Ghana agrees to work with FIFA to tackle corruption," *Africanews.* August 17, 2018. www.africanews.com/2018/08/17/ghana-agrees-to-work-with-fifa-to-tackle-corruption-in-football/

"Trump's decision to cut off aid to 3 Central American countries, explained." *Vox*, April 1, 2019. www.vox.com/2019/4/1/18290443 /aid-central-america-mexico-guatemala-immigration-border

"Tear gas, lobbed at migrants on the southern border, is banned in warfare." *The Washington Post.* November 26, 2018. www.washing-tonpost.com/national-security/2018/11/26/why-tear-gas-lobbed-migrants-southern-border-is-banned-warfare/?noredirect=on

Additional information came from the following studies and reports:

U.S. Department of State, *Country reports on Human Rights Practices—Ghana*, 2008–12.

U.S. Department of State, U.S. Department of Homeland Security, U.S. Department of Health and Human Services, *Proposed Refugee Admissions for Fiscal Year 2018*, 2017.

Immigration and Customs Enforcement, *Human smuggling equals grave danger, big money*, January 16, 2018.

INS Internal Guide, *Asylum Identity Checks Quick Reference Guide* (February 1998); Office of International Affairs Asylum Division,

Affirmative Asylum Procedures Manual, February 2003.

Isacson, Adam, Maureen Meyer, and Gabriela Morales. Washington Office on Latin America, *Mexico's Other Border: Security, Migrations, and the Humanitarian Crisis at the Line with Central America*, August 2014.

McGuirk, Siobhan, Max Niedzwiecki, Temitope Oke, and Anastasia Volkova. *Stronger Together, A Guide to Supporting LGBT Asylum Seekers*. Washington, D.C.: LGBT Freedom and Asylum Network. October 2015.

Newhouse School of Public Communications, Syracuse University. *Asylum Representation Rates Have Fallen Amid Rising Denial Rates*. November 28, 2017.

Refugee Review Tribunal, Australia RRT Research, *Ethnic conflict in Ghana, GHA35648*, November, 2009.

Further research was conducted with the support of the following:

U.S. Department of State: www.state.gov

Immigration & Refugee Board of Canada: www.irb-cisr.gc.ca

UNHCR Refworld: www.refworld.org

All Africa: allafrica.com

Africa Confidential: www.africa-confidential.com/home

Ghana Web: www.ghanaweb.com

© Bo Demsas

SEIDU MOHAMMED was born and raised in Accra, Ghana, where he was a celebrated soccer player and entrepreneur. After leaving Ghana in 2014, he worked a variety of jobs, including as a dishwasher and cook in a Vietnamese restaurant, in order to pursue his plea for asylum abroad. He is now an interpreter living in Winnipeg, Canada, where he is an outspoken advocate for refugee and LGBT rights.

© Bo Demsas

RAZAK IYAL is from the Nima neighborhood of Accra, Ghana, where he was a successful electronics business owner and highly respected member of his community. After running afoul of a Ghanaian member of parliament, he fled his homeland in 2012 to seek asylum in the West. Iyal faced nearly two years of unjust detention in a U.S. facility. While he awaited the results of his asylum appeal, he lived and worked in New York City before traveling to Canada, where his appeal for refugee status was finally accepted. He speaks frequently on matters of the refugee experience and is currently employed in the hotel service industry in Winnipeg, Canada.

JOE MENO is a fiction writer and journalist who lives in Chicago. He is the winner of the Nelson Algren Literary Award, a Pushcart Prize, and the Great Lakes Book Award and was a finalist for the Story Prize. The bestselling author of seven novels and two short story collections, including *Marvel and a Wonder*, *The Boy Detective Fails*, and *Hairstyles of the Damned*, he is a professor in the English and creative writing department at Columbia College Chicago. Find out more at joemeno.com.